W9-BYL-619

DAVID LONGEST

and

MICHAEL STERN

COLLECTOR BOOKS

A Division of Schroeder Publishing Co., Inc.

The current values in this book should be used only as a guide. They are not intended to set prices, which vary from one section of the country to another. Auction prices as well as dealer prices vary greatly and are affected by condition as well as demand. Neither the Authors nor the Publisher assumes responsibility for any losses that might be incurred as a result of consulting this guide.

Searching For A Publisher?

We are always looking for knowledgeable people considered to be experts within their fields. If you feel that there is a real need for a book on your collectible subject and have a large comprehensive collection, contact us.

COLLECTOR BOOKS
P.O. Box 3009
Paducah, Kentucky 42002-3009

Cover Design: Beth Summers

Book Design: Beth Ray

Additional copies of this book may be ordered from:

COLLECTOR BOOKS
P.O. Box 3009
Paducah, Kentucky 42002-3009

@$24.95. Add $2.00 for postage and handling.

1 2 3 4 5 6 7 8 9 0

ACKNOWLEDGMENTS

When we first set out to combine our collections, efforts, and energies into the production of a very large Disneyana collectors guide, it was the summer of 1990. Neither of us had a real idea about how large the task ahead of us was going to be. Michael had written his two paperback versions of *Stern's Guide To Disney Collectibles* and David had written two books on character toys, *Character Toys and Collectibles, Series One* and *Two,* and a general toy price guide, *Toys–Antique And Collectible.* Neither of us were rookies, but neither of us had ever published a work picturing over 1000 toys in nearly 900 photographs. The photography sessions, the UPS packages traveling back and forth, and the lengthy late night long distance phone calls all helped to pull this book together. As the project is now completed, we can both honestly say that the collaboration has been satisfying, enjoyable, and downright fun. And as it goes with any major effort in life, there are significant friends to thank.

George Hattersley of Pennsylvania literally flung open the doors of his home and collection to us. He is a passionate collector of Disneyana who genuinely enjoys each new acquisition like a kid on Christmas morning, and as we "shot" his fantastic collection, he spruced up the showcases shelf by shelf and seemed to have a story for every toy. There is no real way to thank George for his generosity in allowing us to photographically devour his collection except by saying, "You're a pal, George. Your friendship, kindness, and open support will allow thousands of Disneyana collectors to see some great celluloid toys they might never have seen otherwise. If we could imagine that all Disneyana collectors are warm, friendly, and enthusiastic just like you, then you make us all look good. We thank you, and may the fates drop a big chest of 1930's Mickey celluloid toys on your doorstep, all in their original boxes!"

Elmer and Viola Reynolds of Indiana are character toy collectors "extraordinaire" who embody all that is good about toys and people. They anxiously look forward to each weekly antique or toy show in the hopes of snatching up yet another small addition to their absolutely incredible collection. Their "Disney room" is our favorite spot, and without the addition of their toys, dolls, windups and quality Disneyana, this book would not be what it is. David would like to thank them personally for their generous support on all four of his book efforts. So to Elmer and Viola we say, "Thanks. Thanks for all the joy that your toys will bring to the collectors who discover this book. And thank you for the friendship and the love of old toys that we share. May some time machine transport you both back to a dime store in the 1930's for an hour of toy shopping with $200.00 in each of your pockets. And then may it safely return you to us so that we can hear all about it. Thanks, guys."

The authors would like to additionally thank Steve Quertermous and Bill Schroeder at Collector Books for their initial faith in this project, and Lisa Stroup, our editor, for her enthusiasm toward the book and her patience with us when we missed a few deadlines. (Hey! We're collectors, too! We couldn't write ALL THE TIME!)

Also, the authors would like to thank David Smith and his staff at the Walt Disney Archives for their final review of the text.

Only four collections were photographed in the production of this book: the George Hattersley Collection, the Elmer and Viola Reynolds Collection, and the collection of each of the authors.

Michael would like to dedicate this book to his wife, Merrill, and twin daughters, Jenny and Lisa, for their support and encouragement.

David would like to dedicate this book to his wife, Ann, and his daughter, Claire, for their own support and enthusiasm for Disneyana. Claire wishes to say "Hello " to Mickey Mouse!

David Longest & Michael Stern

INTRODUCTION

We have put together what we feel is the most complete and comprehensive Disney price guide available for today's collectors. We have concentrated our efforts on items from the "golden age" of Disney – the 1930's. These items are the rarest and their prices escalate more rapidly because of this rarity.

We have attempted to give equal billing to the many different areas of Disneyana. We have tried to reach each collector and what might be their particular passion. We have shown the magnitude of the different items created by the Disney empire.

There's still no greater thrill than to find a Disneyana collectible not previously seen before. Since the second series of *Stern's Guide to Disney Collectibles* was published, the Disneyana marketplace has gone through quite a transformation. The most basic economic principle of supply and demand has informed the collecting of Disney memorabilia. The demand for these artifacts of the past has grown dramatically and the supply has just as dramatically decreased. This is not to say that one cannot find Disneyana available; it's just that it's more difficult because the number of collectors has grown.

Lack of supply, and more demand for it, has pushed the prices of high-quality, early Disney memorabilia much higher. Who could have fathomed that a black and white cel from "Orphan's Benefit" would have sold for $450,000.00 or that a Knickerbocker Mickey Mouse Cowboy doll would fetch $16,000.00 at auction.

Disneyana is a comic art form and the appreciation of prices of this art form parallels the increase in the values of all forms of artwork. It could be said that Disneyana is, like quality stocks and bonds, an excellent investment that increases in value on a yearly basis.

The added value is that whereas stocks and bonds are tucked away in a safe or vault, your Disneyana collectibles can be displayed and enjoyed on a daily basis. We call it "double appreciation."

Mickey Mouse and the gang continue to be the most sought-after of any characters in the comic collectible field. With the addition of Disney theme parks in Europe and Japan, Disneyana collecting has become international. Each day more and more people join the fold of Mickey Mouse fanatics who live and breathe for that new piece to add to their collection.

All of the photographs in this book are taken from the collections of four die-hard Disneyana collectors. Each has his own particular interest and favorite area of collecting. That's the most exciting aspect of collecting Disneyana – the sheer magnitude of the items that have been produced.

Each of these collectors has put on a lot of miles, showed an abundance of patience, and had a lot of luck in being in the right place at the right time.

Our hope is that this book will help broaden one's scope so that when acquiring a piece of Disney memorabilia, it can be dated and its price put into perspective.

TABLE OF CONTENTS

CHAPTER ONE

MICKEY AND MINNIE MOUSE TOYS OF THE 1930's

When Mickey Mouse first appeared in the black and white comic film short "Steamboat Willie" in 1928, his creator must have hoped for a cartoon character who would at least survive through several short films. Walt Disney may have realized that he had hit upon something special with the creation of Mickey, but he could have had no idea of the genuine cultural phenomenon his little rodent would create.

For over 60 years, Americans have been charmed by Mickey Mouse. His early squeaky voice and rat-like features may have made him appear somewhat bratty, but we all knew that he symbolized the little, regular guy. He was not a hero who won out with physical force. Mickey always got to where he was by hard work (and sometimes even pain) combined with a little bit of luck. He came to stand for us all.

Early in his cartoon animation career, Walt Disney learned the importance of characters having real feeling and emotions which could be displayed on the screen. Without this depth of character, the little fictional beings he created would have been as flat as the celluloid upon which they were penned. Instead of simple cartoon foolery, Disney insisted upon rounded, interesting cartoon characters. Some rather horribly sub-standard competitors could imitate the techniques, but they could not duplicate the characters Disney created. As a result, it is Mickey Mouse above all others who stands as the symbol of popular American culture of the 1930's. Most definitely, there was a host of cartoon characters who arrived on the scene in this decade. But Mickey's appearance in 1928 and his subsequent evolution through the 1930's and 1940's as both a corporate symbol and the subject of American marketing genius makes him the most interesting of all.

Walt Disney may have begun his animation career as an artist, but he quickly developed a reputation as one who could inspire others with his tremendous imagination and the ability to turn ideas into actual film possibilities. He was not a merchandiser or a retailer, yet even in his thirties he had the savvy to realize that the popularity of his mouse was worth more than simply movie rentals or theatre admissions.

Enter a man by the name of Kay Kamen, and the rest is merchandising history. Walt had a studio to run with tight production schedules and an ever-increasing staff. Kamen had the time, energy, and most importantly the business know-how to take a lot of good ideas for potential Mickey Mouse merchandise and turn them into simply fantastic toys! This is not to say Kamen was the toy designer or inventor of the great 1930's Mickey toys – he was the facilitator, the man who put the right toy licensing contracts into the hands of the right toy people. As a result, such big names as Parker Brothers, Whitman Publishing, Louis Marx, Milton-Bradley, Fisher Price, George Borgfeldt Distributors, Lionel Train, and Ohio Art, among many others, quickly jumped on the Disneyana bandwagon.

Collectors of Disneyana quickly realize they are faced with many important choices. Collecting Disneyana in general is quite fulfilling for a while, but the sheer amount of merchandise in the marketplace makes it financially impossible to collect everything that is "out there." Furthermore, space limitations in the average home usually force even novice collectors to decide upon certain specialty areas within a few years. And if there is one common character that nearly every Disneyana collector holds in common, it is Mickey Mouse. Since the early 1930's Mickey toys are the virtual flagships of Disneyana collecting, nearly all collectors try to find at least a few rare 1930's Mickey pieces.

The 1930's may be synonymous with the Great Depression in America, but it certainly did not adversely affect the appearance of hundreds of wonderful Mickey Mouse toys brought onto the market. Maybe they were purchased as a diversion – a way to keep the kids from realizing how bad things really were. Or maybe they were intended to reach the adults, too. After all, the Mickey cartoons were not geared toward only a child audience, adults went nuts over Mickey Mouse too!

Today's collector of 1930's vintage Mickey Mouse memorabilia still faces a wide assortment of interesting toys available. The old folk tale that "the good stuff just isn't out there" is simply untrue. Because Disneyana in general underwent a price renaissance in the late 1980's, with prices on many items seemingly doubling overnight, a cavalcade of dealers and collectors brought wonderful merchandise out onto the market. The supply is still there, and the demand continues to be great. So be prepared to pay for the rare and quality toys that you desire. It's getting harder and harder to find a Mickey Mouse 1930's toy bargain these days.

Another interesting phenomenon that affects the pricing of vintage Mickey Mouse toys is Mickey's cross-collectibility. Because he is such a recognizable character, Mickey toys are passionately sought by general toy collectors, comic character toy collectors, animation art enthusiasts, tin windup collectors, and popular art collectors, in addition to Disneyana enthusiasts. All of this interest in Mickey toys helps to fuel the fires that keep Disneyana prices generally higher than many other similar vintage toys on the market today.

For the sake of the novice collectors who use this book as a basic introduction to Disneyana collecting, several simple identification notes should be helpful. And for the advanced, experienced collector who doesn't want to review what is already known, just skip to the next paragraph. When dealing with identification of vintage Disneyana, three basic and simple copyright markings can help establish the age and date of a toy. The earliest Mickey Mouse toys are simply marked "Walt E. Disney" or "Walter E. Disney." Toys with this copyright marking are from the very late 1920's to the early 1930's. The greatest bulk of vintage 1930's Disneyana items are marked "Walt Disney Enterprises" which was the marketing and licensing branch of the Disney Studio from the mid-1930's until the release of *Pinocchio* in 1939. After *Pinocchio*, the copyright identification switches to the more familiar "Walt Disney Productions." Therefore, the marking of "Walt Disney Productions" should signal to the collector that a toy is from the 1940's or later.

Many novice collectors will make the statement, "I only collect Disneyana marked 'Enterprises'," and that is probably not what they mean to say. Most of these collectors are forgetting that items from the very early 1930's *would not* be marked "Enterprises" since the term did not come into existence until the marketing/licensing branch was established. Hence, these collectors would probably be more than happy to collect any of the very early items marked simply "Walter E. Disney."

The Mickey and Minnie Mouse toys pictured in this chapter take up 403 of the 860 plates pictured in this book. This fact alone should signal to collectors the marketing scope of these two characters. Items pictured here range from the extremely rare to the common, and the price guide at the back of the book reflects how the tremendous rarity affects prices. The MICKEY MOUSE HURDY GURDY pictured in Plate #1 is one of the rarest and most sought-after of all Disney collectibles. This beautiful piece is often found missing the tiny Minnie Mouse dancing figure on top of the windup, so collectors should beware. Aside from the wonderful windup action of the toy, the astounding early rat-like Mickey graphics and the intense color make this an even more impressive toy.

The MICKEY MOUSE DRUMMER by Nifty is a little less rare than the HURDY GURDY, but it is certainly a desirable toy. This toy is pictured in Plate #2. It's action is slightly simpler with Mickey's scissor-like arm mechanism striking the small drum attached to his waist. Once again, however, it is the early graphic style of Mickey and the design of the toy which make it so appealing. The boxed celluloid MICKEY AND MINNIE MOUSE PLAYLAND windup has never, to our knowledge, been pictured anywhere before. As the cardboard cylinder in the center of the toy swings back and forth, the celluloid figures of Mickey and Minnie Mouse spin while ringing a bell. Considering the fragile nature of the celluloid and cardboard construction of this toy, it is a miracle that one has survived in this mint condition. When looking at this toy in Plate #3, notice also the fragile paper canopy which shelters the whole structure. And certainly take a look at the original box for it in Plate #4.

The MICKEY AND MINNIE ON THE MOTORCYCLE TIN WINDUP pictured in Plate #5 is also one of the rarest toys in this book. Manufactured by Tripp, this toy features excellent windup action combined with strikingly graphic early Mickey and Minnie lithography. Some collectors supposedly gauge the "depth" of advanced Disneyana collections by whether or not they contain *this* toy. Out of the four collections contributing to this book, only one collection has this toy. It is a very rare one. The Nifty MICKEY MOUSE SPARKLER shown in Plate #6 is worthy of note because it is shown with its very rare box.

The "king" of all Mickey Mouse lamps is the one pictured in Plate #8. Originally manufactured by Soreng-Manegold in the 1930's, the beautiful plaster composition piece is extremely rare, and even rarer when found in excellent condition. Because of the nature of its plaster based construction, many of these are found badly chipped, broken, and missing much of the original paint finish. Our little fellow pictured in this plate was fortunately spared any significant wear and tear.

The large RAMBLING MICKEY MOUSE CELLULOID WINDUP in Plate #9 is worthy of note because of its impressive size and its fantastic box. A long line of rare and highly desirable celluloid toys is pictured in this chapter. Plate #10 shows HOBBY HORSE MICKEY MOUSE with its colorful jointed celluloid Mickey and the wooden horse. Plate #11 shows a spectacular COWBOY MICKEY RIDING PLUTO CELLULOID WINDUP. This is an extremely rare celluloid windup example. Plates #15 and #17 show two different styles of early 1930's celluloid windup trapeze toys. Because of their fragility, most owner/collectors are often reluctant to actually play with these toys. But the action is worth the risk. Wind one of these up. With a lubricated and free mechanism, they go wild!

The MICKEY IN WAGON PULLED BY PLUTO CELLULOID WINDUP in Plate #18 is particularly colorful and rare. A similar toy but a factory variation is the MICKEY PULLED BY PLUTO CELLULOID WINDUP pictured in Plate #16.

The MICKEY CELLULOID WINDUP DRUMMER shown in Plate #21 is an exceptionally rare celluloid piece. The nature of the mechanical windup action on this toy would tend to bring it almost to the point of destruction over the years. It is an oddity that one of these survived in such fine condition. Another MICKEY MOUSE WALKER CELLULOID WINDUP is pictured in Plate #23. The toy is identical to the one pictured in Plate #9, but the box is a different version. The MICKEY

NODDER CELLULOID WINDUP pictured in Plate #24 (Item A) runs on a simple rubber band mechanism strung from the metal base of the toy and attached at the neck. When the band is wound beneath the base, the tension activates a gear mechanism at the back of Mickey's neck and allows it to "nod."

The ROCKING HORSE MICKEY WOOD AND CELLULOID WINDUP pictured in Plate #26 features Mickey astride a wooden horse. This toy probably best depicts the combination wood and celluloid design found on many of the early 1930's Disney toys. Since both materials, wood and celluloid, were inexpensive, they were combined into some remarkable toys. The HOBBY HORSE MINNIE MOUSE pictured in Plate #25 is another example of the wood and celluloid combination.

A seeming myriad of possibilities exists when it comes to the form of Japanese celluloid windup toys from the early 1930's. Although many of the jointed-arm and jointed-leg Mickeys appear identical, they can be found driving, riding, standing, or twirling on seemingly endless toy designs. Plate #27 shows MICKEY MOUSE PULLED BY PLUTO in yet another windup example. Compare this to the Mickey wagon in Plate #18 and it is easy to see both striking similarities and distinct differences.

The CELLULOID MICKEY AND MINNIE ON TIN TRICYCLE WINDUP of Plate #28 is also a very rare toy. This toy is unique because it not only presents Mickey driving the tricycle mechanism, it also places a cute little Minnie Mouse in the back! Plates #29 and #30 picture two figural Minnies similar in form, but distinctly different. Plate #31 shows the SWINGING EXHIBITION FLIGHTS of Mickey and Minnie Mouse. This toy features Mickey and Minnie Mouse jointed figures which are joined at the hands on the swinging windup mechanism. An interesting point to note here is the unusual name for this toy. Close inspection of the box shows that the illustrated figures are clearly Mickey and Minnie Mouse, yet nowhere does their name appear in the title or box art. If the box was not present, it would be virtually impossible to guess the name of this toy. When the box is not available for any of the toys in this book, we have given the toy the most obvious or useful generic name. Who knows what some of the weird names are for the toys we picture here without boxes! "Swinging Exhibition Flights" would be a tough one to guess!

Two extremely similar MINNIE MOUSE ACROBAT WINDUPS are pictured in Plates #33 and #34. The metal frame is the same on both toys, but they are both pictured here to show one obvious difference. Notice the ears on both Minnies. The ears in Plate #33 are almost twice the size of those on the Minnie in Plate #34. Also, the shape of the head is slightly different.

MICKEY AND MINNIE ON CELLULOID ELEPHANT is another very rare toy, pictured in plate #35. A tiny Minnie Mouse rides straddling the elephant's trunk while a much larger Mickey Mouse rides on the elephant's back. Considering the fact that the Mickey Mouse is jointed and detachable, the elephant was manufactured in two parts – head and body – and the fact that the little Minnie is so small and easily lost, it is easy to understand why so few mint examples of this toy exist today. It is a fortunate collector who owns this complete toy!

The MICKEY MOUSE HOLDING A BALL CELLULOID FIGURE in Plate #37 is a colorful example of the variety found in the Mickey Mouse celluloid figures. In this version, it is obviously a pie-eyed, 1930's Mickey pictured, but he wears a stylish yellow cap, red sport shirt (with a black necktie!) and striped shorts. This is one stylish little ball player! The MINNIE MOUSE HULA DANCER CARNIVAL TOY pictured in Plate #38 is an oddity. Probably manufactured or intended as a crib toy, her arms and legs are made of springs and the "hula skirt" also wiggles with pleasing action. This toy must be hung to be appreciated, as it will not stand on its own.

Plates #39 and #40 show the toy and box for MICKEY AND MINNIE MOUSE AS ACROBATS. Compare this to the box and toy for SWINGING EXHIBITION FLIGHTS in Plate #31. The toys and boxes are identical! Only the name from the factory label is changed. Here stands yet another example of the difficulty of naming particular toys, especially when identical toys carried different names right from the factory! Two slightly different MICKEY MOUSE WHIRLYGIG toys are pictured in Plates #41 and #42. Both toys feature a windup rolling base mechanism which drives the toy in a complete circle and causes the canopy above to spin wildly. These are simple, yet visually exciting toys.

The MICKEY MOUSE THERMOMETER pictured in Plate #46 is particularly worthy of special note. Although it had a very common usage, few can be found today. The graphics on the face of the thermometer are superb, and Mickey's hand moves up and down as a pointer as the temperature rises or falls. The tall MICKEY MOUSE BOXER FIGURES pictured in Plate #47 were originally found on a windup platform toy. They are pictured here because of their unusual rarity showing Mickey Mouse wearing boxing gloves on each hand! The MICKEY AND DONALD IN A ROWBOAT is a much desired and extremely rare celluloid figure. This item, pictured in Plate #48, features a long-billed Donald Duck and a bulbous-nosed Mickey Mouse.

The three EGG TIMERS pictured in Plate #49 are all solid celluloid figures. Mickey Mouse, Donald Duck, and Minnie Mouse are what we believe to be the complete set. Plate #50 shows the CELLULOID MICKEY MOUSE BAND. All five of these little Mickeys wear derby style hats and play different musical instruments.

The large WOODEN FUN-E-FLEX MICKEY DOLL pictured in Plate #53 has hands often referred to as "lollipop hands" because of their unusual shape. As opposed to many later versions of Mickey dolls with wood composition parts, all of the parts that make up this wonderful doll are solid wood. The toy is entirely jointed. The MICKEY MOUSE DOLL pictured in Plate #54 is often credited with being the first Mickey toy ever produced. Because the label bears the earliest copyright date "c. 1928 Walter E. Disney" most collectors assume this is one of the very first Mickey Mouse toy designs. Those collectors who do not own this doll might find it interesting to note that it was not simply a static, figural piece. It also features an interesting (although somewhat crude) mechanical action. When the tail in the back is pushed down like a lever, Mickey's head pops up at the neck.

Beginning with Plate #55, this chapter introduces toys manufactured by Fun-E-Flex. Toys manufactured by this company have wooden heads and bodies with either spring or covered wire flexible arms and legs. Fun-E-Flex figures came in a wide array of sizes and designs. Two of the large versions of Mickey and Minnie Mouse are shown in Plate #55. The BALANCING MICKEY MOUSE pictured in Plate #56 is one of the most unique of all the solid wood jointed figural Mickeys. Because of the weight of Mickey's head and ears, he can balance his entire body on one arm horizontally. This is an amazing feat really, since it would appear that his center of gravity would actually be much further down on his body. This toy has a bright, diagonal label forming a stripe across his chest.

Plate #57 pictures an unusual FUN-E-FLEX MICKEY MOUSE IN ROWBOAT. This lonely looking little Mickey stands in a very realistic looking wooden boat. Plate #58 shows a virtual reunion of Fun-E-Flex figures. Notice the fourth figure from the left – an unusual variety of Minnie Mouse wearing a little cloth skirt. Plate #63 pictures an unusual MICKEY MOUSE ON A SPRINGBOARD wooden spring toy which bounces when tension is applied to it.

Plates #67 through #77 show the component parts of the now famous LIONEL MICKEY MOUSE CIRCUS TRAIN. A nearly mint-in-box version is shown displayed in its original packaging in Plate #68. The original box lid is pictured in Plate #67. This is one of the most aggressively sought-after toys by all Disneyana collectors, and what makes the set even more scarce is the interest in it by toy train collectors and general toy collectors alike. Functionally, the train is simple enough. It consists of three metal cars (Plates #75, #76, and #77) plus a stoker (coal car) with a mechanical "shoveling" Mickey. All of this is pulled around the metal track by a standard red engine, Lionel's popular Commodore Vanderbilt of the mid-1930's. The engine has a windup mechanism.

What makes the train set even more desirable are the "extras" that came along with the set. Also included was a series of cardboard punch-outs which could be assembled into a very large and impressive circus tent to stand in the middle of the oval track. The tent is pictured in Plates #71 through #74. Included was a composition figure of a waving Mickey Mouse, punch-out figures of a circus truck, buildings, a billboard, and further figures of Mickey and Minnie running to meet the train. All of these paper accessories have extremely bright and vivid early Mickey, Minnie, Horace Horsecollar, and Clarabelle Cow graphics. Absolutely complete sets of this toy are extremely hard to find. Consequently, a complete version of the LIONEL MICKEY MOUSE CIRCUS TRAIN in the box commands *big, big money* in the collector's marketplace. But, when considering all of the contents included in this set and the fact that only one missing piece can render it incomplete, the high value is less surprising. What Disneyana collector wouldn't like to step into a time machine and go back to a Christmas morning in the 1930's to pick up a couple of these sets under the Christmas tree? Well, at least we can dream.

Two versions of the LIONEL MICKEY MOUSE HAND CAR are pictured with their original boxes in Plates #78 and #79. Both a green based version and a red one have been pictured. This particular toy has more interesting mechanical action than the much more expensive LIONEL MICKEY MOUSE CIRCUS TRAIN mentioned previously. When this little windup handcar circles the track, the Mickey and Minnie Mouse figures pump up and down on the center handbar furiously. It is quite funny just watching this little toy work, for the figures do, indeed, seem to be propelling themselves madly around the track! Even today, after twenty years of hard Disney collecting has gone on across America, there are still hundreds of these little sets to be found, simply because so many thousands of these popular toys were produced. It is an accepted fact among Disneyana collectors and a well documented history that these toys, along with other Disney items in the Lionel train line, literally saved the toy train corporation from bankruptcy in the 1930's. These toys stand today as a tribute to the great marketing impact that Mickey

Mouse had upon both domestic and foreign manufacturers of toys in the 1930's.

Knickerbocker produced a wide assortment of Mickey Mouse, Minnie Mouse, and Donald Duck dolls in the 1930's. Several beautiful and striking examples are pictured in this section of the book. Plate #80 pictures a sharply dressed MICKEY BANDLEADER in his original coat and hat. Plate #81 pictures a giant version of the standard MICKEY MOUSE DOLL complete with his original tag and permanently attached composition shoes. Plate #82 pictures a pair of medium-sized MICKEY AND MINNIE MOUSE DOLLS, also with original Knickerbocker tags.

Plates #84 and #85 show superbly costumed COWBOY MICKEY AND COWGIRL MINNIE DOLLS. The Mickey Mouse in Plate #84 is missing his tiny toy guns, but appears otherwise complete. He still holds his original lasso. A very similar example of this toy in absolute mint condition sold two years ago in a national mail and phone auction for $16,000! And the darling COWGIRL MINNIE DOLL of Plate #85 complete with her fringed western skirt, hat, and cowgirl gloves is the best example of this toy that we have ever seen photographed!

Most collectors of dolls and teddy bears come into the collecting world with a great respect for the quality and at least a minimal knowledge of the toys manufactured by Steiff of Germany in the 1930's. Many of the Steiff dolls found today still have the distinctive mark that the company placed on them at the factory – a metal button punched through the ear. Many of today's knowledgeable Disneyana collectors could spot a Steiff doll from a tremendous distance even without the button simply because of the wonderful, recognizable design of these dolls. And this is good, because some of the identification buttons were pulled off either by wary mothers or inquisitive youngsters. Consequently, when the button is gone, there is usually a small hole in the ear.

The most common distinction of a Steiff doll is its velvet construction. The dolls are very plush and pleasant to touch and most examples have proved to be quite sturdy considering the effects of 60 years of soil, mold, mildew, and dry rot. Unfortunately, many of the Knickerbocker dolls mentioned earlier did not stand up quite as well since they were constructed of a thinner fabric. Many sizes and varieties of STEIFF MICKEY AND MINNIE MOUSE DOLLS from the 1930's can be found today, and all of them have in common that distinctive Steiff look. Plates #86 through #88 show several fine examples. Plate #89 pictures a rare Steiff hand puppet, still complete with his original tag and button in his ear!

The Dean's Rag Book Company of England manufactured an interesting series of Mickey and Minnie Mouse dolls during the 1930's. Most Disneyana collectors today either love or hate these dolls – there seems to be no in-between. Plate #94 shows a particularly interesting pair of DEAN'S RAG BOOK MICKEYS because the rare original label is shown with them. Plates #95 and #97 also picture DEAN'S RAG BOOK MICKEYS. The very ratty, toothy grin of these dolls is what endears them to some, and alienates them from other collectors. Actually, Mickey Mouse never really looked like the Dean's dolls in *any* of his films, even the early ones. But because many Disneyana collectors hold the particular contention that a ratty looking Mickey is the earliest Mickey, they are permanently bonded with their little English rodent chaps.

The giant MICKEY MOUSE BISQUE FIGURE pictured in Plate #100 is the largest bisque figure of Mickey manufactured in the 1930's. We use this super figure to introduce the section on Mickey and Minnie Mouse bisque figures. A bisque figure is made of fired ceramic material which was never glazed. Most bisque 1930's Disney figures were painted in many wonderful colors, but because a glaze was never applied, the paint is often worn away on early bisque examples.

Plate #101 pictures an absolutely "store stock" mint example of the MICKEY MOUSE MUSICIANS BISQUE SET. Note in particular the super graphics on the top box lid. Bisque sets found in such completely factory fresh condition are a real rarity. THE TWO PALS BISQUE SETS featuring Mickey and Minnie Mouse figures are pictured in Plates #102 and #103. Two identical versions are shown, with only the design of the box being different. Plate #104 pictures an even rarer set, THE THREE PALS, which contains figures of Mickey Mouse, Minnie Mouse, and Pluto. This set is also shown with the original box. Plates #105 through #110 picture a wide variety of Mickey and Minnie Mouse bisque toothbrush holders. Notice the two MINNIE MOUSE FIGURAL BISQUE TOOTHBRUSH HOLDERS shown in Plates #105 and #106. Although both have a looped arm and an indented foot to be used to hold a toothbrush, they are completely different figural designs of Minnie Mouse. The figure in Plate #105 is short and squatty with a more pointed nose, while the Minnie figure in Plate #106 is much taller with a more bulbous nose. Both are shown with 1930's vintage MICKEY MOUSE TOOTHBRUSHES.

Plates #107 and #108 picture two versions of MICKEY AND MINNIE MOUSE DUAL TOOTHBRUSH HOLDERS. Each of these bisque versions has two compartments in the back for toothbrushes. Plates #109 and #110 show additional varieties of standing figural toothbrush holders with jointed arms.

The early MICKEY MOUSE CHINA SUGAR BOWL with miniature mice as salt and pepper shakers is pictured in Plate #111. All are glazed ceramic, and on the back of the Mickey bowl is a small slot with a tiny ceramic sugar spoon in it. The entire set fits neatly on a ceramic tray which is marked on the bottom simply "Germany." This extremely rare piece is from the early 1930's and is even more unusual because of its depiction of Mickey without any color – as he was in the early black and white cartoons!

The MICKEY MOUSE IN THE CANOE BISQUE FIGURE is a rare one, as pictured in Plate #115. The MICKEY MOUSE VIOLIN PLAYER ASHTRAY is another unusual bisque design with a wobbly spring-legged Mickey made of bisque presiding over a glazed ceramic ashtray. The MICKEY AND MINNIE MOUSE SALT AND PEPPER SHAKERS pictured in Plate #123 are worthy of special note because of their unusual depiction of Mickey and Minnie in white clothes (which almost look like underwear!). These are a very rare and highly desirable set. Two lusterware ashtrays pictured in Plates #127 and #128 are also worthy of special attention. These pieces feature Mickey, Pluto, and Minnie figures. The MICKEY BASEBALL PLAYERS BISQUE SET pictured in Plate #130 is very rare and highly prized by today's Disneyana collectors because of the unusual design and its rarity. Pictured are Mickey as a fielder, batter, and catcher complete with mitt and pads!

The MICKEY MOUSE CHINA ALPHABET BOWL pictured in Plate #134 features a rather ratty looking Mickey playing a tambourine and surrounded by tiny figures of Mickey, Minnie, and an early Disney cat. The piece is marked on the reverse as "Bavarian China" and is one of the rarest versions of children's china manufactured in the 1930's. Notice here the absolute mint condition of the figure in the bottom of the bowl, which was often scarred and scratched from everyday use.

Many other examples of MICKEY MOUSE PATRIOT CHINA pieces are found in Plates #135 through #143. Examples of china from this company are desired by collectors because of the clear, full color graphics and high quality of design found on all the pieces manufactured by them. Patriot China is the usual marking on the reverse of most of these pieces, but occasionally pieces will be marked Salem China, which was the name of the actual company of production.

The MINNIE MOUSE CUP AND SAUCER shown in Plate #136 appears identical in design to the Patriot China pieces, but it is shown here only for comparison. This cup and saucer set was actually manufactured in England in the 1930's and is not a Patriot China piece. The FIREMAN MICKEY BOWL AND CUP SET pictured in Plate #140 is a rare and unusual themed set, because Mickey appears as a fireman on both pieces, and because the designs are different from each other.

The French MICKEY MOUSE ART DECO TEA SET pieces are worthy of special note since they represent imported china pieces. Both the large ceramic pitcher pictured in Plate #145 and the smaller creamer pictured in Plate #155 have superior Mickey and Minnie Mouse decals on both sides combined with a striking Art Deco concentric circle silver line design. Both items are beautifully marked on the bottom with French manufacturer names and copyright notations written in French, along with an attractive small graphic of a waving Mickey Mouse. The MICKEY MOUSE AND BETTY BOOP CERAMIC BOWL from the 1930's pictured in Plate #148 is a real oddity and a highly collectible knock-off (unauthorized) piece.

The Marks Brothers Company of Boston, Massachusetts, was responsible for bringing to the 1930's toy marketplace some of the most vivid and graphically appealing Disney toys ever produced. The line of toys manufactured by this company mainly included boxed games, target sets, and small hand-held novelty toys. Collectors often confuse Marks Brothers with Louis Marx Toy Company, which produced great 1930's Disney tin windups among a host of other wonderful windup toys. Louis Marx licensed and produced toys into the 1960's, but the Marks Brothers Company of Boston produced their fine line in the 1930's.

The MICKEY MOUSE HOOP-LA GAME pictured in Plate #157 and the MICKEY MOUSE BAGATELLE GAME pictured in Plate #158 are two of the largest games manufactured by this company. Notice the striking similarity of the two graphics of Mickey shown on the pieces.

One of the most unusual pieces, and probably the most outstanding toy design by this company, is the MICKEY MOUSE PIANO pictured in Plate #159 with its original box. The colors and Disney graphics on the piano are vibrant, and because this little piano not only plays real music but also features the mechanical movement of Mickey and Minnie Mouse jumping up and down whenever the keys are struck, it is the most desired 1930's Disney musical toy among today's Disneyana collectors. The MICKEY MOUSE ROLL'EM GAME pictured in Plate #160 presents six bright Mickey and Minnie figures ready to be bowled over by six solid wood balls. The MICKEY MOUSE SOLDIER SET pictured in Plate #162 is also a fine example of the beautiful full color graphics found in the toys designed by the Marks Brothers Company.

The MICKEY MOUSE CIRCUS GAME also manufactured by the Marks Brothers Company is not only one of the most beautiful graphic Disney designs ever manufactured by this company, it also has the most unique action. When a marble is placed in the cup of the top Mickey Mouse figure, it is then handed down from figure to figure until the marble finally is rolled from the bottom Minnie figure's cup, striking a bell and bouncing onto the lower bagatelle game board to score points. This is by far the rarest of all Marks Brothers games. Plates #163A and #163B picture the MICKEY MOUSE CIRCUS GAME vertical marble drop game board and the lower bagatelle board.

One of the most complete and highly collectible target sets manufactured by Marks Brothers is the MICKEY MOUSE POP GAME pictured in its entirety in Plates #163C and #164. This set is in astonishing near-mint condition and is complete with all targets, wooden support stands, seven original cork "bullets" and the mechanical pop gun. This set also features one of the most beautiful box lids found on any of the Marks Brothers games.

The MICKEY MOUSE SCATTER BALL GAME by Marks Brothers is shown in Plates #165 and #166. Although this is a more common game, the lively 1930's Mickeys printed all over the box and the game board make it a highly prized game collectible among Disney enthusiasts. And the complete set of MICKEY MOUSE PICTURE PUZZLES shown with their original box and storage trays in Plates #167 through #170 is a real rarity in this complete condition. The beauty of this set attests to the fact that this company produced exquisite designs for even simple toys like picture puzzles. The MICKEY MOUSE TARGET GAME found in Plates #171 and #172 is another astonishingly complete set that includes the target, target stand legs, six rubber-tipped darts, original metal dart gun and the original box! These games don't get any better than this!

The MICKEY MOUSE COMING HOME GAME pictured in Plate #176 is still another fine Marks Brothers design. Although the two main items which make up this game were originally not packaged together, the game board and the game tokens box make up the complete set. Evidently, when these items were sold in toy departments in the 1930's, the buyers would find the game boards and the small game boxes stacked separately on the shelves and then would purchase them together. Collectors should note that the small game box is often mistaken for a complete game, when in actuality it merely contained the playing pieces (dice, dice cup, tokens, and instructions) to be used along with the game board. The MICKEY MOUSE COMING HOME GAME is a wonderfully colorful game set with exciting early Mickey Mouse, Minnie Mouse, Clarabelle, Pluto, and Horace graphics.

Mickey Mouse toys manufactured by the Fisher Price Toy Company in the 1930's are highly popular among collectors today. After a very fine identification and price guide to all Fisher Price toys appeared in bookstores several years ago, prices for Fisher Price 1930's Disney items soared! Today, prices finally seem to have stabilized somewhat. But what used to be some of the best bargains in the toy marketplace – wooden pull toys – are bargains no more. All collector contributors to this book easily recall that only about five or six years ago Fisher Price Mickey Mouse toys could be purchased for well under $100, with many examples under $50. Those certainly were the "good old days" because those prices can no longer be found unless an unknowing dealer is selling them. The MICKEY MOUSE XYLOPHONE PLAYER pictured in Plate #188 is a good example of the colorful graphics found in toys manufactured by this company. All are similarly constructed completely of wood with colorful lithographed paper labels glued onto both sides.

The MICKEY MOUSE BAND PULL TOY manufactured by Fisher Price and marked "Walt Disney Enterprises" is pictured in Plate #189. This wonderful design presents Mickey playing a cymbal attached to Pluto's vertical tail and a drum attached to Pluto's feet. The toy is shown in this picture with a small Mickey sand pail to clarify its relative size. Examples of this toy can be found as pull toys or push toys with a long stick connected to the back.

The N.N. Hill Brass Company also manufactured fine Mickey Mouse pull toys in the 1930's. Two of their colorful examples are pictured in Plates #187 and #192. The Fisher Price Mickey toys of the 1930's are often more colorful and detailed, while the N.N. Hill Brass toys were evidently produced in smaller quantity and are much harder to find today.

The Ohio Art Company of Bryan, Ohio, produced a broad line of tin sandbox and beach toys with superb all-over lithography in the 1930's. Sand pails, toy drums, shovels, washing machines, sand sifters, vacuum cleaners, tea sets, and watering cans manufactured by Ohio Art are highly collectible today. We are proud to present in this volume one of the most well-rounded samples of the broad line of Ohio Art Disney toys that have ever been published.

Two superior versions of the prized MICKEY MOUSE WASHER toys are pictured in Plates #194 and #195. The washer shown in Plate #194 is an extremely rare MICKEY MOUSE WASHER with the factory attached wringer mechanism included in the design. There are two cranks on this version: one for the wringer, and one for the plunger mechanism inside the washer. The more standard yet still very rare MICKEY MOUSE WASHER without the wringer is pictured in Plate #195. Because the wonderful, practical design of a washer that actually held water and actually had a cranking plunger/agitator mechanism must have presented a great temptation to 1930's children to actually *use* these toys with a load of water, doll clothes, and soap, many examples of these toys are found badly rusted inside and outside. When purchasing one of these, always be sure to look inside. Collectors may be pleasantly surprised by a near mint example, or they may be stricken with horror when they find one nearly rusted-through.

The MICKEY AND MINNIE MOUSE SAND PAIL picturing Mickey and Minnie floating in a gondola down an Italian canal is a rare lithographed tin pail design. It shows the sophistication of the intricate lithography on Ohio Art toys and is pictured in Plate #193. The MICKEY MOUSE SWEEPER shown in Plate #198 exemplifies the company's vibrant use of bright primary colors in their lithographed designs and presents strong graphics of an early 1930's Mickey and Minnie Mouse. The MICKEY MOUSE SAND PAIL pictured in Plates #201 and #202 is one of the most colorful examples of all the sand pails. The MICKEY AND MINNIE MOUSE IN A ROWBOAT TEA TRAY pictured in Plate #205 shows how striking the colorful graphics can be! And the tea tray pictured in Plate #206 is unusual because it pictures all of the early Disney characters: Mickey, Minnie, Donald, Pluto, Horace, Clarabelle, and Goofy.

Two OHIO ART MICKEY MOUSE WATERING CAN examples are pictured in Plates #207 and #208. Once again, collectors should always check inside toys that may have been used with water. Severe rust on the inside is usually impossible to correct. Three different examples of MICKEY MOUSE SAND SIFTERS are pictured in Plates #211, #212, and #213.

A very beautiful and large TIN DRUM by Ohio Art is pictured in Plates #219 and #220. This design pictures all of the very early Disney characters (pre-1935, before Donald Duck) playing musical instruments and marching. Note the bright colors used on this particular design. Three other Ohio Art drum designs are pictured in Plates #221, #222, and #225.

The George Borgfeldt Corporation of New York was responsible for marketing several beautiful lithographed tin top designs decorated with Disney characters manufactured by Lackawanna Manufacturing Company of Hackettstown, New Jersey. These bright orange tin tops are pictured, smallest to largest, in Plates #226, #227, and #228.

The Geuder, Paeschke, and Frey Company also manufactured several attractive tin lithographed pieces with Disney character designs in the 1930's. The rarest of their items is the MICKEY MOUSE LUNCH KIT pictured in Plate #238. This company also manufactured several different DISNEY WASTEBASKETS. One of these examples is pictured in Plate #237.

The photographic section on 1930's Mickey Mouse items continues with an extensive sampling of the line of merchandise manufactured by the Joseph Dixon Company, which specialized in school supplies. Plates #254 to #261 display many of the schoolboxes and pencil cases with early Mickey Mouse and Disney designs. It is a rare treat when collectors stumble upon any of these pencil cases complete with their original contents of erasers, Mickey Mouse pencils, Mickey Mouse rulers, and in some cases, Mickey Mouse maps!

Several extremely rare books lead off the section of printed material highlighted in this chapter. The *MICKEY MOUSE WADDLE BOOK*, published by Blue Ribbon Books in 1934, is by far the rarest of all the books pictured here when found complete with its punch-out waddles. Even without the waddles intact it is dynamically colorful and attractive, but the addition of the complete punch-out waddles and their graphic downhill slope makes this a fantastic collectible piece. The book is pictured in Plate #262, and the waddle figures are in Plate #263. Note the wrap-around paper belt pictured along with the cover in Plate #262. It helped to hold the detachable waddle section into the book until the waddles were ready to be punched out.

Also pictured in the book section of this chapter is the extremely beautiful pop-up book, *MICKEY MOUSE IN KING ARTHUR'S COURT*, also published by Blue Ribbon Books. The front and back covers of this book are pictured in Plates #264 and #265, while the absolutely gorgeous inside pop-up figures are pictured in Plates #266 through #269. Other more common but equally attractive books published by Blue Ribbon Books are *THE POP-UP MICKEY MOUSE* pictured in Plate #270 and *THE POP-UP MINNIE MOUSE* pictured in Plates #272 and #273. Many other fine 1930's Mickey Mouse books are pictured in this chapter. Most are by Whitman Publishing, but several were published by the Saalfield Publishing Company of Ohio. The die-cut *MICKEY MOUSE BOOK FOR COLORING* published by Saalfield is worthy of note because of the unusual shape of the cover. Also worthy of special attention is *THE STORY OF MICKEY MOUSE, THE BIG BIG BOOK* pictured in Plate #276 with its highly colorful cover. The *MICKEY MOUSE ILLUSTRATED MOVIE STORIES* hardcover book published by David McKay in 1931 is particularly interesting because of its very attractive cover, its huge thickness (190 very heavy pages), and its inclusion of animated "flip pages" which allowed children to flip the bottom corners of the pages to watch Mickey Mouse dance. This latter feature was nice for the 1930's children who owned the books, but it often caused the pages to wear out quickly or tear, much to the dismay of modern collectors. This book is pictured in Plate #277.

The three MICKEY MOUSE LAMPS in Plates #310 through #312 were all manufactured by the Soreng-Manegold Company and are worthy of special attention. The examples in Plates #310 and #312 both are identical except they each have a different design of the original shade. Examples of these lamps with the original shade are extremely rare and hard to find in the collectors' marketplace. The lamp pictured in Plate #311 is extremely rare with its unusual long-billed Donald decal on the base of the Mickey Mouse filament bulb.

The MICKEY MOUSE TAMBOURINE, manufactured by Noble and Cooley in the 1930's, has very bright and clear graphics of both Mickey and Minnie, as is pictured in Plate #314. The MICKEY MOUSE PARTY HORN, NOISE MAKER, and GIANT PARTY HORN which were all manufactured by Marks Brothers of Boston and are pictured in Plates #315A and #315B represent one common item (the small party horn) along with two rarer variations.

Micro-Lite manufactured the wonderful little MICKEY MOUSE NIGHT LIGHT pictured in Plate #334. This small tin piece is unusual because it represents a battery-operated light item even as early as the 1930's. The MICKEY MOUSE FLASHLIGHT manufactured by USA Light in the 1930's and shown in Plate #335 with its original box is extremely rare with superb box graphics and beautiful tin lithography on the flashlight itself.

The MICKEY MOUSE TALKIE JECKTOR complete boxed set as pictured in Plate #336 along with the display box of MOVIE-JECKTOR FILMS shown in Plate #337 features an actual sound recording added to simple animation. When the Talkie-Jecktor is cranked, an internal mechanism allows two slightly different Mickey Mouse pictures to be shown through two different projection lenses in rapid sequence, thus producing a crude but effective animation effect. The Talkie-Jecktor has a built-in record player to include sound. The sheer novelty of this item combined with its interesting action and wonderful film and box graphics makes it very desirable among today's collectors.

Certainly the MICKEY MOUSE EMERSON RADIO pictured in plate #341 is worthy of note (shown here with original box!). The wood composition cabinet of the radio has a woodcarved look and is one of the most sought-after early Disney items. The SEIBERLING LATEX HARD RUBBER MICKEY MOUSE FIGURES pictured in Plates #348 and #349 are excellent likenesses of the 1930's Mickey. Because the rubber structure of these solid figures tends to degrade with age, it is hard to find examples of these in mint condition that still stand.

The MICKEY MOUSE SILVERPLATE SPOON AND FORK SET, manufactured by the William Rogers and Son International Silver Company and shown in Plate #352, includes the original gift presentation box decorated with a bright Mickey Mouse graphic inside and little black and white Mickeys all over the top of the orange box lid. A companion piece to this set is the MICKEY MOUSE SILVERPLATE PORRINGER pictured in Plate #364 (it originally sold for $2.00). It is also pictured complete with its original box and original Mickey Mouse price card. These items are rarely found boxed.

The store display for the PAAS EASTER PARADE MICKEY MOUSE TRANSFER-O-S is pictured in Plate #374. Although the packaged transfers themselves are not an uncommon item, the original store display is extremely rare! A piece such as this is sought mainly for its bright graphics and particular rarity.

Two beautiful MICKEY MOUSE WATCHES manufactured by the Ingersoll Company in the 1930's are pictured in Plates #384 and #385. Both are shown with their original boxes. The addition of a graphically interesting box for a watch in mint condition can sometimes nearly double its value! The INGERSOLL MICKEY MOUSE POCKET WATCH complete with fob and original box is pictured in Plate #386. Notice the difference in design of the two watches shown in Plates #385 and #386. Mickey Mouse watches from the 1930's are considered the "Cadillacs" of all character watch collectibles because their popularity and design in the 1930's inspired so many of the later character watches.

We have attempted to take both the novice and the advanced collector on a whirlwind tour of over 400 "golden age" vintage Mickey and Minnie Mouse toys. The trip may seem overwhelming at first, but the sheer scope of vintage items that are still out at the flea markets, toy shows, antique shows, and antique malls waiting to be collected is absolutely mind-boggling. To paraphrase a quite popular toy collecting adage, "There is so little time ... and so many toys!" The vintage Mickey Mouse toys are certainly still out there. They may cost a little or a lot more than they did a few years ago. And if a collector is willing to wait a little longer, there are still occasional bargains. We hope our chapter on Mickey and Minnie Mouse collectibles from the 1930's has been helpful to Disneyana collectors of all levels. Now, may the great "Mouse Hunt" begin – or continue!

PLATE I: MICKEY MOUSE HURDY GURDY is a German windup probably made by the Distler Company. Minnie is rarely found on this toy.

PLATE 2: MICKEY MOUSE DRUMMER was manufactured by Nifty Toys. When the lever is depressed, the arms move to beat the drum.

PLATE 3: MICKEY AND MINNIE MOUSE PLAYLAND is one of the rarest of all Disney toys. It was distributed by the George Borgfeldt Corporation.

PLATE 4: MICKEY AND MINNIE PLAYLAND BOX was produced in Japan.

PLATE 5: MICKEY AND MINNIE ON THE MOTORCYCLE TIN WINDUP was produced in Germany by the Tripp Company. It is one of the earliest examples of Disney tin lithography.

PLATE 6: MICKEY MOUSE SPARKLER was made by the Nifty Toy Company. Note the "Luna" face, which is the trademark of Nifty, on the box.

PLATE 7: MICKEY MOUSE DRUMMER by Nifty. This is a slightly different version of the toy in Plate #2.

PLATE 8: MICKEY MOUSE PLASTER COMPOSITION LAMP manufactured by Soreng-Manegold, 1930's. This is one of the most desirable of the early Disney lamps. The sculpture of Mickey in the chair is an excellent likeness.

PLATE 9: RAMBLING MICKEY MOUSE CELLULOID WINDUP was distributed by the George Borgfeldt Company in 1934. The windup mechanism is encased in his body.

PLATE 10: HOBBY HORSE MICKEY MOUSE is made of celluloid and uses a spring mechanism. The hobby horse is made of wood.

PLATE 11: COWBOY MICKEY RIDING ON PLUTO is an unusual celluloid windup with a wooden base. It features a very simple early windup mechanism that simulates the rocking motion.

PLATE 12: COWBOY MICKEY MOUSE CELLUOID ON WOODEN HORSE is a very unusual toy. Pushing down on the tail propels the toy.

PLATE 13: MICKEY AND MINNIE CELLUOID NURSERY DOLLS are made in vibrant colors. It is rare to find Minnie's original flowers.

PLATE 14: MICKEY MOUSE ON A TRICYCLE celluloid and tin windup toy, 1930's manufactured in Japan.

PLATE 15: DONALD AND MINNIE ON TRAPEZE is a very rare celluloid windup toy. This combination of characters in rarely seen.

PLATE 16: MICKEY PULLED BY PLUTO CELLULOID TIN WINDUP utilizes a mechanism under Pluto.

PLATE 17: MICKEY AND MINNIE ACROBATS were made in Occupied Japan. The figures are celluloid.

PLATE 18: MICKEY IN WAGON PULLED BY PLUTO CELLULOID WINDUP cart is English but was produced in Japan for the English market.

PLATE 19: MICKEY MOUSE BALANCING WHIRLYGIG is made of celluloid. When the toy is wound Mickey turns.

PLATE 20: MINNIE MOUSE CELLULOID WHIRLYGIG ON CART was made in Japan in the 1930's. The umbrella and balls are also celluloid.

PLATE 21: MICKEY MOUSE WINDUP DRUMMER utilizes a celluloid Mickey. This is an extremely rare celluloid toy.

PLATE 22: MICKEY MOUSE INGERSOLL WRIST WATCH and original store display, 1930's. Display card is cardboard.

PLATE 23: MICKEY MOUSE WALKER CELLULOID WINDUP. 7" tall. This is the rarer of the two boxes for this toy.

PLATE 24: ITEM A - MICKEY MOUSE CELLULOID WINDUP NODDER, circa early 1930's, is made in Japan. When wound, Mickey "nods" his head. ITEM B - MICKEY MOUSE CELLULOID PENCIL SHARPENER, 1930's. Metal sharpener is in base.

PLATE 25: HOBBY HORSE MINNIE MOUSE is a simple toy that was made popular by adding Minnie to it.

PLATE 26: ROCKING HORSE MICKEY MOUSE is one of the few hand painted wooden windups featuring Mickey Mouse that were produced in the 1930's.

PLATE 27: MICKEY PULLED BY PLUTO WINDUP. When wound the cart goes along the floor and Pluto bobs up and down.

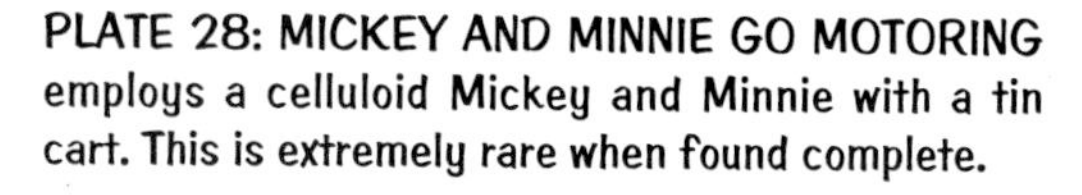

PLATE 28: MICKEY AND MINNIE GO MOTORING employs a celluloid Mickey and Minnie with a tin cart. This is extremely rare when found complete.

PLATE 29: MINNIE MOUSE CELLULOID NURSERY DOLL has a string tail. Note design of eyelashes.

PLATE 30: MINNIE MOUSE CELLULOID NURSERY DOLL has movable arms. Notice how this design differs from Minnie in Plate #29.

PLATE 31: SWINGING EXHIBITION FLIGHTS MICKEY AND MINNIE ACROBATS are made of celluloid. This is a very rare and unusual box.

PLATE 32: MICKEY ON WOODEN SCOOTER is one of the few celluloid toys that utilizes a vehicle of this sort.

PLATE 33: MINNIE MOUSE ACROBAT was made in Japan and imported into the United States.

PLATE 34: MINNIE MOUSE ACROBAT is made of celluloid and goes over metal bar when wound.

PLATE 35: MICKEY AND MINNIE ON CELLULOID ELEPHANT was made in Japan in 1934. The elephant is 10" long and 8" high, making it one of the largest celluloid toys.

PLATE 36: MICKEY MOUSE COWBOY ON WOODEN HORSE. This toy shows the unique combination of a celluloid figure on an interesting wooden toy.

PLATE 37: MICKEY MOUSE HOLDING A BALL. This is a most unusual celluloid design.

PLATE 38: MINNIE MOUSE HULA DANCER CARNIVAL TOY has spring arms and a string skirt. Her hands are composition.

PLATE 39: MICKEY AND MINNIE AS ACROBATS BOX is one variation of the box for this toy.

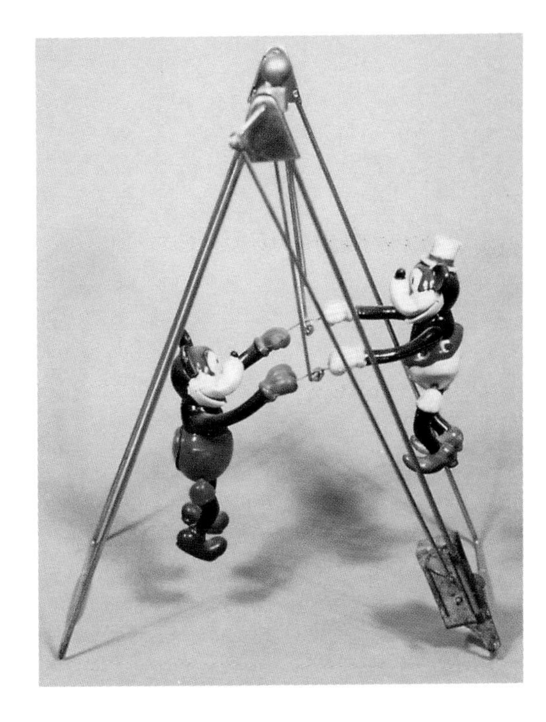

PLATE 40: MICKEY AND MINNIE AS ACROBATS are both made of celluloid.

PLATE 41: MICKEY MOUSE WHIRLYGIG CELLULOID WIND-UP. As this toy moves in a circle the canopy above rotates. This toy exhibits excellent action for a relatively simple design.

PLATE 42: MICKEY MOUSE ON CART is an early celluloid windup. This is a slightly different version from the one pictured in Plate #41.

PLATE 43: MICKEY MOUSE NURSERY DOLL has movable arms. The head is referred to as bulbous, oversized in comparison to the body.

PLATE 44: ROLLOVER MICKEY was made by the Schuco Company in Germany.

PLATE 45: CELLULOID MINNIE ON CELLULOID BALL is an unusual example of an all celluloid toy.

PLATE 46: MICKEY THERMOMETER is an example of an everyday item that featured Mickey Mouse.

PLATE 47: LARGE 8" CELLULOID MICKEY MOUSE BOXERS (from a 1930's platform toy). One figure wears red trunks and the other wears green ones.

PLATE 48: MICKEY AND DONALD IN A ROWBOAT is all celluloid and is one of the few celluloids that feature Mickey and Donald together.

PLATE 51: MICKEY MOUSE CRIB TOY is made of wood and makes noises when shaken.

PLATE 49: CELLULOID EGG TIMERS were used in kitchens everywhere in the 1930's. These examples are English.

PLATE 52: MICKEY MOUSE RATTLE is made of celluloid and utilizes bead-like hands and ears.

PLATE 50: CELLULOID MICKEY MOUSE BAND figures in vibrant colors.

PLATE 53: **WOODEN FUN-E-FLEX MICKEY** identified by his hands, referred to as "lollipop hands."

PLATE 54: **MICKEY MOUSE WOODEN TOY** is thought to be the first American made Disney toy. It is made of wood, leatherette and rope.

PLATE 55: **FUN-E-FLEX MICKEY AND MINNIE** are 7" tall and made of wood. They are marked "Walt E. Disney."

PLATE 56: BALANCING MICKEY MOUSE is the only wooden Mickey Mouse that can be positioned into a variety of stances. He is 4½" tall.

PLATE 59: MICKEY AND MINNIE FUN-E-FLEX FIGURES are 5" tall and were made in Japan. It is difficult to find Minnie with her dress intact.

PLATE 57: MICKEY IN ROWBOAT has a Fun-E-Flex Mickey in a wooden rowboat with words "Mickey Mouse 28" on boat.

PLATE 58: FUN-E-FLEX MICKEYS AND MINNIES are all 3½" tall, made of wood, and have "boxing glove" hands.

PLATE 60: MICKEY AND MINNIE FUN-E-FLEX are 7" tall. These larger Fun-E-Flex figures are much rarer than the smaller ones.

PLATE 61: MICKEY MOUSE CANES. Both utilize Fun-E-Flex heads. Note identification by Fun-E-Flex decals on handles.

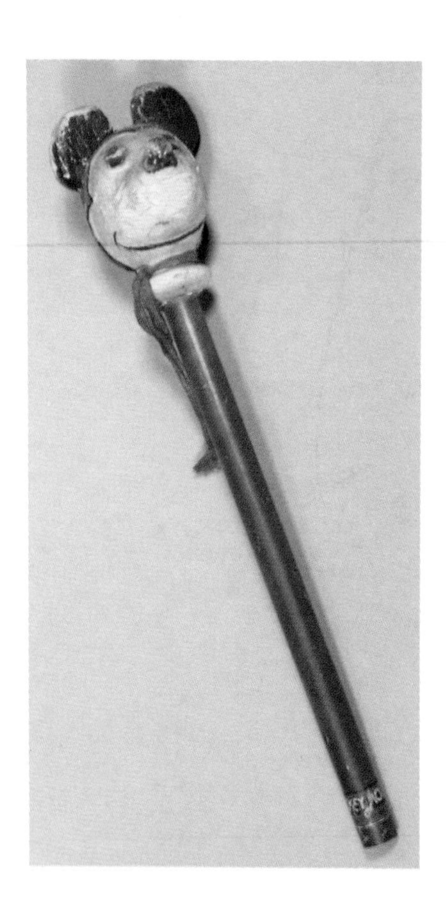

PLATE 62: MICKEY MOUSE BATON has a composition head. The label on the bottom is marked Walt Disney.

PLATE 63: MICKEY MOUSE SPRINGBOARD shows the many toys that used Fun-E-Flex figures.

PLATE 64: FUN-E-FLEX MINNIE that has "four-fingered" hands is made of wood.

PLATE 65: MINNIE MOUSE WOOD FIGURES show the many sizes of Fun-E-Flex.

PLATE 66: MICKEY MOUSE WOOD FIGURES show different hand configurations that were used.

PLATE 67: LIONEL MICKEY MOUSE CIRCUS TRAIN BOX. Note how box lid pictures all component parts of the complete set.

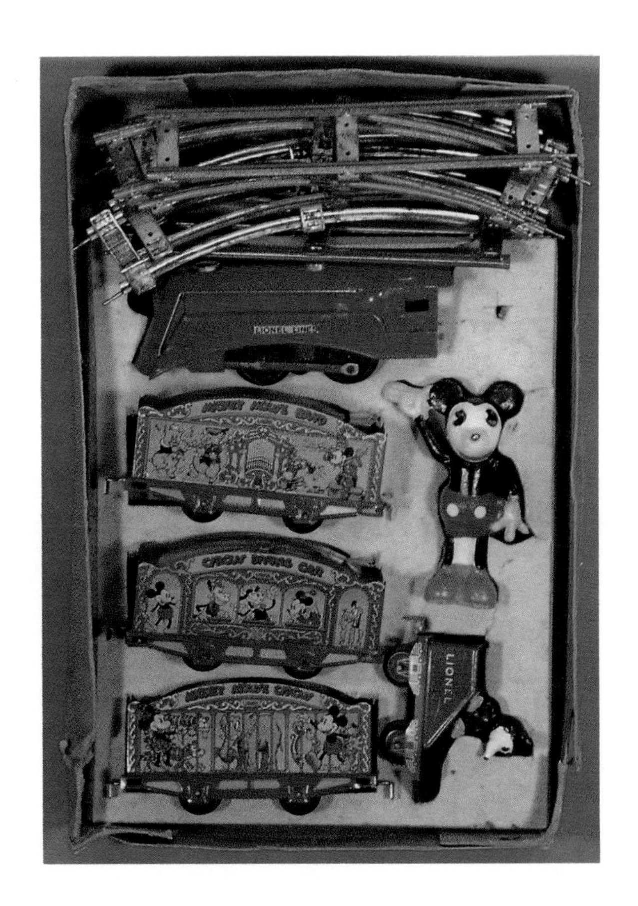

PLATE 68: LIONEL MICKEY MOUSE CIRCUS TRAIN and waving Mickey Barker figure. This set contains its original packaging card.

PLATE 69: MICKEY MOUSE CIRCUS TRAIN by Lionel is an early example of beautiful tin lithography.

PLATE 70: PAPER CUT OUTS that went with circus train produced by Lionel in the 1930's.

PLATE 71: MICKEY MOUSE LIONEL CIRCUS TRAIN CARDBOARD TENT (front view).

PLATE 73: MICKEY MOUSE CIRCUS TRAIN TENT shows incredible detailed graphics (side view).

PLATE 72: MICKEY MOUSE LIONEL CIRCUS TRAIN TENT (rear view).

PLATE 74: MICKEY MOUSE CIRCUS TENT from Mickey Lion Circus Train, 1930's (other side view.)

PLATE 75: MICKEY MOUSE CIRCUS DINING CAR of the Lionel Circus Train.

PLATE 76: MICKEY MOUSE CIRCUS CAR from Lionel Mickey Circus Train, 1930's.

PLATE 77: MICKEY MOUSE BAND CAR from the 1930's Mickey Lionel Circus Train.

PLATE 78: LIONEL MICKEY MOUSE HAND CAR, 1930's, c. Walt Disney Enterprises. Shown here is the red body version. Mickey and Minnie pump the handcar bar up and down as it moves around the track.

PLATE 79: LIONEL MICKEY MOUSE HAND CAR, 1930's c. Walt Disney Enterprises. Green body version is shown.

PLATE 80: GIANT MICKEY MOUSE 1930's BAND LEADER DOLL with composition shoes, by Knickerbocker Toy Company.

PLATE 81: MICKEY MOUSE KNICKERBOCKER DOLL is 21" tall with composition shoes. It is the largest Knickerbocker doll.

PLATE 82: MICKEY AND MINNIE KNICKERBOCKER DOLLS are 14" tall. Both have original store tags.

PLATE 83: SMALL COWBOY MICKEY was made by the Knickerbocker Doll Company in 1936. Mickey has tufted chaps which held two guns.

PLATE 84: LARGE COWBOY MICKEY MOUSE was produced by the Knickerbocker Toy Company. The shoes are composition.

PLATE 85: COWGIRL MINNIE is the companion doll to Cowboy Mickey. Her holster is made of leather.

PLATE 86: MICKEY MOUSE STEIFF DOLL was made by the Margarete Steiff Company of Germany. The doll is 7" tall and has original tag.

PLATE 87: MICKEY MOUSE STEIFF DOLL is 9" tall and made of velvet. The Steiff trademark is a metal button and tag punched into the left ear.

PLATE 88: MICKEY MOUSE STEIFF DOLL is 11" tall. The doll has both the metal tag and paper tag. All buttons on Steiff dolls are mother-of-pearl.

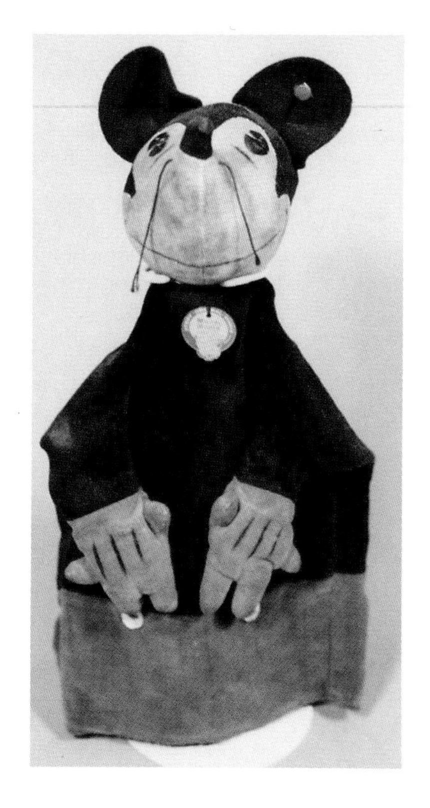

PLATE 89: MICKEY MOUSE STEIFF HAND PUPPET is made of sateen and velvet material and wood pulp. The mouth is drawn on and the whiskers are made of string.

PLATE 90: MICKEY MOUSE LARGE FUN-E-FLEX is 9¼" high. The head is composition. The wire tail is cloth covered and the body is jointed and fully flexible.

PLATE 91: MICKEY MOUSE FRENCH BANK was made of aluminum by the Depeche Company.

PLATE 92: MICKEY MOUSE CLOTH DOLL by Knickerbocker, 1930's, 14" with compostition shoes. This is a standard version of the doll. Note the stitched together fingers.

PLATE 93: MICKEY MOUSE CLOTH DOLL by Knickerbocker, 1930's, with starched felt shoes, 12" tall. Mickey's head can turn to the left or right on this doll.

PLATE 94: DEAN'S RAG BOOK MICKEY MOUSES are 5" tall. The tag reads "A1 toys are hygienic, Mickey Mouse, Made in England by Dean's Rag Book Co. LTD."

PLATE 95: DEAN'S RAG BOOK MICKEY MOUSE is 8" tall. These dolls are noted for their thinner bodies, five-fingered hands and their toothy sneer.

PLATE 96: MICKEY MOUSE DIXON COMPOSITION PEN AND PENCIL HOLDER, 1930's, shown with original fountain pen.

PLATE 97: DEAN'S RAG BOOK MICKEY MOUSE was discontinued by Walt Disney because the rat-like look frightened children.

PLATE 98: MICKEY MOUSE WOOD COMPOSITION DOLL WITH JOINTED HEAD AND ARMS, 1930's by Knickerbocker. This is the standard version of this doll. Other versions are Mickey wearing additional costumes.

PLATE 99: MICKEY MOUSE STEIFF DOLL has original store tag and Steiff button.

PLATE 100: MICKEY MOUSE BISQUE is the largest Mickey Mouse bisque produced. Mickey is 9½" tall and both arms are movable.

PLATE 101: MUSICAN BOXED BISQUE SET was manufactured in Japan. The figures are hand painted and are 3½" tall.

PLATE 102: THE TWO PALS BOXED BISQUE SET was made in Japan. The original sticker on Mickey's foot is marked "Mickey Mouse copy. 1928, 1930 by Walter Disney."

PLATE 103: MICKEY AND MINNIE THE TWO PALS BISQUE FIGURES, c. Walt Disney Enterprises, dist. by George Borgfeldt, 1930's. Boxed examples in mint condition are very hard to find.

PLATE 104: THE THREE PALS BOXED BISQUE SET is an excellent example of the colorful and graphic box used.

PLATE 105: MINNIE MOUSE TOOTHBRUSH HOLDER is referred to as "bulbous" because of her oversized head.

PLATE 106: ITEM A – MINNIE MOUSE BISQUE TOOTHBRUSH HOLDER figure with movable arm, 1930's. **ITEM B – ORIGINAL CELLULOID MICKEY MOUSE BAKELITE TOOTHBRUSH,** 1930's.

PLATE 107: MICKEY AND MINNIE MOUSE BISQUE TOOTHBRUSH HOLDER, 1930's 5" tall. This held two toothbrushes. Copyright Walt E. Disney. This is one of the most common toothbrush holders.

PLATE 108: MICKEY, MINNIE AND PLUTO BISQUE TOOTHBRUSH HOLDER was made in Japan. It is marked "Walt E. Disney" on the back.

PLATE 109: MICKEY AND MINNIE TOOTHBRUSH HOLDERS each have one movable arm.

PLATE 110: MICKEY MOUSE TOOTHBRUSH HOLDERS are called "bulbous" because of the oversized head.

PLATE 111: MICKEY MOUSE GLAZED CHINA SUGAR BOWL, TRAY, SALT AND PEPPER SHAKERS, 1930's, marked "made in Germany" on bottom. The Mickey sugar bowl in this rare set is 4" tall.

PLATE 112: ITEM A - MICKEY MOUSE JOINTED ARM 5" BISQUE TOOTHBRUSH HOLDER, 1930's, Walt E. Disney. ITEM B - MINNIE MOUSE 5" BISQUE TOOTHBRUSH HOLDER WITH JOINTED ARM, 1930's, Walt E. Disney.

PLATE 113: MICKEY MOUSE, DONALD DUCK, AND MINNIE MOUSE BISQUE TOOTHBRUSH HOLDER, 1930's, c. Walt E. Disney. This is the only bisque toothbrush holder design that unites Mickey, Minnie and Donald.

PLATE 114: ITEM A - MICKEY MOUSE STANDING FIGURAL BISQUE TOOTHBRUSH HOLDER with jointed arm, 5", 1930's. ITEM B - 3" MICKEY MOUSE FIGURE, BISQUE, WITH BULBOUS NOSE, 1930's, playing French horn.

PLATE 115: BISQUE MICKEY MOUSE IN BISQUE CANOE was made in Japan. The canoe is 5" long, which is oversized.

PLATE 116: ITEM A - MICKEY WITH CANE AND HAT 1930's bisque. ITEM B - MICKEY MOUSE CERAMIC ASHTRAY, 1930's, with wobbly spring-legged fiddler Mickey.

PLATE 117: GIANT MICKEY MOUSE CREAM PITCHER, made out of glazed ceramic. This pitcher shows the design of an early Mickey Mouse and measures approximately 8" tall.

PLATE 118: MICKEY MOUSE BANJO PLAYER BISQUE FIGURE, 5½" tall. made in Japan. This musical fellow is one of an entire set of musical Mickeys.

PLATE 119: ITEM A - MICKEY MOUSE BASEBALL CATCHER BISQUE FIGURE, 1930's. ITEM B - MICKEY MOUSE RIDING PLUTO BISQUE FIGURE, Japan 1930's. Both bisque figures still have excellent original paint.

PLATE 120: MICKEY MOUSE PLAYING THE SAXOPHONE Japanese bisque figure is approximately 3½" tall. The rounded nose in this great 1930's example is often refered to as "bulbous" Mickey.

PLATE 121: MICKEY AND MINNIE IN NIGHTSHIRTS BISQUES were made as a pair. Note how the figures face each other by design.

PLATE 122: SET OF FOUR MICKEY AND MINNIE MOUSE MUSICIANS. All are 3½" bisque figures made in Japan in the 1930's. Note that each figure plays a different musical instrument.

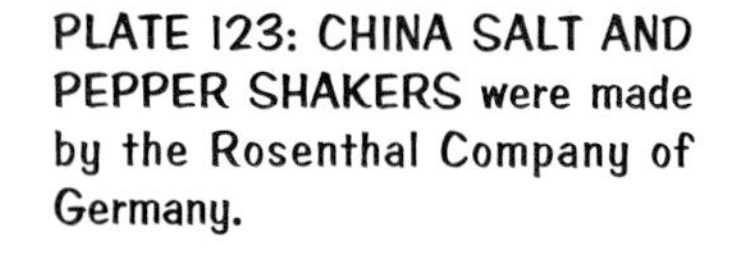

PLATE 123: CHINA SALT AND PEPPER SHAKERS were made by the Rosenthal Company of Germany.

PLATE 124: MICKEY MOUSE CELLULOID SPRING ARMED FIGURE. Notice Mickey's unusual red-striped pants.

PLATE 125: MINNIE MOUSE PINCUSHION is a rare bisque piece. It is unusual to find a bisque figurine that features an inanimate object with Mickey or Minnie.

PLATE 126: MICKEY MOUSE CERAMIC ASHTRAY is marked "Walt Disney Enterprises" on the bottom. Ashtray has a lusterware finish.

PLATE 127: MINNIE MOUSE GLAZED CERAMIC ASHTRAY, Japan, 1930's. This wonderfully graphic version of Minnie is glazed with a "Lusterware" finish and is designed with 1930's art deco styling.

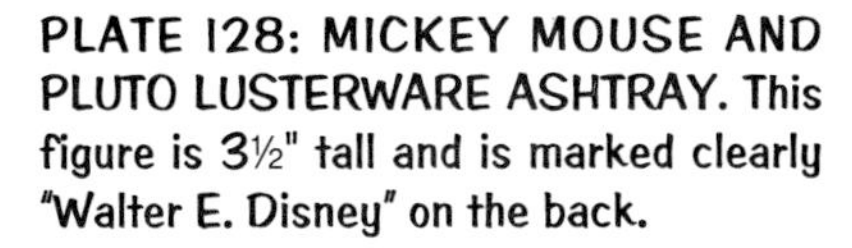

PLATE 128: MICKEY MOUSE AND PLUTO LUSTERWARE ASHTRAY. This figure is 3½" tall and is marked clearly "Walter E. Disney" on the back.

PLATE 130: MICKEY MOUSE BISQUE BASEBALL SET is composed of three 3¼" figures, each depicting a different baseball position.

PLATE 129: MICKEY MOUSE MUSICIAN BISQUES are 5" tall. They have string tails. Shown are Mickey playing the horn and the banjo.

PLATE 131: MICKEY MOUSE CERAMIC EGG TIMER was made in Czechoslovakia. Mickey plays a banjo on this design.

PLATE 132: MICKEY MOUSE CERAMIC ASHTRAY utilizes the early rat-faced Mickey.

PLATE 133: MINNIE MOUSE CHILD'S CERAMIC PLATE manufactured by Patriot China, of Salem, Massachusetts, in the 1930's. This particular pink-rimmed design is very rare, as most ceramics by this company had a thin orange stripe on the rim. It is marked c. Walt Disney Enterprises.

PLATE 134: MICKEY MOUSE BAVARIAN CHINA CHILD'S ALPHABET BOWL. Pictured here is a rather ratty looking Mickey with the unusual five fingered glove design found on some early imported pieces. Tiny figures of Mickey, Minnie, Horace, and an early Disney cat surround the inside bowl rim.

PLATE 135: MINNIE MOUSE PATRIOT CHINA PLATE manufactured by Salem China in the 1930's. This particular piece shows the vibrant graphics of Minnie Mouse with the standard orange decorative rim. Marked c. Walt Disney Enterprises.

PLATE 136: MINNIE MOUSE CHILD'S CUP AND SAUCER, made in the 1930's. A cute little Minnie Mouse is pictured reading a letter on this design. The matching saucer is plain.

PLATE 137: MINNIE MOUSE CHILD'S GLAZED CUP by Patriot China, the children's ceramic line of the Salem China Company. This colorful 1930's design pictures Minnie brushing her mouse "hair." Marked c. Walt Disney Enterprises.

PLATE 138: MICKEY MOUSE CHILD'S CERAMIC BOWL by Patriot China, and manufactured in the 1930's. The underglaze decals used on all Patriot China pieces are extremely bright and graphic. Marked c. Walt Disney Enterprises.

PLATE 139: MICKEY, MINNIE, DONALD, AND PLUTO GLAZED CERAMIC CHILD'S MUG by Patriot China in the 1930's. This is one of the more unusual designs since it shows so many early Disney characters. Of particular interest to collectors is the long-billed Donald pictured in this scene. Marked Walt Disney Enterprises.

PLATE 140: MICKEY MOUSE "FIREMAN MICKEY" CHILD'S GLAZED CERAMIC MUG AND BOWL by Patriot China in the 1930's. It is a proud collector who can own a matched set of any of the more unusual Patriot China designs! Marked c. Walt Disney Enterprises.

PLATE 141: MINNIE MOUSE CUP AND SAUCER CHILD'S GLAZED CHINA SET manufactured by Patriot China in the 1930's. The Minnie Mouse decal designs are identical. Marked c. Walt Disney Enterprises.

PLATE 142: MICKEY MOUSE CHILD'S DIVIDED DISH by Patriot China. This dish was manufactured in the 1930's and is marked on the back "c. Walt Disney Enterprises."

PLATE 143: MICKEY MOUSE AND PLUTO GLAZED CERAMIC CHILD'S PLATE by Patriot China of the Salem China Company in the 1930's. This is a particularly desirable design because of the appearance of both Mickey and Pluto on the plate. Marked c. Walt Disney Enterprises.

PLATE 144: MICKEY MOUSE BOXED TEA SET was made in Japan and the pieces are lusterware.

PLATE 146: MICKEY AND MINNIE MOUSE GLAZED CHINA PITCHER from France in the 1930's. This picture shows the Minnie figure on the reverse of the design in Plate #145. This beautiful ceramic piece has exceptional Art Deco trim.

PLATE 145: MICKEY AND MINNIE MOUSE CERAMIC PITCHER. This giant 10" glazed ceramic pitcher was manufactured in France during the 1930's and pictures a wonderful graphic of Mickey stirring his tea.

PLATE 147: MICKEY MOUSE CERAMIC CUP was manufactured by the Krueger Company in Germany.

PLATE 148: MICKEY MOUSE AND BETTY BOOP GLAZED CHINA BOWL, circa 1930's. This unique bowl pictures an unusual pairing of Mickey and Betty (what would Minnie think!?) on a pretty, fluted edge ceramic bowl.

PLATE 149: ITEM A - MICKEY AND MINNIE MOUSE LUSTERWARE TEAPOT c. Walt E. Disney, Japan, 1930's. ITEM B - MICKEY AND MINNIE MOUSE LUSTERWARE PLATE, Japan, 1930's. Both pieces have the identical design of Mickey and Minnie in a rowboat.

PLATE 150: MICKEY MOUSE LUSTERWARE DIVIDED DISH from Japan in the 1930's. This small dish measures only 5" in diameter. It was probably used as a doll dish.

PLATE 151: MICKEY MOUSE MINIATURE CREAM PITCHER AND SUGAR BOWL produced in Japanese Lusterware in the 1930's. Both pieces measure approximately 2" in height.

PLATE 152: MICKEY MOUSE 1930's LUSTERWARE CUP AND SAUCER. The plate showing Mickey at a radio microphone from the 1930's is an unusual design.

PLATE 153: MICKEY AND MINNIE GLASSES were made by the Libbey Glass Company.

PLATE 154: MICKEY MOUSE ASHTRAY is an example of Bavarian china. Note Mickey's ratty appearance and the decorative gold rim.

PLATE 155: MICKEY MOUSE GLAZED CERAMIC PITCHER, manufactured in France in the 1930's. Mickey is pictured on one side and Minnie is on the other. This Art Deco styled piece is a companion to the large pitcher pictured in Plate #145.

PLATE 156: MICKEY MOUSE POCKET BEAD GAME manufactured by the Marks Brothers Company of Boston, Massachusetts, in the 1930's. The game is sealed under glass. It is an interesting adaptation of what is actually one of the Marks sewing cards.

PLATE 157: MICKEY MOUSE HOOP-LA GAME was made by the Marks Brothers Company. The hoops are made of wood.

PLATE 158: MICKEY MOUSE BAGATELLE was made by the Marks Brothers Company. This game is made of wood and was played with marbles. The piece is over two feet tall.

PLATE 159: MICKEY MOUSE PIANO manufactured by Marks Brothers of Boston. The piano pictured here is absolutely mint and is shown with its original box. The Mickey and Minnie figures jump about when the keys are played. Marked c. Walt Disney Enterprises.

PLATE 160: MICKEY MOUSE ROLL'EM GAME by the Marks Brothers Company of Boston, Massachusetts, c. Walt Disney. On the back of each figure is printed a large numeral for the target value.

PLATE 161: MICKEY MOUSE HOME FOUNDRY QUALITY CASTING SET. This colorful box contains a hot plate and casting molds to make lead cast Disney figures. Marked c. Walt Disney Enterprises, 1930's.

PLATE 162: MICKEY MOUSE SOLDIER SET manufactured by Marks Brothers of Boston in the 1930's. This set features beautiful graphics on the box and set of soldiers.

PLATE 163 A: MICKEY MOUSE CIRCUS GAME manufactured by Marks Brothers of Boston, Massachusetts. Shown here is the vertical game board with marble action and a ringing bell. This toy features superior Mickey and Minnie graphics.

PLATE 163 C: MICKEY MOUSE POP GAME by the Marks Brothers Company of Boston, Massachusetts and marked "c. by Special Permission Walt Disney Enterprises." The bright box graphics are found on many of the toys manufactured by Marks Brothers.

PLATE 163 B: MICKEY MOUSE CIRCUS GAME by Marks Brothers, 1930's. Shown here is the bottom, horizontal game board with target holes and the bright circus Mickey graphics. Standard marbles are used with this game.

PLATE 164: MICKEY MOUSE POP GAME inside of box showing pop gun, original corks, target, and wooden target stands. Rarely is this set found in such complete condition!

PLATE 165: MICKEY MOUSE SCATTER BALL GAME by Marks Brothers of Boston. This plate shows the fantastic graphics of the game's box lid.

PLATE 166: MICKEY MOUSE SCATTER BALL GAME box (inside). This plate shows the box interior including a spinning wooden top and small wooden game balls.

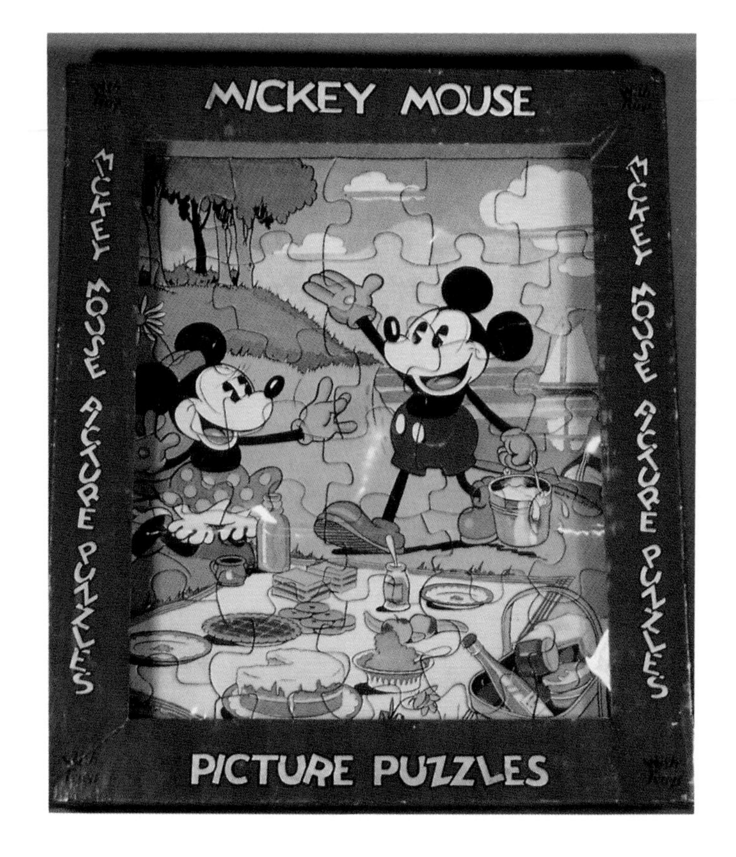

PLATE 167: MICKEY MOUSE PICTURE PUZZLES. Boxed set manufactured by the Marks Brothers Company of Boston marked c. Walt E. Disney.

PLATE 168: MICKEY AND MINNIE MOUSE PUZZLE by Marks Brothers of Boston, marked "c. Walt E. Disney." Puzzle is shown in its original tray, which was a part of the original packaging of the box in Plate #167.

PLATE 169: MICKEY MOUSE AND MINNIE MOUSE LOCOMOTIVE PUZZLE in its original tray, manufactured by Marks Brothers. All four puzzles pictured in Plates #167 through #170 were shipped in trays which "nested" one inside of the other.

PLATE 170: MICKEY MOUSE WATERSKIING PUZZLE manufactured by Marks Brothers pictures Mickey in a striped bathing suit being pulled by Minnie driving a speedboat. Marked "c. Walt E. Disney."

PLATE 171: MICKEY MOUSE TARGET GAME was made by the Marks Brothers Company. Shown with the target are the enameled steel, spring-loaded gun and six rubber-tipped vacuum cup darts.

PLATE 172: MICKEY MOUSE TARGET GAME BOX featuring strong 1930's line graphics.

PLATE 173: MICKEY MOUSE PLAYING CARDS from the 1930's marked "c. Walt Disney Enterprises." The card backs all have identical Mickey logos. The card faces are standard playing cards.

PLATE 174: MICKEY MOUSE PLAYING CARDS are marked "Walt Disney Enterprises" on each card.

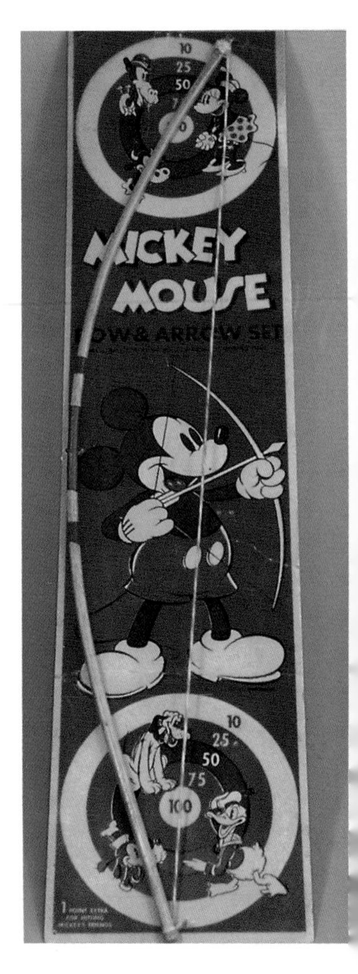

PLATE 175: MICKEY MOUSE BOW AND ARROW SET, circa late 1930's and marked c. "Walt Disney Enterprises." This particular example displays the bow on its original card, but has no arrows.

PLATE 176: MICKEY MOUSE COMING HOME GAME manufactured by Marks Brothers of Boston. Shown here is the complete 1930's game set including the large game board and the small box of dice, instructions, dice cup, and game tokens.

PLATE 177: MICKEY MOUSE OLD MAID CARDS manufactured by Whitman Publishing and c. 1937 Walt Disney Enterprises. All cards were printed in pairs except for Clarabelle Cow, who was the old maid.

PLATE 178: WALT DISNEY'S SILLY SYMPHONY SNAP CARDS manufactured by Chad Valley of England in the 1930's. The box is marked "Copyright Walt Disney Mickey Mouse LTD." Cards are extremely bright and colorful.

PLATE 179: MICKEY MOUSE DOMINOES manufactured by Halsam in the 1930's. The box features bright graphics of Mickey and Pluto running, while each individual domino is molded with a 1930's Mickey figure on the back.

PLATE 181: MICKEY MOUSE PUZZLE manufactured by Marks Brothers and marked "Walt Disney Enterprises copyright 1933." This puzzle measures 8"x10" and is shown in a standard frame.

PLATE 180: MICKEY MOUSE SAFETY BLOCKS by Halsam, 1930's. The set pictured in this plate was never played with and the box along with the blocks are all in pristine condition – factory fresh!

PLATE 182: MICKEY MOUSE MUSICAL BAND PUZZLE by Marks Brothers of Boston. This puzzle is dated "c. 1933 Walt Disney Enterprises" and features wonderfully vivid graphics.

PLATE 183: MICKEY MOUSE OLD MAID CARDS were made by the Whitman Publishing Company.

PLATE 184: MICKEY MOUSE PICNIC PUZZLE by Marks Brothers of Boston, 1933. This puzzle measures 8"x10".

PLATE 185: "SHUFFLED SYMPHONIES" MICKEY MOUSE CARDS manufactured in England and marked "By Permission Walt Disney Mickey Mouse LTD and Mickey Mouse Weekly." These early cards are printed in spectacular colors!

PLATE 186: MICKEY AND MINNIE MOUSE PILLOW COVER, 1930's, from a kit manufactured by McCall's Patterns. The graphics printed on the cloth are lively.

PLATE 187: MICKEY MOUSE PULL TOY by N.N. Hill Brass, 1930's. This toy is marked "Walt Disney Enterprises" and features a circular bell attached to the wheel axle which makes the moving toy "ring."

PLATE 188: MICKEY MOUSE XYLOPHONE PLAYER by Fisher Price. This wooden pull toy is marked "c. 1939 W.D.P." When pulled along Mickey stikes the xylophone keys with the mallets in excellent action.

PLATE 189: ITEM A - MICKEY MOUSE AND PLUTO PULL TOY by Fisher Price marked "Mickey Mouse Band" on the drum. This toy features great mechanical action and is one of the most desirable early Fisher Price toys. ITEM B - Mickey Mouse 3" pail by Ohio Art, 1930's.

PLATE 190: MICKEY MOUSE ROLLING TOY by Fisher Price, from the 1930's. This unusual toy measures 6" in length and is one of the harder to find small Fisher Price designs.

PLATE 191: MICKEY MOUSE TARGET by Marks Brothers of Boston used with a 1930's dart gun target set. The colors and graphics on these targets are extremely bright.

PLATE 192: MICKEY MOUSE PULL TOY by N.N. Hill Brass. This 1930's toy presents a large, excellent likeness of Mickey with rolling action. Note the paper wheel cover with three tiny running Mickeys.

PLATE 193: MICKEY AND MINNIE MOUSE SAND PAIL by Ohio Art, 1930's. Marked "c. Walt Disney Enterprises." This rare pail pictures a wonderfully colorful scene of Mickey and Minnie in Italy floating in a gondola on a canal. Pluto stands on shore barking.

PLATE 194: MICKEY MOUSE WASHER by Ohio Art. This is the rarest of all versions of this extremely colorful tin toy because of the inclusion of the attached wringer mechanism on top. This is an exquisite example of Ohio Art's superb tin lithography.

PLATE 195: MICKEY MOUSE TIN WASHING MACHINE was produced by the Ohio Art Company.

PLATE 196A: MICKEY'S GARDEN TIN SAND PAIL. This pail was manufactured by the Ohio Art Company of Bryan, Ohio, and is marked "Walt Disney Enterprises." This bright pail is 8" tall.

PLATE 196 B: MICKEY AND MINNIE MOUSE FRENCH LITHOGRAPHED TIN CONTAINER from the 1930's. Mickey, Minnie, and Pluto are shown watching a black cat.

PLATE 197: MICKEY MOUSE ENGLISH TIN picturing Mickey, Minnie, and a long-billed Donald Duck watching a very early television. Circa late 1930's when T.V. actually began to appear in England. This is one of the most beautifully colorful of all Disney tins.

PLATE 198: MICKEY MOUSE SWEEPER by Ohio Art, 1930's. This tin and wood toy is marked "c. Walt Disney." It actually will sweep up large particles of dirt.

PLATE 199: MICKEY MOUSE BAND SAND PAIL manfactured by Ohio Art of Bryan, Ohio, in the 1930's and marked c. Walt Disney Enterprises.

PLATE 200: MICKEY MOUSE SAND PAIL by Ohio Art, 1930's. This pail is marked "c. Walt Disney Enterprises" and is 8" tall. The pail pictures Mickey, Minnie, Pluto and Donald riding in a rowboat.

PLATE 201: MICKEY MOUSE BUILDING A SAND CASTLE large 8" pail by Ohio Art, 1930's. The bright colors and early graphics of Mickey Mouse make this a most dynamic tin lithographed sand pail.

PLATE 202: MICKEY MOUSE SAND PAIL, by Ohio Art, 1930's. This plate shows the reverse side of the pail picturing Minnie Mouse and Pluto building a sand castle on the beach.

PLATE 203: MICKEY MOUSE ON AN ISLAND TIN SAND PAIL, 1930's by Ohio Art. This 5" pail is marked "c. Walt Disney Enterprises" and pictures Mickey on an island signalling to "admiral Donald" in a boat offshore.

PLATE 204: MICKEY MOUSE MINIATURE WATERING CAN by Ohio Art, 1930's. This tiny can is only 3½" tall and pictures black and white Mickey and Minnie Mouse graphics.

PLATE 205: MICKEY MOUSE TIN TEA TRAY by Ohio Art of Bryan, Ohio. This early tin piece is from a tea set and is simply marked "c. Walt Disney." The highly colorful graphics makes this one of the most attractive of all Ohio Art pieces.

PLATE 206: MICKEY MOUSE TIN TEA TRAY by Ohio Art, 1930's. Tray is marked "c. Walt Disney Enterprises" and pictures Mickey, Minnie, and Pluto being announced by a long-billed Donald Duck as the doorman.

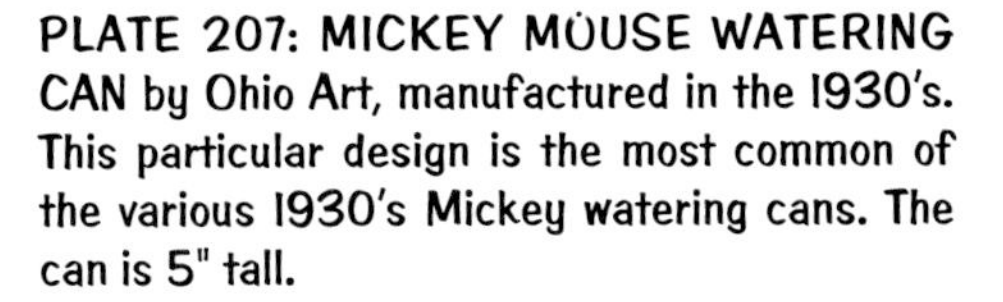

PLATE 207: MICKEY MOUSE WATERING CAN by Ohio Art, manufactured in the 1930's. This particular design is the most common of the various 1930's Mickey watering cans. The can is 5" tall.

PLATE 208: MICKEY MOUSE NARROW SPOUT WATERING CAN by Ohio Art. This colorful tin item is a more unusual watering can style which stands 6" tall.

PLATE 209: MICKEY AND MINNIE MOUSE WITH A BEACH UMBRELLA SAND PAIL by Ohio Art, 1930's. This striking design measures 5" tall.

PLATE 210: MICKEY ON ROLLER SKATES TIN SAND PAIL by Ohio Art, 1930's, is shown with its original red sand shovel. This pail measures approximately 4" in height and shows Mickey on skates being pulled by Pluto.

PLATE 212: LARGE MICKEY MOUSE SAND SIFTER by Ohio Art picturing various multi-color scenes. This is the largest of all sand sifter designs, measuring approximately 8" in diameter.

PLATE 211: MICKEY AND MINNIE MOUSE SAND SIFTER, by Ohio Art in the 1930's. This 6" diameter tin toy pictures Mickey and Minnie at play in the sand on the beach.

PLATE 213: MICKEY MOUSE LITHOGRAPHED TIN SAND SIFTER from the 1930's marked "c. Walt Disney Enterprises."

PLATE 214: MICKEY MOUSE SAND PAIL by Happynak of England, manufactured in the 1930's. This 5" pail features unusual color variations on Mickey and several other early Disney characters.

PLATE 215: MICKEY MOUSE WASH TUB by Ohio Art, 1930's, shown with original attached wringer mechanism. This example is 5" in diameter with black and white Mickey and Minnie figures all around.

PLATE 216: MICKEY AND MINNIE MOUSE WASH TUB by Ohio Art shown with original washboard. This is the more common variety of the tub pictured in Plate #215.

PLATE 217: MICKEY AND MINNIE MOUSE TREASURE ISLAND pail by Ohio Art, 1930's. This pail features a colorful scene of Mickey and Minnie finding buried treasure on the beach.

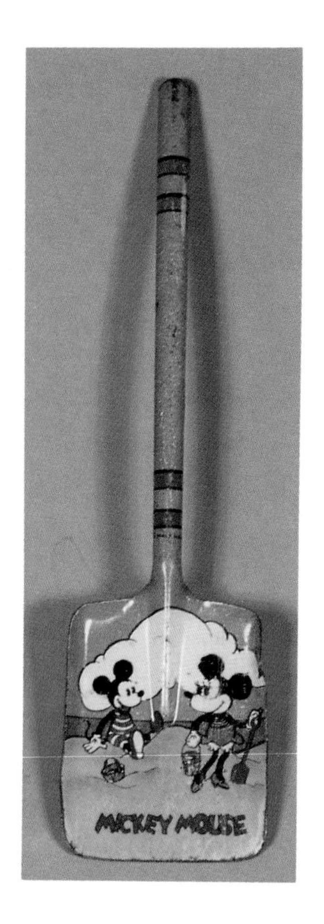

PLATE 219: GIANT MICKEY MOUSE TIN DRUM by the Ohio Art Company of Bryan, Ohio, measures 11" in diameter and is the most impressive of all Ohio Art drums. This early drum is marked "c. Walt Disney" and dates before Donald Duck's origin as he is not pictured among the many characters.

PLATE 218: MICKEY MOUSE SAND SHOVEL by Ohio Art, 1930's is marked "c. Walt Disney" and measures 8" long.

PLATE 221: MICKEY MOUSE DRUM is made by the Ohio Art Company. This is a more unusual design and is extremely colorful.

PLATE 220: GIANT MICKEY MOUSE TIN DRUM by Ohio Art, 1930's. This is another view of the drum pictured in Plate #219.

PLATE 222: MICKEY MOUSE TIN DRUM by Ohio Art, 1930's. This drum measures approximately 8" in diameter and features lively full-color graphics.

PLATE 223: "MICKEY MOUSE BAND" CLOTH HEAD DRUM is circa 1930's. The body of the drum is lithographed tin with all of the early Disney characters marching in a parade.

PLATE 224: MICKEY MOUSE DRUM highlights the Mickey Mouse Band. This is the largest of any drum produced.

PLATE 225: MICKEY MOUSE DRUM manufactured by Ohio Art, 1930's. This drum pictures Mickey and Minnie with solid black oval eyes and a later Donald Duck. It is marked "c. Walt Disney Enterprises."

PLATE 226: MICKEY MOUSE TOP picturing Mickey running with a salt shaker being chased by an angry Minnie Mouse with a rolling pin. This bright orange metal top is circa 1930's and is 8" in diameter.

PLATE 227: MICKEY MOUSE SPINNING TOP was made by the Fritz Bueschel Company in the 1930's.

PLATE 228: MICKEY MOUSE TOP, circa 1930's picturing Mickey Mouse, Minnie, Pluto, Big Bad Wolf, and the Three Pigs. This is the largest of all tops, measuring 11" in diameter.

PLATE 229: MICKEY MOUSE TOP marketed by the George Borgfeldt Corporation of New York in the 1930's. This is a smaller version top marked "c. Walt Disney Enterprises."

PLATE 230: MICKEY MOUSE TOP from the 1930's picturing a long-billed Donald and marked c. Walt Disney Enterprises. This is the larger 10" version of the top shown in Plate #229.

PLATE 231: MICKEY AND MINNIE MOUSE PIRATES SAND PAIL by Ohio Art. This pail measures 8" tall and shows Mickey and Minnie Mouse on a raft with a pirate's Jolly Roger flag.

PLATE 232: MICKEY AND MINNIE MOUSE GIANT 10" SAND PAIL, 1930's. This is one of the largest of all Disney 1930's pails.

PLATE 233: MICKEY MOUSE AND DONALD DUCK GOLFERS TIN SAND PAIL by Ohio Art, c. 1938 Walt Disney Enterprises. This pail is 8" tall.

PLATE 234: MICKEY MOUSE SAND SHOVEL, by Ohio Art Co. of Bryan Ohio, c. Walt Disney Enterprises.

PLATE 235: MICKEY MOUSE AND MINNIE MOUSE HELPMATES TEA SET manufactured by Ohio Art, 1930's. Plates are each marked "c. Walt Disney." This set is shown with its original box.

PLATE 236: MICKEY MOUSE TEA SET, CHINA, distributed by George Borgfeldt, 1930's. Shown in original box decorated with many colorful Mickey and Minnies.

PLATE 237: MICKEY MOUSE WASTEBASKET manufactured by the Geuder, Paeschke and Frey Company in 1936. Because so many examples of these were used as actual wastebaskets, it is hard to find these in mint condition.

PLATE 238: MICKEY MOUSE LUNCH KIT manufactured by the Geuder, Paeschke and Frey Company of Milwaukee in 1935. This kit features superb graphics of early Mickey, Minnie, Donald, and others. This is a rare lunch pail.

PLATE 239: MICKEY MOUSE GIANT WATERING CAN by Ohio Art, circa 1930's. This is the largest of the Mickey sprinklers and pictures Mickey playing a saxophone for Minnie Mouse.

PLATE 240: MICKEY MOUSE SAND PAIL by Ohio Art, 1930's. This small sand pail is only 3" tall and pictures Mickey selling lemonade at a lemonade stand.

PLATE 241: MICKEY MOUSE SAND PAIL, made in France in the 1930's. This is an unusual foreign tin beach toy.

PLATE 242: MICKEY MOUSE SAND PAIL was made by the Ohio Art Company. The figures actually stand out from the pail.

PLATE 243: MICKEY AND MINNIE MOUSE SAND PAIL, 1930's, manufactured by Happynak of England. This tall 8" pail pictures Mickey and Minnie fishing from a rowboat.

PLATE 244: MICKEY MOUSE "ATLANTIC CITY" SAND PAIL, 1930's by Ohio Art. This is one of the rarest designs of all the 1930's pails.

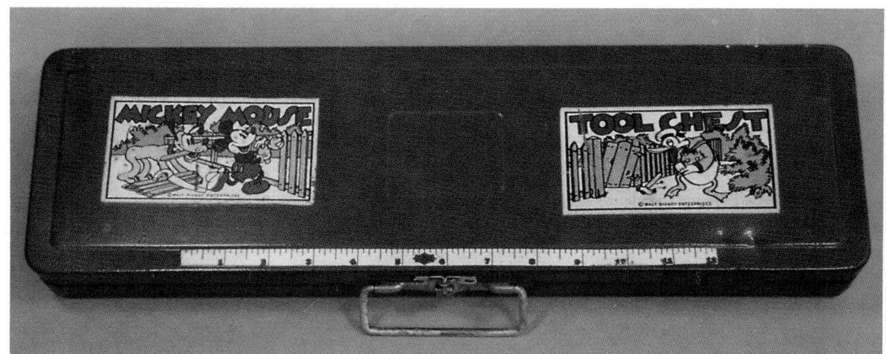

PLATE 245: MICKEY MOUSE TOOL CHEST, 1930's hinged tool box picturing an early, long-billed Donald Duck along with Mickey and Pluto. Marked "Walt Disney Enterprises." The tool box is 18" long.

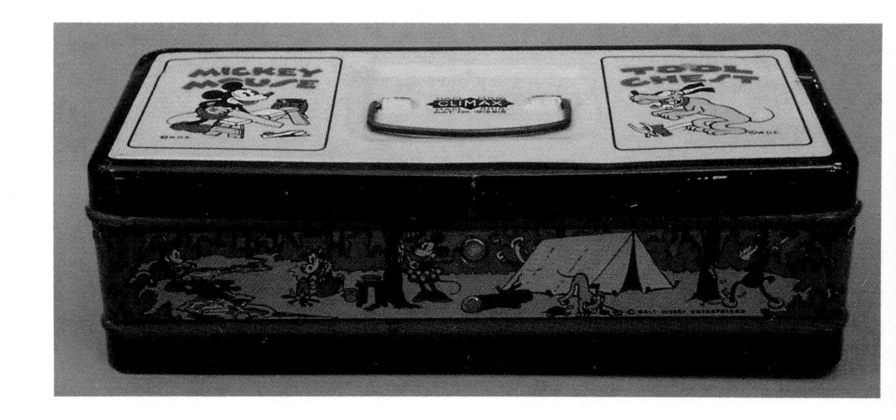

PLATE 246: MICKEY MOUSE TOOL CHEST, 1936, manufactured by the Hamilton Metal Products Company of Hamilton, Ohio. This box features full color tin lithography on all sides and is marked "c. Walt Disney Enterprises."

PLATE 247: MICKEY MOUSE CHILD'S POTTY is porcelain-clad metal made in Germany by the Richard G. Krueger Company.

PLATE 248: MICKEY MOUSE CHILD'S CHAMBER POT, 1930's, made of porcelain over metal. The chipping on the edge of this example is obviously from being emptied.

PLATE 249: MICKEY MOUSE TELEPHONE BANK was made by the N.N. Hill Brass Company. Mickey is made of hard cardboard.

PLATE 251: MICKEY MOUSE PENCIL BOX by Dixon, 1930's and marked "c. Walt Disney." Because these were made only of cardboard and paper, few survive in excellent condition today.

PLATE 250: MICKEY MOUSE TELEPHONE has a Mickey that pops up and down when receiver is picked up.

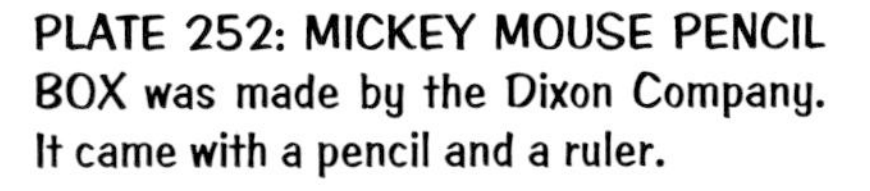

PLATE 252: MICKEY MOUSE PENCIL BOX was made by the Dixon Company. It came with a pencil and a ruler.

PLATE 253: MICKEY MOUSE PICTURE PRINTING SET, 1930's, by the Fulton Specialty Company of Elizabeth, New Jersey. This set is labelled as "Artistamp Picture Set No. 795" and includes letter and picture blocks along with a stamp pad.

PLATE 254: MICKEY MOUSE DIXON PENCIL BOX with original ruler, c. Walt Disney Enterprises, 1930's.

PLATE 255: MICKEY MOUSE PENCIL BOX by Dixon, 1930's. This particular example contains two drawers for storage.

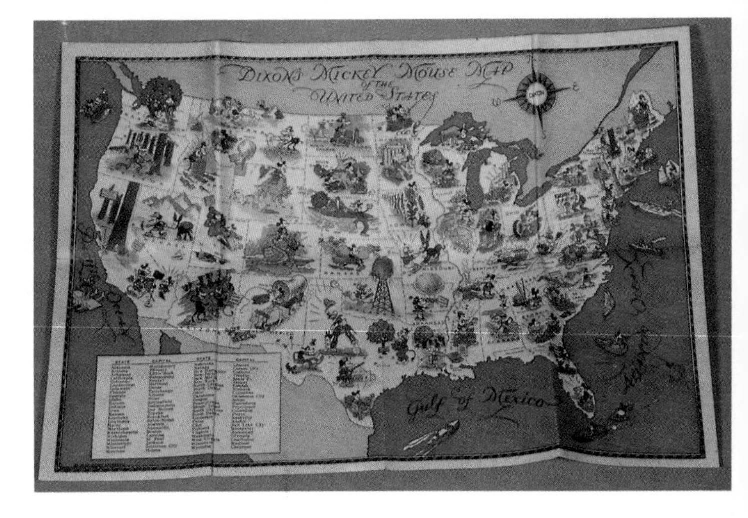

PLATE 256: "DIXON'S MICKEY MOUSE MAP OF THE UNITED STATES" came folded inside some deluxe Dixon pencil boxes of the 1930's. This is a very small map.

PLATE 257: ITEMS A AND B - MICKEY MOUSE PENCIL BOXES by Dixon, 1930's.

PLATE 258: MICKEY MOUSE PENCIL BOX by Dixon, 1930's. Pictures the back of this box.

PLATE 261: MICKEY MOUSE PENCIL BOX has the unusual color label attached to the box.

PLATE 259: ITEMS A, B, AND C - THREE VARIETIES OF MICKEY MOUSE DIXON PENCIL BOXES c. Walt Disney Enterprises, 1930's.

PLATE 260: ITEM A - LARGE MICKEY MOUSE PENCIL BOX by Dixon, 1930's. ITEM B - SMALLER BLUE PENCIL BOX manufactured by Dixon in the 1930's.

PLATE 262: *MICKEY MOUSE WADDLE BOOK* came with cutout characters and included a ramp.

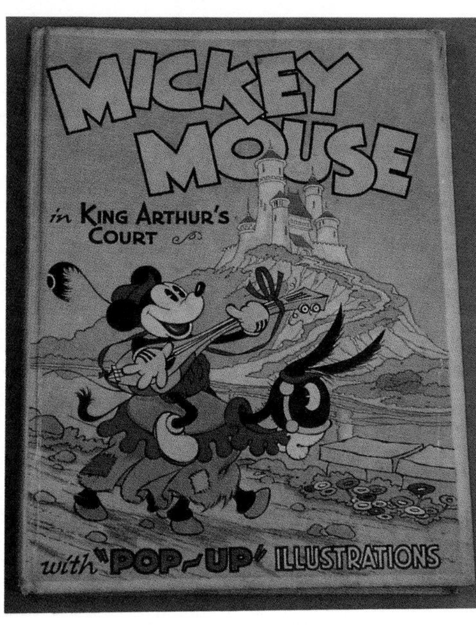

PLATE 264: *MICKEY MOUSE IN KING ARTHUR'S COURT* pop-up book by Blue Ribbon Books, 1934. This is the most beautiful of all the pop-up books.

PLATE 263: MICKEY MOUSE WADDLES found in waddle book.

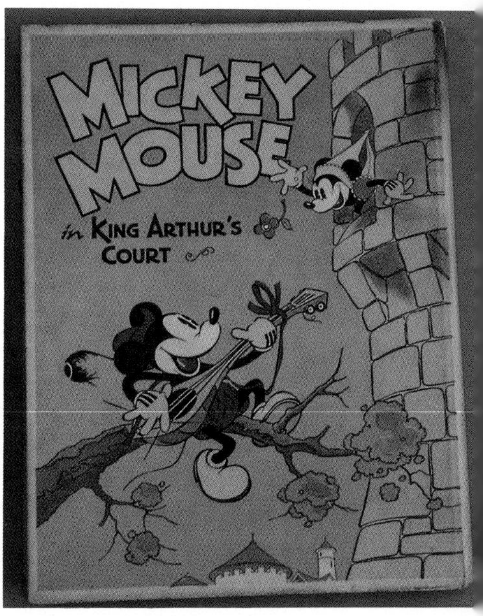

PLATE 265: REAR COVER OF BOOK SHOWN IN PLATE 264. Showing Mickey serenading Princess Minnie.

PLATE 266: MICKEY MOUSE JOUSTING POP-UP SCENE from Blue Ribbon Books' *Mickey Mouse in King Arthur's Court.*

PLATE 267: MICKEY AND MINNIE MOUSE POP-UP from *Mickey Mouse in King Arthur's Court.*

PLATE 268: MICKEY AND MINNIE MOUSE WITH THE KING POP-UP from *Mickey Mouse in King Arthur's Court,* 1930's.

PLATE 269: MICKEY MOUSE SERENADING MINNIE POP-UP PAGES from *Mickey Mouse In King Arthur's Court* by Blue Ribbon Books.

PLATE 270: *THE POP-UP MICKEY MOUSE* by Blue Ribbon books. The book contained three different pop-up scenes.

PLATE 271: MICKEY AND MINNIE POP-UP FIGURE from *The Pop-Up Mickey Mouse.*

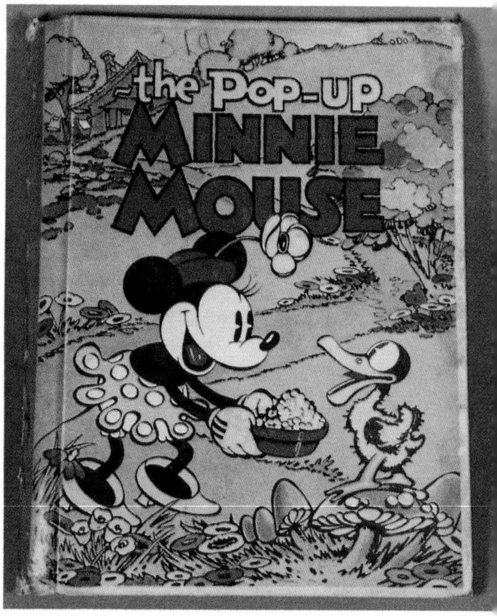

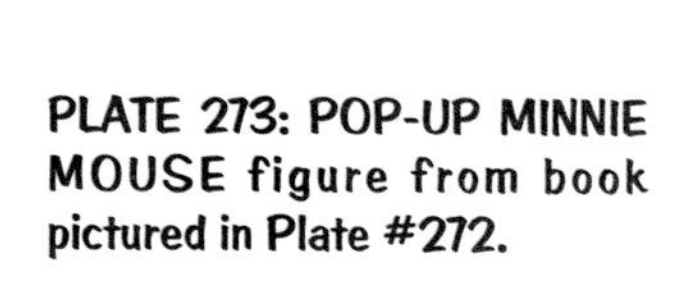

PLATE 273: POP-UP MINNIE MOUSE figure from book pictured in Plate #272.

PLATE 272: *THE POP-UP MINNIE MOUSE* published by Blue Ribbon Books, 1930's.

PLATE 274: *MICKEY MOUSE BOOK FOR COLORING* published by Saalfield, 1930's. Notice the die-cut top edge of book.

PLATE 275: MICKEY MOUSE COMPOSITION BOOK manufactured by the Powers Paper Company, c. Walt Disney Enterprises. Note the long-billed Donald on the cover.

PLATE 276: *THE STORY OF MICKEY MOUSE, THE BIG, BIG BOOK* c. Walt Disney Enterprises. This book features a vibrantly'colorful cover.

PLATE 277: *MICKEY MOUSE ILLUSTRATED MOVIE STORIES* hardcover story book, c. 1931. This book features black and white illustrations taken directly from early Mickey Mouse films.

PLATE 278: *A MICKEY MOUSE ALPHABET BOOK FROM A TO Z* published by Whitman Publishing, c. Walt Disney Enterprises.

PLATE 279: *THE WALT DISNEY PAINT BOOK,* c. 1938 by Whitm[illegible] Publishing. This is one of the largest of all Mickey Mouse colori[illegible] books.

PLATE 280: *MICKEY MOUSE COLORING BOOK* published by Saalfield, 1930's. This is one of the earliest Mickey coloring books.

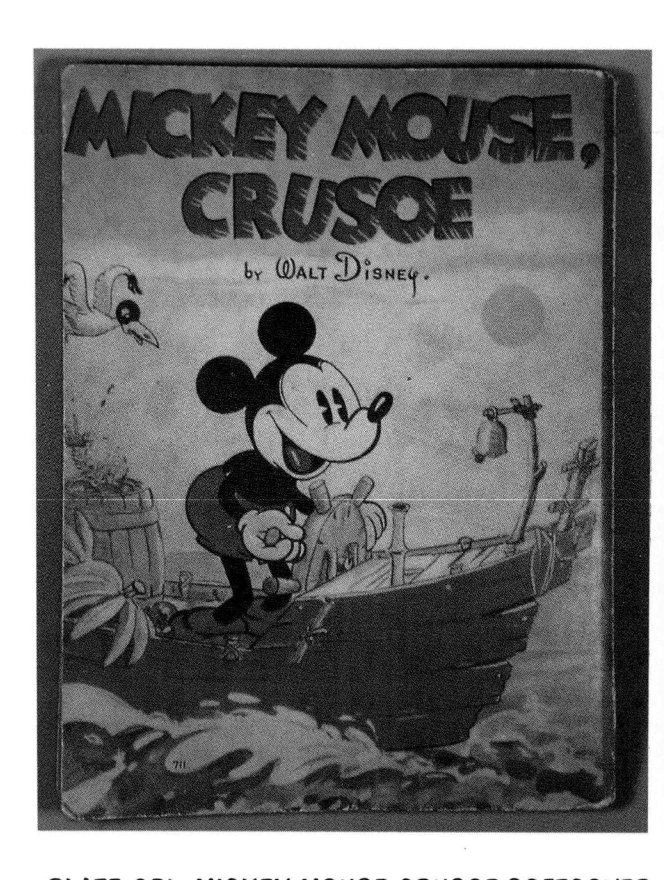

PLATE 281: *MICKEY MOUSE CRUSOE* SOFTCOVER STORYBOOK published by Whitman and copyright Walt Disney Enterprises.

'LATE 282: SIX MICKEY MOUSE WEE LITTLE BOOKS, manufactured in 1935 by Whitman 'ublishing. The set of six books is shown with its original cardboard slipcase, c. Walt Disney nterprises.

PLATE 284: *A MICKEY MOUSE ABC STORY* by Walt Disney, hardcover storybook, 1930's c. Walt Disney Enterprises.

'LATE 283: MICKEY MOUSE COOKIES HAT PREMIUM, from the 1930's ıarked "c. Walt Disney Enterprises." This paper hat was a give-away associated ʻith Mickey Mouse Cookies in the 1930's.

PLATE 285: *THE MICKEY MOUSE FIRE BRIGADE* storybook by Walt Disney, 1930's. Note the early style of Mickey and Donald on the cover.

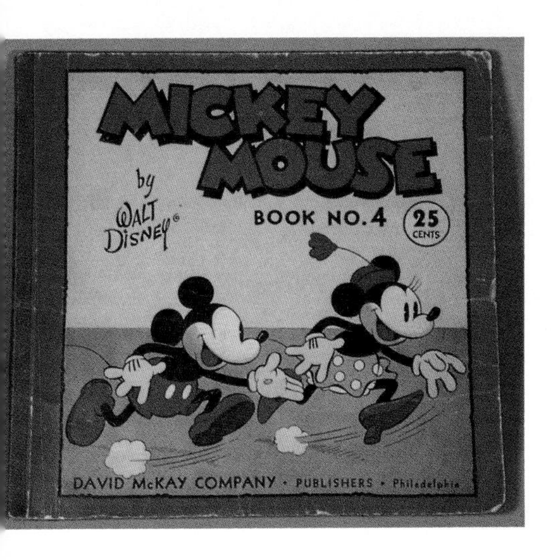

PLATE 286: *MICKEY MOUSE BOOK NO. 4* by Walt Disney, published by David McKay Company of Philadelphia in the 1930's. This book originally sold for 25¢.

PLATE 287: ITEM A - MICKEY MOUSE COMING HOME GAME BOX (only) from 1930's Marks Brothers Game. ITEM B - *MICKEY MOUSE IN YE OLDEN DAYS* small pop-up book with one center pop-up inside, 1930's.

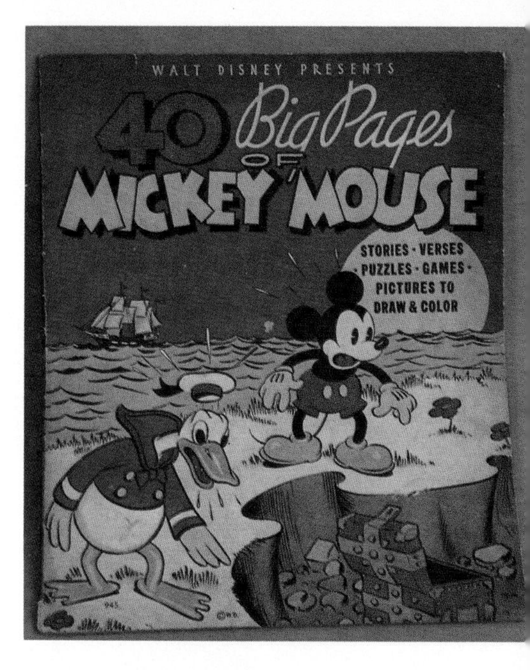

PLATE 288: *WALT DISNEY PRESENTS 40 BI PAGES OF MICKEY MOUSE* large format activit book from the 1930's including stories, poem games, puzzles, and pictures to color.

PLATE 289: *THE ADVENTURES OF MICKEY MOUSE BOOK NUMBER 2,* hardcover storybook. Published by David McKay of Philadelphia. This little book is circa 1933 and contains wonderful color pictures.

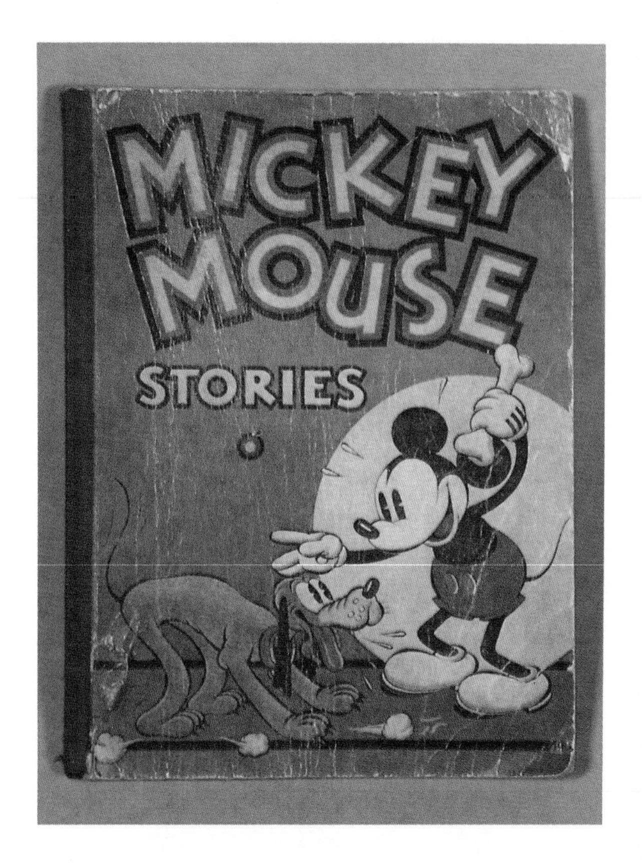

PLATE 290: *MICKEY MOUSE STORIES* book published by David McKay of Philadelphia in 1934.

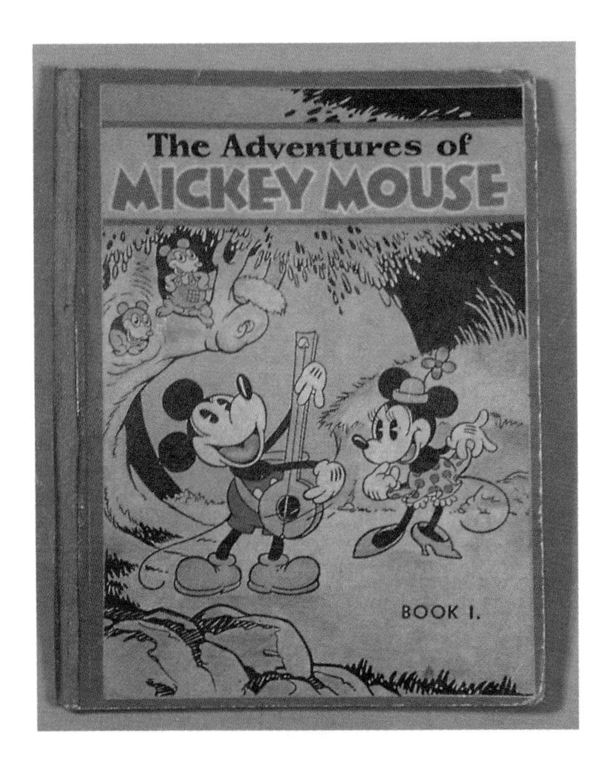

PLATE 291: *THE ADVENTURES OF MICKEY MOUSE BOOK I,* published by David McKay. This book contains illustrations taken directly from black and white Mickey Mouse cartoons.

PLATE 292: *MICKEY MOUSE HAS A BUSY DAY, A WALT DISNEY PICTURE STORY BOOK* published by Whitman in 1938. This is a soft cover picture book.

PLATE 293: *WALT DISNEY SILLY SYMPHONY, MICKEY'S MAGIC HAT AND COOKIE CARNIVAL.* This is a full color soft cover illustrated storybook.

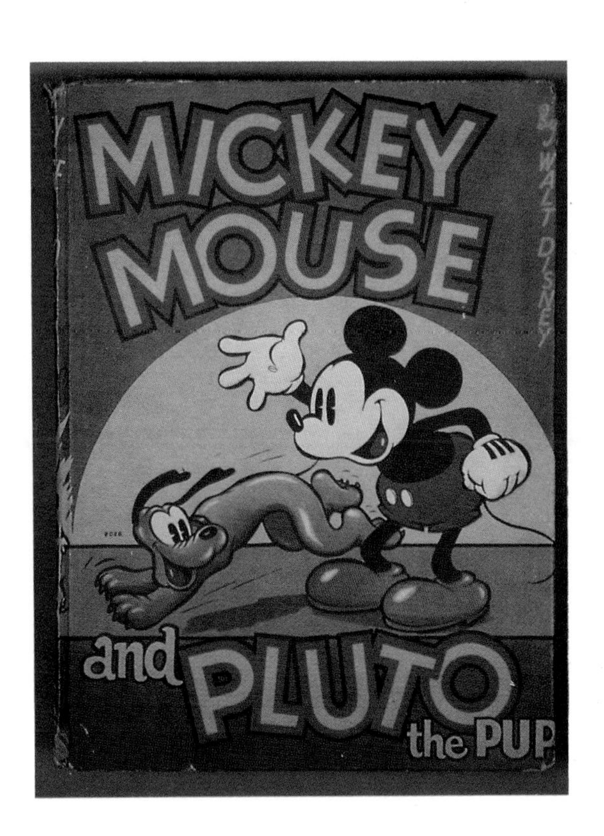

PLATE 294: *MICKEY MOUSE AND PLUTO THE PUP* storybook by Walt Disney, 1930's. This hardcover book features a gorgeous color cover and was published by Whitman Publishing.

PLATE 295: *MICKEY MOUSE IN GIANTLAND* hardcover storybook with full color illustrations published by David McKay Publishers in the 1930's.

PLATE 296: ITEM A - *MICKEY MOUSE AND THE MAGIC CARPE* small paperback book used as a store giveaway or radio premium. ITEM B - MICKEY MOUSE CINE ART FILMS BOX with one small 16mr Mickey Mouse film from the 1930's.

PLATE 297: *WALT DISNEY'S STORY OF MICKEY MOUSE* smal hardcover storybook, circa. 1930's.

PLATE 298: MICKEY MOUSE PRINT SHOP NO. 195 by Fulton Faultless Educational Toys of Elizabeth, New Jersey. This set includes stamp pad, paper, rubber stamps, and stamp holder. The set is from the 1930's and is copyright "Walt Disney Enterprises."

PLATE 299: MICKEY MOUSE BREAD RECIPE CARDS, 1930's. Marked c. Walt Disney.

PLATE 299B: MICKEY MOUSE BREAD CARDS, c. Walt Disney. These were packaged inside loaves of bread.

PLATE 299C: MICKEY MOUSE BREAD CARDS, 1930's c. Walt Disney. Each postcard sized bread card has a recipe on the reverse.

PLATE 300: ITEM A - WALT DISNEY'S MICKEY MOUSE TO DRAW AND COLOR, THE BIG LITTLE SET manufactured by Whitman in the 1930's. This set includes 320 loose leaf pictures and a set of crayons. **ITEM B - MICKEY MOUSE RECIPE SCRAP BOOK**, c. Walt Disney Enterprises, 1930's premium.

PLATE 301: MICKEY MOUSE PIN THE TAIL ON MICKEY PARTY GAME manufactured by Marks Brothers Co. of Boston and sold in the 1930's c. Walt Disney Enterprises.

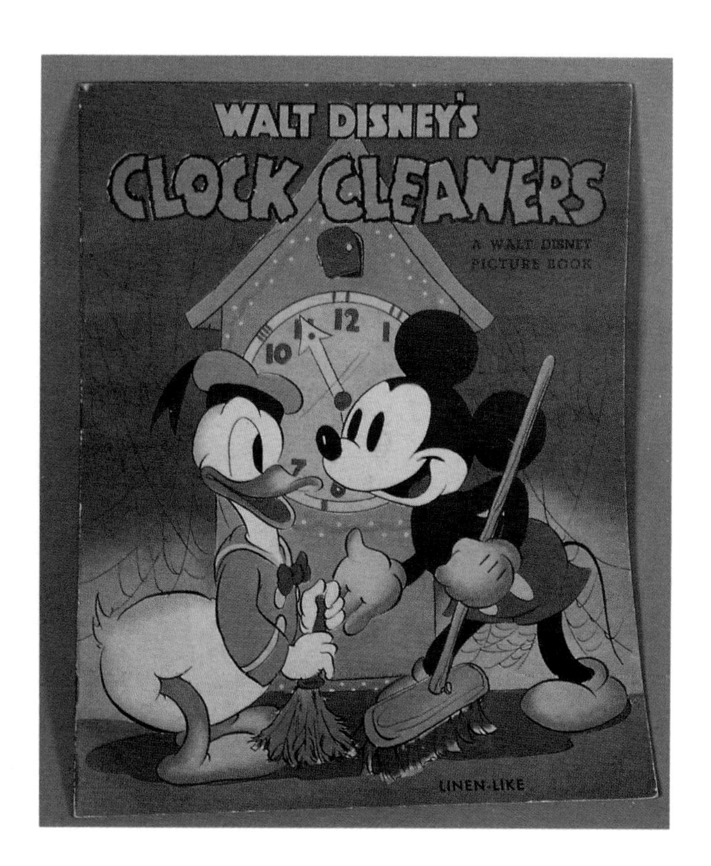

PLATE 302: *WALT DISNEY'S CLOCK CLEANERS* A WALT DISNEY PICTURE BOOK published in the 1930's and designed in full color on linen-like stiff paper.

PLATE 303: *WALT DISNEY ANNUAL* large 1930's storybook featuring many Disney characters.

PLATE 304: MICKEY AND MINNIE MOUSE VALENTINE by Hall Brothers Cards, 1930's and copyright Walt Disney Enterprises.

PLATE 305: ITEM A - MICKEY MOUSE BRAVE LITTLE TAILOR HEART SHAPED VALENTINE, c. 1939 Walt Disney Productions. ITEM B - MINNIE MOUSE HULA DANCER MECHANICAL VALENTINE, c. 1939 Walt Disney Productions.

PLATE 306: MINNIE MOUSE VALENTINE by Hall Brothers in the 1930's.

PLATE 307: MICKEY MOUSE CHRISTMAS CARD by Hall Brothers in the 1930's. c. Walt Disney Enterprises.

PLATE 308: *WHAT! NO MICKEY MOUSE? WHAT KIND OF A PARTY IS THIS?* Early Mickey Mouse sheet music copy when Mickey was distributed by United Artists.

PLATE 309: *MICKEY MOUSE'S BIRTHDAY PARTY* SHEET MUSIC published by Irving Berlin, Inc. of New York. This is a very desirable Disney paper collectible.

PLATE 310: MICKEY MOUSE LAMP shown with original shade picturing Mickey walking with a lantern. Manufactured in the 1930's by Soreng-Manegold.

PLATE 311: MICKEY MOUSE LAMP FILAMENT when plugged in provides a neon-like effect.

PLATE 312: MICKEY MOUSE LAMP with original shade by Soreng-Manegold, 1930's, c. Walt Disney Enterprises.

PLATE 313: MICKEY MOUSE CELLULOID BABY RATTLE c. Walt Disney Enterprises.

PLATE 314: MICKEY MOUSE TAMBOURINE manufactured by Noble and Cooley in the 1930's and marked "c. Walt Disney Enterprises."

PLATE 315A: ITEM A - MICKEY MOUSE NOISE MAKER, 1930's, by Marks Brothers. When spun with wooden handle, it makes a ratchet sound. ITEM B - MICKEY MOUSE PARTY HORN by Marks Brothers of Boston, 1930's.

PLATE 315B: TALL HORN made by Marks Brothers, 1930's.

PLATE 316: MICKEY MOUSE SILLY SYMPHONY LIGHTS were produced by the Noma Light Company.

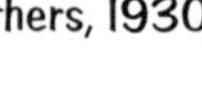

PLATE 317: "MICKEY MOUSE BELLS BY NOMA," illustrated Christmas lamp covers. The set included in this box shows scenes of Silly Symphony characters; c. Walt Disney Enterprises.

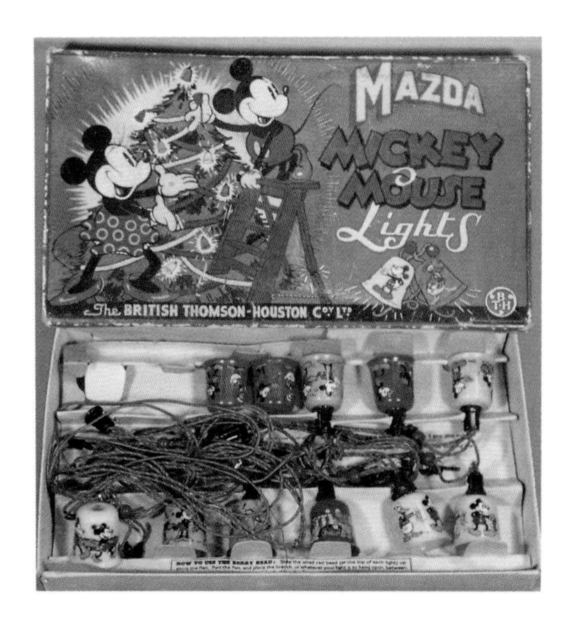

PLATE 318: MAZDA MICKEY MOUSE LIGHTS were produced by the Thomson-Houston Company. These are the English version of the Noma Christmas lights.

PLATE 319: MICKEY MOUSE BLACKBOARD manufactured by the Richmond School Furniture Company of Muncie, Indiana, in the 1930's. Marked "c. Walt Disney."

PLATE 320: MICKEY MOUSE ELECTRIC ALARM CLOCK was made by Ingersoll-Waterbury Company. It is 4" square and has a paper band stretching around the top and sides.

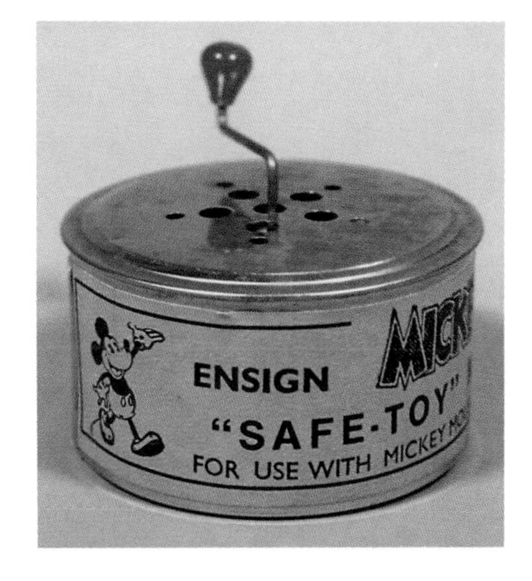

PLATE 321: MICKEY MOUSE MUSIC BOX was made by Ensign and used to create the musical background when showing a "Safe-Toy" film.

PLATE 322: RUBBER MICKEY MOUSE was made by the Seiberling Latex Rubber Company. Shown with a Rolatoy crib toy featured in Plate #323.

PLATE 323: MICKEY MOUSE ROLATOY. Hollow celluloid crib toy from the 1930's. Such examples are hard to find because of their fragile construction.

PLATE 324: MICKEY MOUSE JAM JAR BANK was manufactured by the Glaser Crandell Company of Chicago. Jam was actually sold in the jar.

PLATE 325: MICKEY MOUSE POST OFFICE BANK was made in England by the Happynak Company.

PLATE 326: MICKEY MOUSE COMPOSITION BANK manufactured by the Crown Toy And Novelty Company in the 1930's. Mickey's head turns from side to side. Marked "Walt Disney Enterprises."

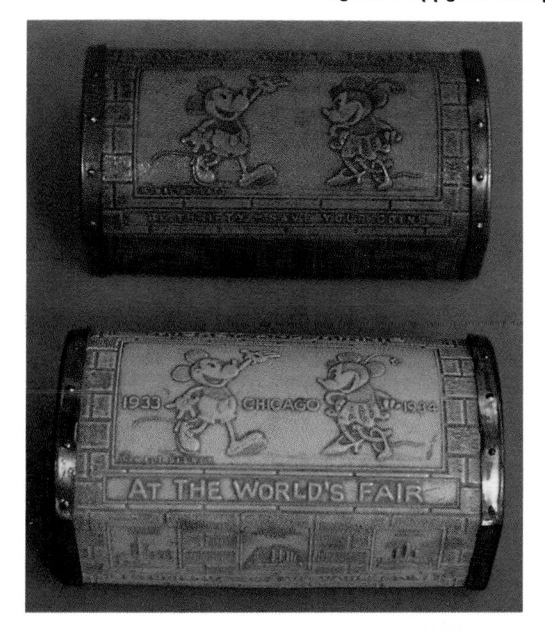

PLATE 327: MICKEY MOUSE TREASURE CHEST BANKS FROM THE 1930's. The bottom example is a 1933-1934 Chicago World's Fair commemorative piece.

PLATE 328: MICKEY MOUSE MECHANICAL RACING CAR, c. Walt Disney Enterprises, 1930's. Shown with original box. This is a small 3" tin windup car. Note tiny Mickey figure in car.

PLATE 329: MICKEY MOUSE WINDUP TIN RACE CAR. Green version of same race car shown in Plate 328.

PLATE 330: MICKEY MOUSE SOAP from the 1930's, c. Walt Disney Enterprises. This is one of the most graphic of all Mickey soap box designs.

PLATE 331: MICKEY MOUSE SOAP was made by Weco Products Company. The box is marked © Walt Disney Enterprises.

PLATE 332: MICKEY MOUSE TOILET SOAP was made by Pictorial Products, Inc. and features beautiful color graphic designs.

PLATE 333: BACK OF MICKEY MOUSE SOAP BOX as shown in Plate #332.

PLATE 334: MICKEY MOUSE NIGHT LIGHT was made by the Micro-Lite Company. This "Kiddy-Lite" is battery operated.

PLATE 335: MICKEY MOUSE FLASHLIGHT was made by the USA Lite Company. It is a great example of early tin lithography.

PLATE 336: MICKEY MOUSE TALKIE JECKTOR complete 1930's set pictured with films, record, turntable, speaker horn, "Talkie Jecktor" projector and original box. Manufactured by the Movie Jecktor Company of New York in 1935.

PLATE 337: MICKEY MOUSE MOVIE-JECKTOR FILMS in original display box, c. Walt Disney Enterprises. Film boxes have wonderful graphics on all sides.

PLATE 338: MICKEY MOUSE CINE ART FILM STORE DISPLAY containing four original Cine Art films.

PLATE 339: MICKEY MOUSE INGERSOLL WRIST WATCH BOX (only). A good watch box with superb graphics can often double the value of the watch inside.

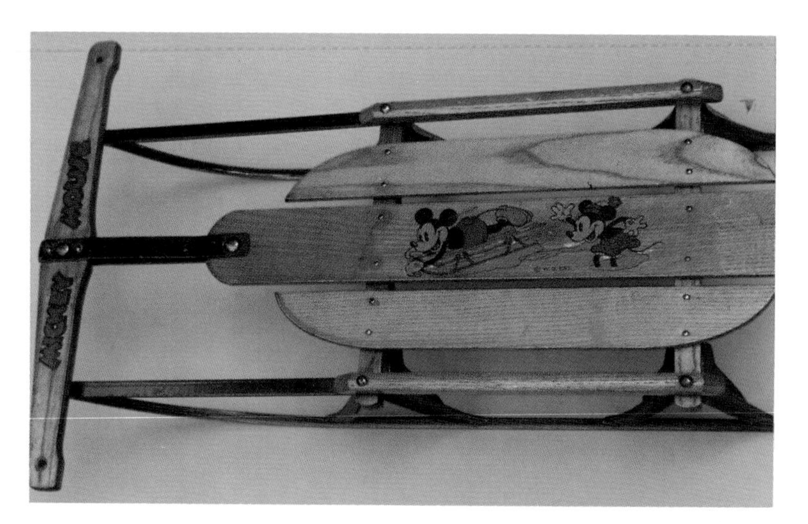

PLATE 340: MICKEY MOUSE SLED, 1930's marked "c. Walt Disney Enterprises." This particular example is in mint condition. Notice the colorful decal in the middle of the sled.

PLATE 341: MICKEY MOUSE RADIO was manufactured by the Emerson Company. It is made of wood.

PLATE 342: MICKEY MOUSE SHORT WAVE RADIO was made in Australia by Astor. This is the only Mickey Mouse radio known to be made of Bakelite.

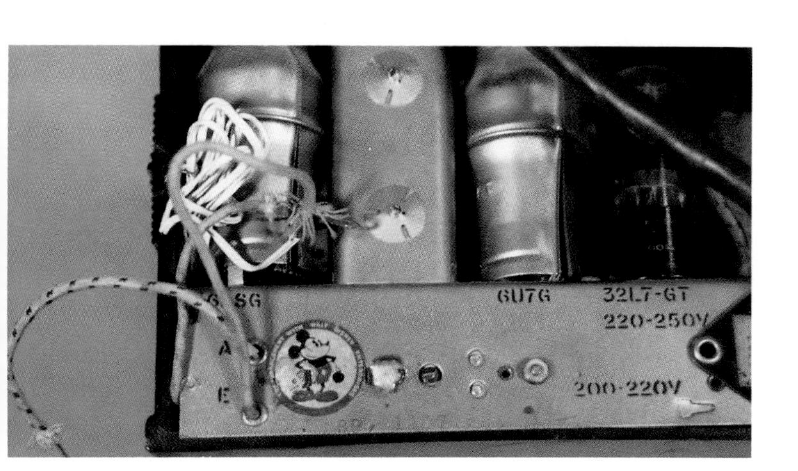

PLATE 343: REVERSE AND ENLARGED VIEW of Mickey Mouse short wave radio pictured in Plate #342.

PLATE 344: MINNIE AND MICKEY MOUSE SOAPS, 1930's, with black painted details (on wooden stand.)

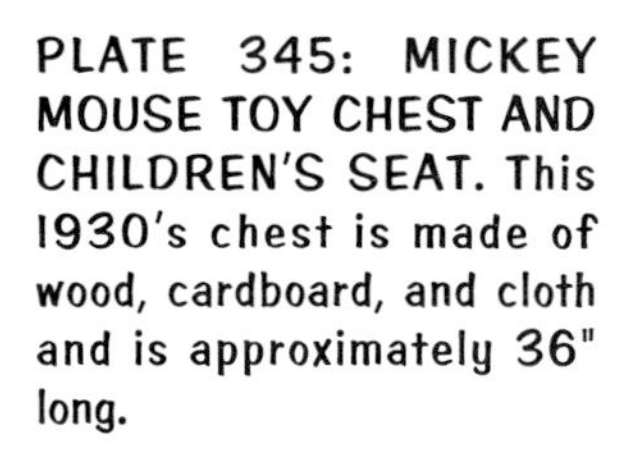

PLATE 345: MICKEY MOUSE TOY CHEST AND CHILDREN'S SEAT. This 1930's chest is made of wood, cardboard, and cloth and is approximately 36" long.

PLATE 346: MICKEY MOUSE PRINT SHOP No. 35 by the Fulton Specialty Company of Elizabeth, New Jersey. This brightly colorful box contains a small alphabet set and stamp pad. From the 1930's, marked "c. Walt Disney Enterprises."

PLATE 347: BABY MICKEY MOUSE FORK AND SPOON WITH HOLDER was made by the International Silver Company and was given as a baby gift in the 1930's.

PLATE 348: MICKIE MOUSE RUBBER FIGURE was made by the Seiberling Latex Rubber Company.

PLATE 349: MICKEY MOUSE SEIBERLING FIGURE.

PLATE 350: ITEM A - SMALL MICKEY RUBBER FIGURE by Seiberling Latex Products. ITEM B - LARGE MICKEY MOUSE Seiberling figure from the 1930's.

PLATE 351: ITEM A - MICKEY MOUSE BEETLEWARE BOWL, red plastic, alphabet rim, 1930's. ITEM B - DONALD DUCK BEETLEWARE BOWL yellow plastic, alphabet rim, 1930's.

PLATE 352: MICKEY MOUSE SILVERPLATE FORK AND SPOON SET, 1930's. Manufactured by William Rogers and Son International Silver Company. "c. Walt Disney Enterprises." In original display box.

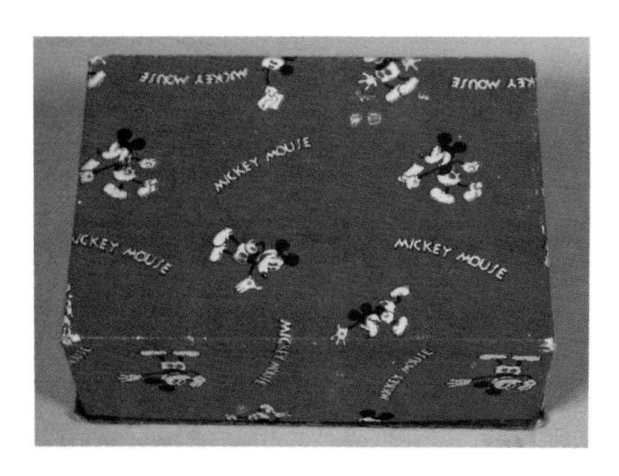

PLATE 353: MICKEY MOUSE SILVERPLATE SET BOX LID showing attractive Mickey graphics on top.

PLATE 354: MICKEY MOUSE 1930'S BRUSH SET by The Hughes-Autograf Brush Company of New York. The brushes have wooden handles with metal trim, c. Walt Disney Enterprises.

PLATE 355: MICKEY MOUSE WOODEN HANDLE BRUSHES manufactured by the Hughes-Autograf Brush Company. Brushes are copyright Walt Disney Enterprises.

PLATE 356: ITEM A - WOODEN BRUSH with 1930's Mickey decal, manufactured by Hughes-Autograf, c. Walt Disney Enterprises. ITEM B - WOODEN AND METAL MICKEY BRUSH by Hughes-Autograf, 1930's.

PLATE 357: MICKEY MOUSE WOODEN AND METAL 1930's BRUSHES by Hughes-Autograf Brush Company of New York.

PLATE 358: MICKEY MOUSE BIRTHDAY CANDLE HOLDERS, manufactured by Cypress Novelty Corporation of Brooklyn, New York. The coils in the holders were to grip the candle and hold it upright.

PLATE 359: MICKEY MOUSE BRUSH, 1930's in unusual character decorated cellophane display box, c. Walt Disney Enterprises.

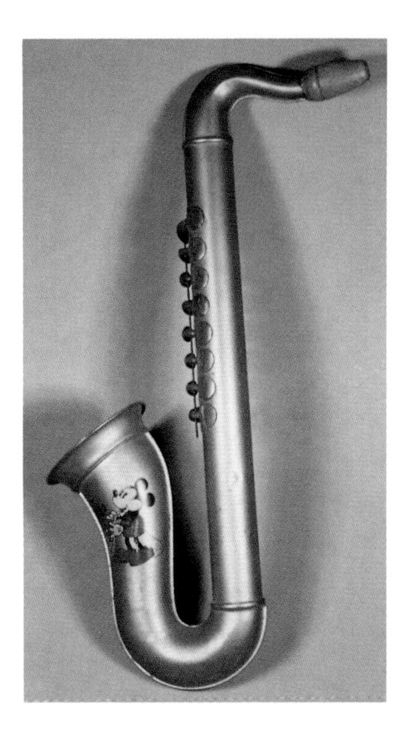

PLATE 360: MICKEY MOUSE SAXOPHONE from the 1930's was made in Czechoslovakia and actually plays an entire octave. Copyright Walt Disney.

PLATE 361: MICKEY MOUSE BANJO was manufactured by the Noble and Cooley Company.

PLATE 364: MICKEY MOUSE SILVERPLATE PORRINGER was made by the International Silver Company. It sold for $2.50, making it an expensive gift.

PLATE 362: MICKEY MOUSE BUBBLE BUSTER was made by the Kilgore Company. The metal gun shot bubble buster bullets.

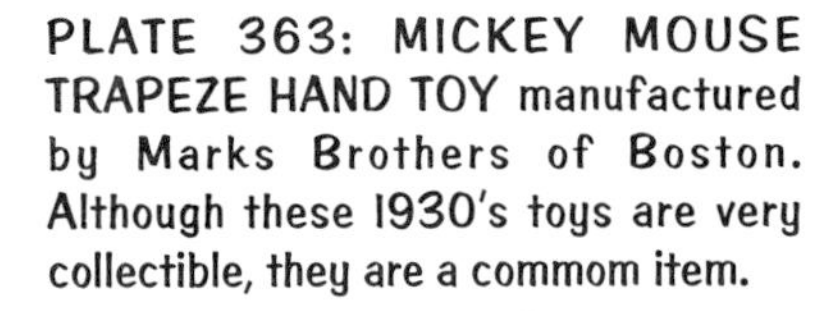

PLATE 363: MICKEY MOUSE TRAPEZE HAND TOY manufactured by Marks Brothers of Boston. Although these 1930's toys are very collectible, they are a commom item.

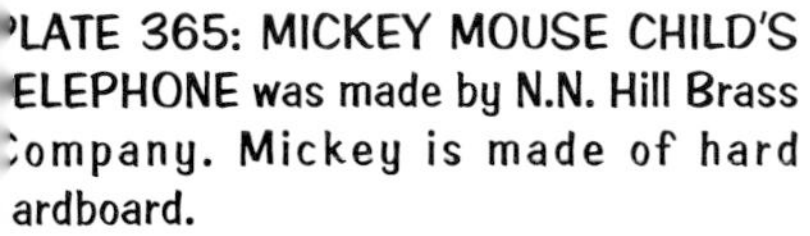

'LATE 365: MICKEY MOUSE CHILD'S
ELEPHONE was made by N.N. Hill Brass
ompany. Mickey is made of hard
ardboard.

'LATE 366: MICKEY MOUSE TUNNEL is made of
apier-maché. It is 1' long by 11" high.

PLATE 368: MICKEY MOUSE ASHTRAY is made of metal. This rat-faced, black and white Mickey is very collectible.

PLATE 367: MICKEY MOUSE CAP was made for the Parisian Company, a Birmingham, Alabama, department store.

PLATE 369: RAT-FACED GERMAN MICKEY MOUSE is made of pressed wood. The label of the foot reads "Mickey Mouse, Walt E. Disney."

PLATE 370: ITEM A - MICKEY MOUSE MAGIC SLATE, 1930's c. Walt Disney Enterprises. ITEM B - MINNIE MOUSE BAKELITE PENCIL SHARPENER, 1930's. ITEM C - MICKEY MOUSE BAKELITE PENCIL SHARPENER, 1930's.

PLATE 371: ITEMS A THROUGH D - MICKEY MOUSE, DONALD DUCK AND PLUTO PENCIL SHARPENERS made of Bakelite in the 1930's.

PLATE 372: MICKEY MOUSE RUG was manufactured by the Alexander Smith and Sons Company.

PLATE 373: MICKEY MOUSE RUG from the 1930's picturing Mickey, Donald, and Pluto playing and dancing to music.

PLATE 374: MICKEY MOUSE TRANSFER-O-S STORE DISPLAY made by the Paas Dye Company.

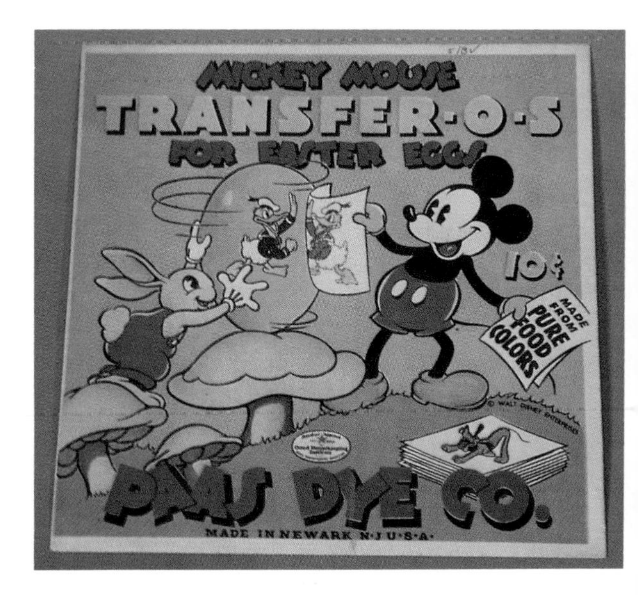

PLATE 375: MICKEY MOUSE TRANSFER-O-S Easter egg transfers (food color decals), c. 1930's Walt Disney Enterprises and manufactured by Paas Dye Company of Newark, N.J.

PLATE 376: MICKEY MOUSE RECIPE SCRAP BOOK c. Walt Disney Enterprises. Shown are original order card, mailing envelope, recipe cards and book. A highly collectible mail order premium set.

PLATE 377: ITEM A - MICKEY MOUSE LAPEL WATCH made by Ingersoll. **ITEM B - MICKEY MOUSE BOOK BANK** was made by the Bell Company.

PLATE 378: MICKEY MOUSE RECIPE LABELS to be used with set pictured in Plate #376. Both are c. Walt Disney Enterprises.

PLATE 379: MICKEY MOUSE DIME REGISTER BANK, c. 1939 Walt Disney Productions. This metal register bank holds up to $5.00 in dimes.

PLATE 380: MICKEY MOUSE CANDY WRAPPER for Mickey Mouse Toasted Nut Chocolate, 1930's, manufactured by Wilbur-Suchard Chocolate Company of Philadelphia, Pennsylvania.

PLATE 381: MICKEY MOUSE SLIDE PICTURES made by Ensign Limited, London.

PLATE 382: MICKEY MOUSE SAFETY FILM AND BOX, 1930's, c. Walt Disney Enterprises, containing one 16mm Mickey Mouse film. Manufactured by Keystone MFG of Boston.

PLATE 383: ITEMS A AND B - MICKEY MOUSE CINE ART FILMS 1930's 16mm films made to fit all standard home projectors.

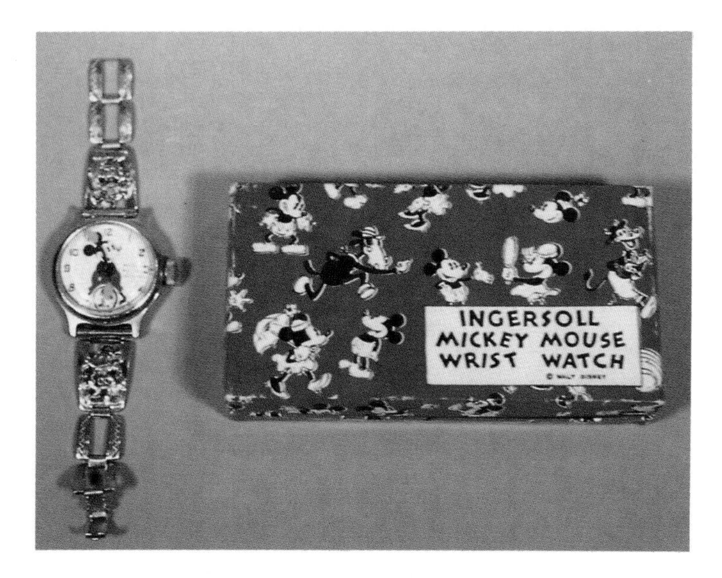

PLATE 384: MICKEY MOUSE WRIST WATCH was made by the Ingersoll Company. This is the first Mickey Mouse watch produced.

PLATE 385: ENGLISH MICKEY MOUSE POCKET WATCH was made by the Ingersoll Company. It features a pink-faced Mickey wearing five-fingered gloves. The watch is marked "Foreign."

PLATE 386: MICKEY MOUSE INGERSOLL POCKET WATCH AND WATCH FOB, 1930's pictured in original box. c. Walt Disney.

PLATE 387: MICKEY MOUSE INGERSOLL WRIST WATCH, 1930's, in original box. Watch sets in boxed displays are prized by all collectors.

PLATE 388: MICKEY MOUSE 1930'S BLACK ENAMELED LAPEL WATCH. Manufactured by Ingersoll and marked c. Walt Disney Enterprises.

PLATE 389: REVERSE OF MICKEY MOUSE LAPEL WATCH pictured in plate #388.

PLATE 390: MICKEY MOUSE COMPACT was made by Cohn and Rosenberger Company. It is made of enamel and tin.

PLATE 391: ITEM A - MICKEY MOUSE POCKET KNIFE c. Walt Disney Enterprises. ITEM B - MICKEY MOUSE SCISSORS, 1930's c. Walt Disney Enterprises.

PLATE 393: MICKEY CELLULOID FIGURES are on a thin base.

PLATE 392: MICKEY AND MINNIE CELLULOID FIGURES were made in Japan.

PLATE 394: MICKEY CELLULOID FIGURES are on a bridge. The figures are hard celluloid. These figures have solid tails, while a hollow tail variation of the same toy appears in Plate #397.

PLATE 396: MICKEY MOUSE AND DONALD DUCK CELLULOID CONTAINERS, 1930's with figural celluloid decorations on top.

PLATE 395: MICKEY MOUSE CELLULOID ON BRIDGE.

PLATE 397: MICKEY MOUSE SOLID CELLULOID FIGURE showing Mickey followed by four tiny little Mickeys. In this variation, Mickey has a hollow tail

PLATE 398: MICKEY MOUSE RATTLE is made of celluloid with bells for hands.

PLATE 399: MICKEY MOUSE CELLULOID FIGURE, human-type hands, circa 1930's.

PLATE 400: MINNIE MOUSE MINIATURE METAL FIGURE, circa 1930's.

PLATE 401: MICKEY MOUSE CELLULOID TOY from the 1930's.

PLATE 402: MINNIE MOUSE PURSE was made by the Cohn and Rosenberger Company. The purse is mesh with an enameled Mickey pin.

PLATE 403: MICKEY MOUSE 1930'S CHILD'S RING with original box showing Mickey running with a letter. This is a rare jewelry item.

CHAPTER TWO

DONALD DUCK AND FRIENDS

Although Mickey and Minnie Mouse were considered Walt Disney's leading man and lady (or leading mice!) in the early 1930's, the Disney Studio quickly realized that simple plots based around two mice and a single villain would be too thin. So very shortly after the creation of Mickey and Minnie Mouse in the late 1920's, an interesting ensemble of other characters emerged from the Disney "stable." First appearing were Pluto the Pup, Clarabelle Cow, Horace Horsecollar, and Dippy the Goof, later to be known as simply "Goofy." The last of the major Disney comic characters to enter the movie scene was Donald Duck, who didn't appear on the screen or in toy merchandising until 1934. Prior to that time, nearly all of the early Disney character items would picture Mickey, Minnie, Pluto, Horace, Dippy, and Clarabelle. If Donald is missing from the design of the item, it is a good bet the toy is pre-1935.

All of the Disney comic characters afforded studio artists the chance to expand plot lines, gags, and movie bits to include a greater variety of action and story possibilities. Because each animal's personality was built around certain character traits of his particular species, these new characters opened up the gate on a stampede of barnyard humor in the early films.

The Disney studios utilized the awkward lankiness of Horace Horsecollar and the somewhat homely clumsiness of Clarabelle Cow to their best advantage. No matter how they drew her or what she wore, Clarabelle was never pretty. But we loved her for what she was – a cow! And Pluto was a peculiar oddity since the studio chose to present him as a smaller companion to Mickey Mouse. In most early illustrations and merchandise, Mickey and Minnie were presented as about two-thirds the height of Horace and Clarabelle. Since the mouse-to-horse and mouse-to-cow scale was already totally unrealistic, Disney artists were free to draw Pluto as Mickey's shorter companion. However, it should be noted, on a few of the early Japanese celluloid Mickey Mouse and Pluto toys, Mickey is presented as a much smaller creature as compared to Pluto (See Chapter One).

But regardless of the popularity of the early characters of Horace, Clarabelle, Dippy, and Pluto, none could claim the real title of "supporting actor" from Donald Duck. Aside from Mickey and Minnie, Donald was the most developed animation character of the Walt Disney Studios. Donald played the frustrated, volatile, unfortunate clown to Mickey Mouse's straight man, or mouse. If an early "Oscar" would have been given to the best actor/animation character in the 1930's, it should certainly have gone to Donald Duck. Although we may never have realized it, Donald's temperamental personality brought a very human dimension to the cartoon screen. He was the little guy who always got the pie in the face, the webbed foot squashed, the bill smashed, or was generally out-smarted. In a sense, he was us. And we laughed at him and cheered for him. On the screen, Donald brought forth a unique, humorously dramatic personality – something that was missing from the cartoons of competing studios in the 1930's.

It is fitting that we begin our photo section beyond Mickey and Minnie Mouse with the cartoon "actor" who so justly deserved at least the "Number Three" spot: Donald Duck. The Donald Duck toy designs are a beautiful complement for and contrast to the 1930's Mickey and Minnie Mouse toys. Whereas Mickey and Minnie were usually designed into toys with colors of red, yellow, black, and white, the Donald Duck toys of the 1930's picture him with bright or navy blue, lots of white, yellow and/or bright orange. In regard to color and design, Donald is as nearly diametrically opposite of Mickey Mouse as he could possibly be. This great contrast is what makes Disneyana collectors dearly love toy examples of both!

The DONALD DUCK CELLULOID WINDUP pictured in Plate #404 is one of the best Donald toy designs of all time! Pictured along with its graphically striking multi-colored original box, this toy is hard to beat. Donald is depicted in this

toy in his familiar early 1930's long-billed, winking style. When wound, the toy waddles neatly along. Celluloid toys of such an early vintage in such mint condition are rarely found. According to many of today's advanced Disneyana collectors, the box nearly doubles the value of this toy! Plate #405 pictures DONALD DUCK ON TRAPEZE along with its original box. Although such windup celluloid trapeze toys are not uncommon, the graphic box design showing a medium-billed Donald is unusual. Plate #407 pictures a much smaller celluloid windup Donald.

Another very attractive celluloid Donald windup is the DONALD DUCK NODDER, pictured in Plate #408. Although this toy utilizes a very simple elastic rubber band windup mechanism, the nodding action of the long-billed head is very humorous and quite pleasing to watch. Although most of the original rubber bands found with these have long ago rotted away, new replacements work very nicely.

The DONALD DUCK CELLULOID ON THE CART is another desirable long-billed Donald celluloid windup toy. This toy is pictured in Plate #410. When wound, the Donald cart wheels around in a neat circle while the miniature character canopy spins wildly. Note that the canopy has miniature figures of Mickey, Minnie, Donald, and Pluto suspended from it. These original canopies are very hard to find and make this a wonderfully complete toy. THE DONALD DUCK IN THE CART PULLED BY PLUTO celluloid windup pictured in Plate #412 is another unique Japanese celluloid toy.

Several fine Donald Duck character dolls are pictured in this chapter. The DONALD DUCK DRUM MAJOR DOLL manufactured by the Knickerbocker Toy Company in the 1930's is pictured in Plate #414. The example pictured is a mint condition toy and is of cloth and felt construction. Another Knickerbocker doll, the DONALD DUCK COMPOSITION DOLL, pictured in Plate #415 and shown wearing his original vest, is a particularly striking design which very closely resembles the cartoon star. Made entirely of wood composition, this Donald has a jointed head and jointed legs. The Knickerbocker DONALD DUCK SAILOR DOLLS pictured in Plates #416 and #417 are a more common variety of 1930's Donald cloth dolls, but they are still desired because of their bright colors, early vintage, and long-billed depiction of Donald.

A wide variety of DONALD DUCK BISQUE FIGURES were produced in Japan in the 1930's and imported into this country. Earlier examples present the desirable long-billed Donald while many others depict him with the more standard mid to late 1930's medium bill. Plate #418 shows a side by side contrast of both bill lengths and designs. Both the DONALD DUCK ON A TRICYCLE and the DONALD DUCK ON A SCOOTER bisques pictured in Plate #419 are hard to find examples. Anytime a Donald figure is associated with another object (rocking horse, paint can, etc.) the bisque is much rarer and more valuable than a plain standing bisque figure.

One of the rarest of all the Disney character 1930's bisque toothbrush holders is pictured in Plate #420. Most Disney collectors are fortunate if they have even just seen this bisque figure for sale. It's almost a miracle to own one! The DONALD DUCK PLAYING A VIOLIN BISQUE FIGURE pictured in Plate #421 is an excellent example of a larger Donald Duck bisque figure. This 4" tall figure was a part of an interesting musical set. Another figure from this musical set is the DONALD DUCK ACCORDION PLAYER BISQUE figure pictured in Plate #422.

The DOUBLE DONALD TOOTHBRUSH HOLDER in Plate #424 is one of the most unique designs among all the Disney character toothbrush holders of the 1930's. No one is really quite sure why there are two Donald figures side by side, but the result of one long bill facing one way and another facing the other way is quite funny. If a collector looks at it long enough, it almost appears to be a sort of frozen "double take." Regardless of why it was produced, it is one of the most sought-after Donald bisque items. An interesting imitation of this toothbrush holder is the DOUBLE DONALD LUSTERWARE ASHTRAY pictured in Plate #425. Although the figures are much smaller and slightly different than those of the toothbrush holder, the concept is still the same. This, too, is a most unusual piece.

Donald Duck was a wonderful subject for many great pull toys. Simply the idea of a temperamental duck pulling along a wagon or cart behind him must have given toymakers countless ideas for toy possibilities. As a result, collectors are afforded the opportunity to collect wonderful 1930's Donald Duck pull toys manufactured by both Fisher Price and the N.N. Hill Brass Company.

Aside from their different trademarks, Fisher Price toys have a distinctly different look than their N.N. Hill Brass counterparts. Most Fisher Price toys have wonderfully multi-colored paper lithographed labels drawn against a colorful background. N.N. Hill Brass toys are nearly always designed against a white background, whether it be Mickey Mouse or Donald. Also, Fisher Price toys usually have small wooden wheels attached to wooden platform bases. N.N. Hill Brass toys usually have the main body of the toy out in front pulling a pair of large metal wheels with a bell on the center axle. The DONALD DUCK PULL TOY by Fisher Price pictured in Plate #426 and the DONALD DUCK N.N. HILL BRASS PULL TOY pictured in Plate #427 show an interesting contrast of similar toys designed by the two different manufacturers. The DONALD DUCK PULL TOY by FIsher Price pictured in Plate #428 has a simple but effective action when rolled. Because the axles are inserted into the wheels off center, the toy bounces up and down when pulled along. This causes the wings, which are mounted to the toy on a rubber strip, to flap as the toy moves along.

The DONALD DUCK CERAMIC PLANTER is one of the most beautiful of all Donald ceramic designs. A perfect likeness of the winking, long-billed squatty duck is depicted standing in front of a wooden fence. Because this piece is glazed ceramic and not simply unglazed bisque, it is even more attractive to collectors. Oddly enough, there are absolutely no markings of identification on this toy, but because of its quality, it must certainly have been an authorized piece. Plates #432 through #434 picture four different paint styles of the popular DONALD DUCK COMPOSITION BANK by Crown Toy and Novelty. These banks are relatively common but are highly collectible because they present an excellent likeness of a mid-1930's Donald. The unique color variations as shown in these examples makes them also interesting to collect as a set. Each has a metal trap door on a hinge in the bottom along with a jointed head which will move from side to side.

Another unusual Fisher Price toy is the DONALD DUCK POP-UP PADDLE toy pictured in Plate #435. This is the rarest of all the paddle toys manufactured by that company and is extremely hard to find with the original wings. The English CERAMIC LONG-BILLED DONALD PITCHER pictured in Plate #436 is another interesting early Donald Duck ceramic design. Three different varieties of SEIBERLING DONALD DUCKS are pictured in Plate #438. The hollow DONALD SQUEAK TOY on the left is the rarest of the three versions because of its fragile hollow construction. Many of these examples either flattened or disintegrated over the years. The two solid Donalds also pictured are wonderful versions of the early Donald and each has a jointed head. Collectors should be especially aware that not all Seiberling figures stand up well even though they may appear to be in mint condition. Before purchasing such examples, always try to stand the figure up. As the hard rubber in these toys ages, it often forces the flat feet to curl upward slightly. Minor off-balance imperfections can be fixed by placing a dab of putty or a coin under the feet. Badly distorted figures should be passed up unless the collector plans to display them lying down in a case.

The WALT DISNEY'S EASTER PARADE as pictured in Plate #439 is one of the rarest Fisher Price toys pictured in this book. Manufactured and marketed as an Easter toy, the set contains three Easter rabbits with eggs, one Donald Duck figure, and one Clara Cluck figure. The whole set is neatly packaged in an attractive "bunny coach" style box. Boxed Fisher Price toys, especially multi-toy sets, are extremely rare and valuable when found today. This toy presents another interesting marketing facet of Donald. Being a duck, he fit right in with the theme of Easter. The Fisher Price toy designers certainly recognized this fact and put his popularity to full use. (Note the Donald toy pulling the little Easter cart with tiny chicks all around it in Plate #426. The cart was undoubtedly designed to be filled with candy and presented as an Easter gift!)

The SCHUCO WINDUP DONALD DUCK pictured in Plate #440 is one of the rarest of all Donald Duck windup toys. The example shown is with its original box and identification tag. The toy is made of a tin body and windup mechanism with the addition of felt clothes and hat. Plate #441 pictures the DONALD DUCK RAIL CAR manufactured by Lionel in the 1930's. Since the first Lionel rail car featured Mickey and Minnie Mouse, it was only fitting that Donald should be featured in his own design. In the Donald handcar version, he is pictured pushing along Pluto and his dog house. The handcar handle moves up and down as Donald pushes Pluto along.

The DONALD DUCK NIGHT LIGHT by the Micro-Lite Company of New York pictured in Plate #446 is worthy of note. This little light is an identical companion to the Mickey Mouse night light pictured in Chapter One and it utilizes the identical tin lithographed cylinder found on the Mickey version. The DONALD DUCK TELEPHONE BANK pictured in Plate #447 is also an interesting piece because it has a double function as both a toy telephone and a savings bank.

The DONALD DUCK ROWBOAT pictured in Plate #451 was manufactured in England by Chad Valley. Shown with its original box, it is an unusual late 1930's Donald toy. Designed as a floor pull toy, Donald "rows" with the oars as the toy is pulled along. Another unique Donald item is the DONALD DUCK ON THE SLED figure by Fun-E-Flex pictured in Plate #455. Any Donald Duck Fun-E-Flex toys are far more rare than Mickey and Minnie versions because fewer were produced. The Donald on the sled combination toy is an extremely rare Fun-E-Flex design.

The DONALD DUCK STORYBOOK pictured in Plate #462 was one of the very first Donald Duck books. It was marketed as a "linen-like" book and features wonderfully colorful heavy paper pages. One of the rarest of all Fun-E-Flex Disney figures pictured in this book is pictured in Plate #465. The HORACE HORSECOLLAR FIGURE is probably the hardest to find of all character toys manufactured by Fun-E-Flex. Although Horace was normally depicted as having a black and white body like Mickey Mouse, he is done in a red hue on this toy. Notice his original cowboy hat!

Pluto rounds out the "Big Four" of early Disney characters. Although Horace and Clarabelle were often pictured as part of a group in the 1930's toys, they were rarely fashioned into toys alone. Therefore, Pluto follows closely behind Donald as the fourth major Disney cartoon character of the 1930's. Once again, Pluto's variety and bright coloring makes him desired by today's Disneyana collectors. Mickey and Minnie toys have lots of red coloring, Donald is done with bright blue, and Pluto adds the third primary color to a Disney toy collection – *yellow!* Most collectors anxiously seek out Pluto toys to round out their Disneyana collection.

The FISHER PRICE TOY PLUTO pictured in Plate #468 is an unusual rolling toy depicting a wonderfully graphic 1930's Pluto. The three different versions of Louis Marx Plutos shown in Plate #469 give evidence to the great variety of 1930's Pluto toys manufactured by that company. One of the toys is a simple tin windup, and the second is a lever action toy which uses Pluto's red tail as a windup mechanism to wind the toy, and a third is a "Rollover Pluto" which moves forward and rolls completely over. All three are fine examples of the colorful designs typical of 1930's Marx toys.

The DONALD DUCK AND ELMER ELEPHANT TEA SET pictured in Plate #477 is an interesting child's china set. Although Mickey Mouse is also a part of the design, what makes the set highly unusual is the addition of Elmer Elephant. Since Elmer was generally considered only a minor Disney character even in the 1930's, it is rare to find more than a handful of examples of Elmer Elephant toys. And to find him "sharing the billing" on a 1930's tea set with the superstars Mickey and Donald is even more unusual. Another interesting Elmer collectible is the ELMER ELEPHANT BISQUE TOOTHBRUSH HOLDER pictured in Plate #478. This is another extremely hard to find Disney bisque toothbrush holder example. Other Elmer toys pictured along with the toothbrush holder in this chapter are a linen-like storybook (Plate #479), a musical stuffed toy (Plate #480), and a box of ELMER THE ELEPHANT SOAP (Plate #481).

Several small highly collectible Disney items conclude this chapter. The DISNEY CHARACTER 1930's FIGURAL BAKELITE PENCIL SHARPENERS pictured in Plate #488 are only a tiny sampling of the many varieties of these available to collectors today. Because they are small and handy to display and collect combined with the fact that they all feature wonderfully colorful decals and attractive Bakelite bodies, examples of these are extremely popular among today's Disneyana collectors. The FIGURAL CELLULOID PENCIL SHARPENERS and TAPE MEASURES as pictured in Plate #489 are also very valuable today and prized by even advanced collectors.

Although the "Donald and Friends" sampling of items in this chapter represents only about one fourth of the quantity of Mickey and Minnie Mouse items pictured, that distribution is nearly proportional to the number of items produced and available to today's collectors.

Most collectors of Disneyana begin with their focus on Mickey and Minnie Mouse, and most inevitably branch out to collect Donald Duck and Pluto. Because Donald is probably the most "human" of all the Disney characters, many collectors hold an especially dear place in their hearts for him. He is the eternal underdog, and that may be why we love him.

PLATE 404: DONALD DUCK CELLULOID WINDUP was made in Japan. The tin windup mechanism is encased in his body.

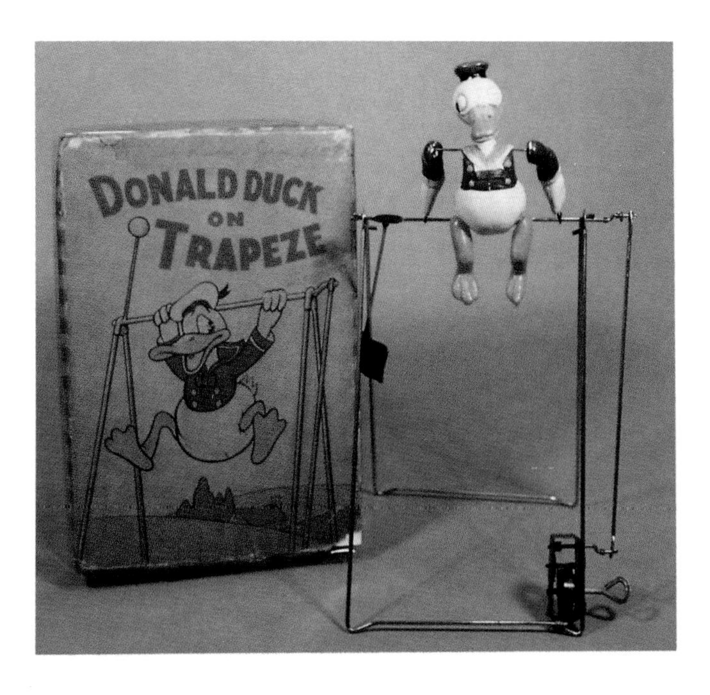

PLATE 405: DONALD DUCK ON TRAPEZE is made of celluloid and was distributed by the George Borgfeldt Company.

PLATE 406: DONALD DUCK WADDLER.

PLATE 407: DONALD DUCK WINDUP is made of celluloid and tin.

PLATE 408: DONALD DUCK CELLULOID NODDER WINDUP featuring a long-billed Donald Duck. Circa 1930's.

PLATE 409: DONALD DUCK CELLULOID ACROBAT.

PLATE 410: DONALD DUCK CELLULOID ON CART is the rarer version known for its hanging figural celluloids.

PLATE 411: DONALD DUCK CELLULOID FIGURE.

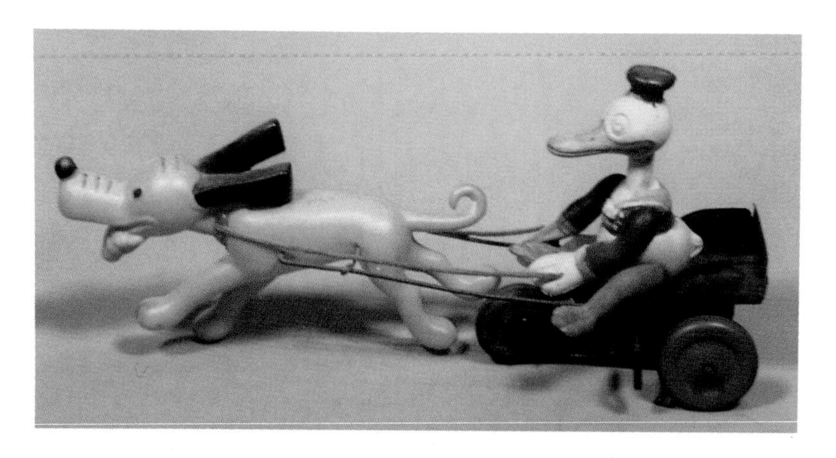

PLATE 412: DONALD DUCK AND PLUTO CELLULOID CART.

PLATE 413, ITEMS A - D: DONALD DUCK CELLULOIDS from the 1930's. Item A - pencil sharpener. Item B - tape measure. Items C & D - jointed figures.

PLATE 414: DONALD DUCK DRUM MAJOR DOLL manufactured by Knickerbocker Toy Company in the 1930's. Costumed dolls in such mint condition are a rarity.

PLATE 415: DONALD DUCK COMPOSITION DOLL is 9" tall and was produced by the Knickerbocker Toy Company. He is wearing his original vest.

PLATE 416: DONALD DUCK CLOTH DOLL was made by the Knickerbocker Toy Company. It is 12" tall.

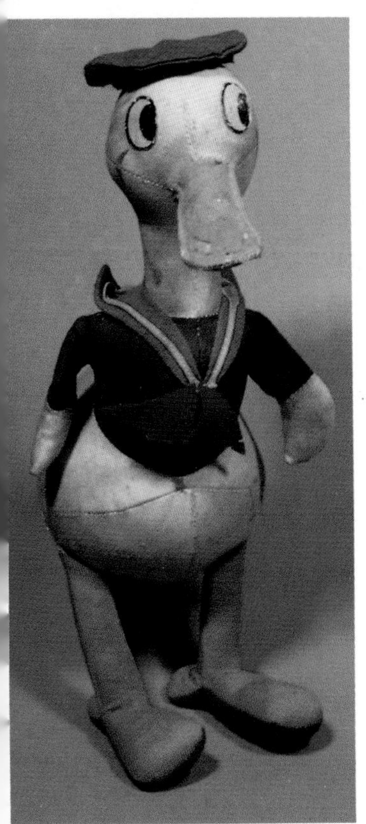

PLATE 417: DONALD DUCK CLOTH DOLL manufactured by Knickerbocker Toy Company in the 1930's. Similar doll to one pictured in Plate #417.

PLATE 418: ITEMS A THROUGH C – DONALD DUCK BISQUE FIGURES, 1930's, Japan, each 3½" tall.

PLATE 419: ITEM A – DONALD DUCK ON A TRICYCLE BISQUE FIGURE, 1930's. ITEM B - DONALD ON A SCOOTER BISQUE FIGURE, 1930's, Japan.

PLATE 420: DONALD DUCK TOOTHBRUSH HOLDER is the rarest of all the toothbrush holders.

PLATE 421: DONALD DUCK PLAYING A VIOLIN BISQUE is 4" tall.

PLATE 422: DONALD DUCK ACCORDION PLAYER BISQUE.

PLATE 423: DONALD DUCK BISQUE is 4¼" tall.

PLATE 424: DONALD DUCK TOOTHBRUSH HOLDER is referred to as "Siamese Donald" or "Double Donald" toothbrush holder.

PLATE 425: DONALD DUCK LUSTERWARE GLAZED CERAMIC ASHTRAY, 1930's, Walt E. Disney, picturing a pair of side by side long-billed Donalds.

PLATE 426: DONALD DUCK FISHER PRICE PULL TOY, 1930's, showing Donald with a long bill and pulling a basket decorated with chicks. C. Walt Disney Enterprises.

PLATE 427: DONALD DUCK BELL RINGER PULL TOY manufactured by N.N. Hill Brass Company. Bell ringing mechanism is located on axle between large wheels.

PLATE 428: LONG-BILLED DONALD DUCK PULL TOY manufactured by Fisher Price Toys, 1930's, c. Walt Disney Enterprises. Off-center axles on wheels cause toy to bob up and down forcing rubber mounted wings to flap.

PLATE 429: DONALD DUCK ROLLING TOY by Fisher Price toys in the 1930's. This cute long-billed Donald toy is only 4" tall.

PLATE 430: LONG BILLED DONALD DUCK BISQUE TOOTHBRUSH HOLDER, Japan, 1930's, Walt E. Disney copyright.

PLATE 431: DONALD DUCK GLAZED CERAMIC PLANTER, 1930's, measures 6" tall and features an excellent design of a long-billed, winking Donald.

PLATE 432: DONALD DUCK COMPOSITIO BANK WITH JOINTED HEAD maunfactured b Crown Toy and Novelty, 1930's, c. Walt Disne Enterprises. Bright blue suit version.

PLATE 433: DONALD DUCK CROWN TOY COMPOSITION BANK, 1930's, showing yellow-suited Donald.

PLATE 434: ITEMS A AND B - DONALD DUCK COMPOSITION BANKS by Crown Toy and Novelty, 1930's, showing navy blue- and pink-suited Donalds.

PLATE 435: DONALD DUCK POP-UP PADDLE was made by Fisher Price. The wings are made of rubber and rarely found with the toy.

PLATE 436: DONALD DUCK LONG-BILLED CREAM PITCHER, English, by Wade Heath of England. The lid to this pitcher is on Donald's back between his wings.

PLATE 437: DONALD DUCK PLATE was part of the Patriot line of the Salem China Company.

PLATE 438: SEIBERLING DONALD DUCKS are all made of rubber.

PLATE 439: WALT DISNEY'S EASTER PARADE manufactured by Fisher Price Toys and copyright Walt Disney Enterprises. This is one of the rarest boxed Fisher Price toy sets.

PLATE 440: SCHUCO WINDUP LONG-BILLED DONALD, circa 1930's. Metal construction with cloth torso and hat. Makes quacking noise. Pictured with original box.

PLATE 441: DONALD DUCK AND PLUTO WINDUP HAND CAR by Lionel Train Corp., 1930's. Pictured with original box.

PLATE 442: DONALD DUCK AND CLARA CLUCK CHILD'S TEA TRAY from 1930's Ohio Art Tea Set, c. Walt Disney Enterprises.

PLATE 443: DONALD DUCK TIN PAIL was made by the Ohio Art Company.

PLATE 444: DONALD DUCK WATERING CAN by Ohio Art Company of Bryan, Ohio, 1930's. c. Walt Disney Enterprises. Pictures Donald watering his garden on reverse.

PLATE 445: DONALD DUCK WATERING CAN by Ohio Art, 1930's, c. Walt Disney Enterprises.

PLATE 446: DONALD DUCK NIGHT LIGHT by Micro-Lite Co. of New York, 1938. c. Walt Disney Enterprises,

PLATE 447: DONALD DUCK TOY TELEPHONE AND BANK manufactured by N.N. Hill Brass of East Hampton, Connecticut. c. Walt Disney enterprises, 1930's.

PLATE 448: DONALD DUCK AND MICKEY MOUSE TIN AND PAPER DRUM c. Walt Disney Enterprises, 1930's.

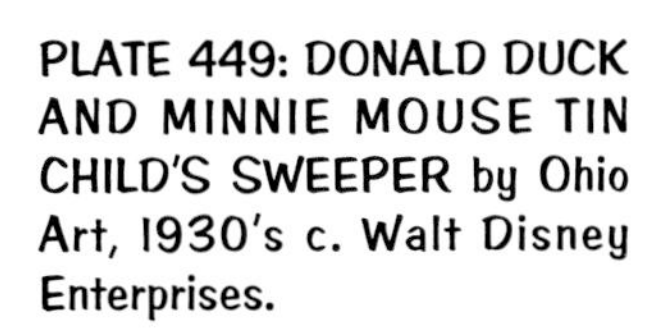

PLATE 449: DONALD DUCK AND MINNIE MOUSE TIN CHILD'S SWEEPER by Ohio Art, 1930's c. Walt Disney Enterprises.

PLATE 450: DONALD DUCK SOAP and original 1930's boxes by Lightfoot Shultz Company, c. Walt Disney Enterprises.

PLATE 451: DONALD DUCK ROWBOAT was made by the Chad Valley Company, circa late 1930's, England.

PLATE 452: ITEM A - DONALD DUCK CELLULOID PENCIL SHARPENER. ITEM B - DONALD DUCK CELLULOID TAPE MEASURE.

PLATE 453: ITEM A - DONALD DUCK HAIR BRUSH. ITEM B - DONALD DUCK CELLULOID.

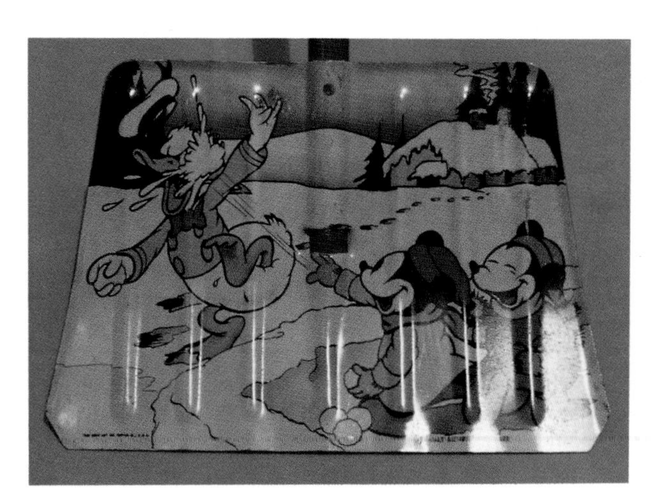

PLATE 454: GIANT CHILD'S TIN SNOW SHOVEL by Ohio Art Company picturing Mickey's nephews throwing snowballs at an angry Donald Duck, c. Walt Disney Enterprises.

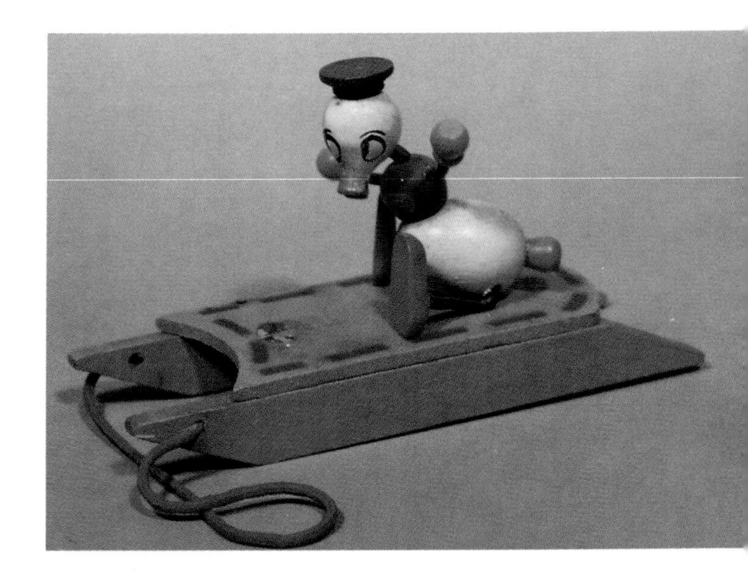

PLATE 455: DONALD DUCK ON SLED is a Fun-E-Flex product. Both the sled and Donald have separate Fun-E-Flex labels.

PLATE 456: DONALD DUCK LARGE SAND SHOVEL by Ohio Art, 1938 Walt Disney Enterprises. Tin shovel with wooden handle.

PLATE 457: DONALD DUCK WINDUP was made in France. It is made of composition and aluminum and is 7" tall.

PLATE 458: DONALD DUCK BRUSHES by Hughes-Autograf Brush Company of New York, circa 1930's and c. Walt Disney Enterprises.

PLATE 459: DONALD DUCK TIN PAINT BOX, copyright Walt Disney Enterprises and manufactured by Transogram, 1930's.

PLATE 460: *DONALD DUCK HAS HIS UPS AND DOWNS*, a Walt Disney Picture Storybook, 1930's, Walt Disney Enterprises.

PLATE 461: MICKEY MOUSE AND DONALD DUCK SKI JUMP TARGET SET by American Toy Works of New York, c. Walt Disney Enterprises – Hollywood, California.

PLATE 462: DONALD DUCK LINEN-LIKE STORYBOOK c. Walt Disney Enterprises, 1930's.

PLATE 463: DONALD DUCK UMBRELLA was made by the Louis Weiss Company.

PLATE 464: MICKEY MOUSE MAGAZINE, May 1936, picturing an angry long-billed Donald on the cover.

PLATE 465: HORACE HORSE-COLLAR WOOD FIGURE is a rare Fun-E-Flex figure. His tail is made of rope.

PLATE 466: ITEM A – GOOFY BISQUE, 1930's 3½" tall. ITEM B – HORACE HORSECOLLAR BISQUE figure, 1930's 3½" tall. Both figures c. Walt Disney.

PLATE 467: *WALT DISNEY'S STORY OF CLARABELLE COW* small storybook, by Whitman Publishing, c. 1938 Walt Disney Enterprises.

PLATE 468: PLUTO FISHER PRICE PUSH TOY, 9" long with wood construction and lithographed paper labels on both sides, c. Walt Disney Enterprises.

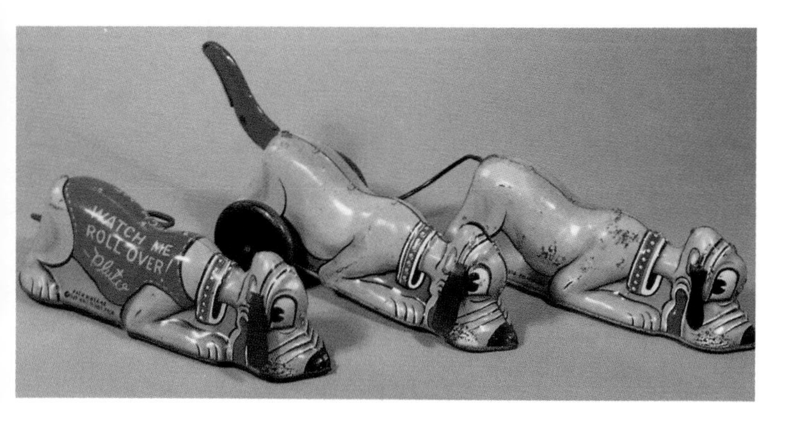

PLATE 469: PLUTO TIN WINDUPS were all made by the Louis Marx Company.

PLATE 470: PLUTO THE PUP AND HIS HOUSE. Both pieces were manufactured by Fun-E-Flex in the 1930's.

PLATE 471: PLUTO THE PUP FIGURES by Fun-E-Flex in the 1930's, c. Walt Disney Enterprises.

PLATE 472: "MICKEY MOUSE'S PAL PLUTO MODELED IN CASTILE SOAP" c. Walt Disney Enterprises, 1930's.

PLATE 473: GIANT PLUTO FUN-E-FLEX figure from the 1930's, c. Walt Disney Enterprises.

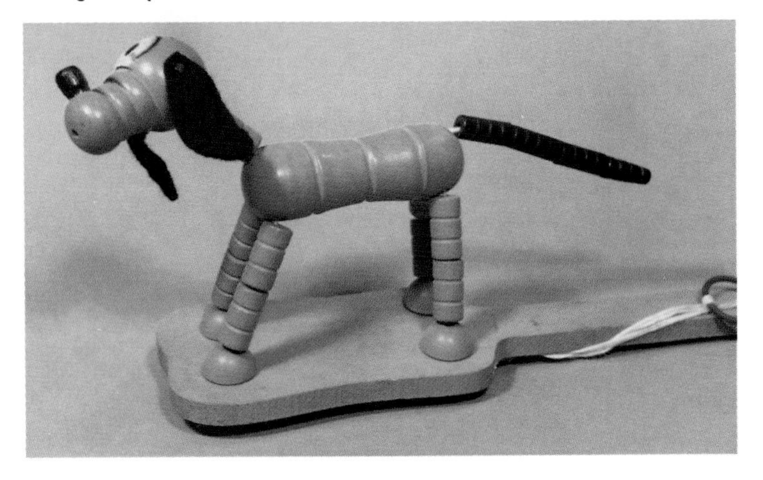

PLATE 474: POP-UP PLUTO PADDLE TOY manufactured by Fisher Price in the 1930's.

PLATE 475: LARGE STUFFED VELVET PLUTO, no tags or markings but factory manufactured and circa 1930's.

PLATE 476: PLUTO THE PUP CUP by Patriot China, c. Walt Disney Enterprises.

PLATE 477: DONALD DUCK, MICKEY MOUSE, AND ELMER THE ELEPHANT TEA SET, glazed china circa 1930's. Made in Japan.

PLATE 478: ELMER THE ELEPHANT BISQUE TOOTHBRUSH HOLDER, 1930's, c. Walt Disney Enterprises.

PLATE 479: ELMER THE ELEPHANT LINEN-LIKE BOOK, c. Walt Disney Enterprises.

PLATE 480: ELMER THE ELEPHANT stuffed doll with jointed head and musical windup mechanism, circa 1930's.

LATE 481: ELMER THE LEPHANT MODELED IN 'OAP, boxed, 5" tall, c. Walt 'isney.

PLATE 482: *PLUTO THE PUP: A WALT DISNEY PICTURE STORY*, c. 1937 by Walt Disney Enterprises, Hollywood, California. Linen-like book.

PLATE 483: ITEMS A THROUGH E – SMALL DISNEY CHARACTER STORYBOOKS, c. Walt Disney Enterprises.

PLATE 484: "WALT DISNEY CHARACTERS MOVIE STUDIO TO COLOR AND ERECT" c. 1939 Walt Disney Productions. Set contains figures, set, and script along with crayons.

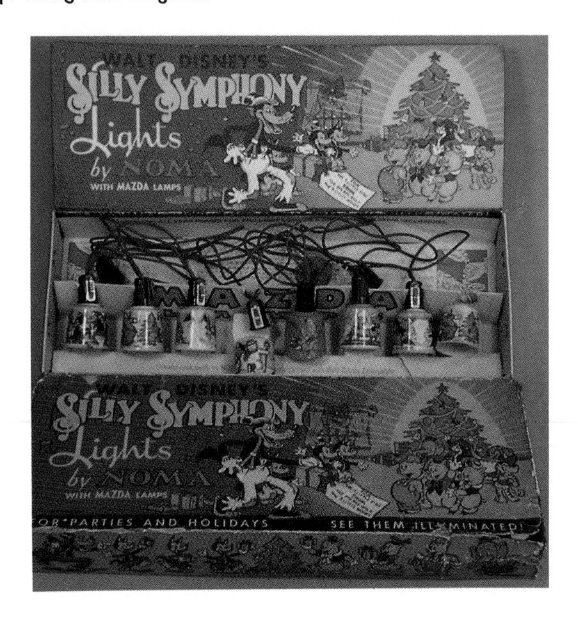

PLATE 486: "WALT DISNEY'S SILLY SYMPHONY LIGHTS BY NOMA" c. Walt Disney Enterprises, 1930's. Features Three Pigs, Big Bad Wolf, Little Wolves, Robber Kitten and Elmer Elephant on lamp covers.

PLATE 489: CELLULOID PENCIL SHARPENERS have the sharpeners encased in their bodies.

PLATE 485: DISNEY CHARACTER CELLULOID CHARMS, circa 1930's.

PLATE 487: SILLY SYMPHONY FAN, c. Walt Disney Enterprises. Has advertising on back and was a giveaway.

PLATE 488: WALT DISNEY CHARACTER BAKELITE PENCIL SHARPENERS. Donald Duck, Pinocchio, Dopey, Snow White, Long-Billed Donald, and Ferdinand.

CHAPTER THREE

DISNEY FEATURE FILM COLLECTIBLES

Walt Disney may have founded and financed his studio on the popularity of Mickey Mouse in the 1930's, but it was his unique experimentation with the featurette and feature length cartoon that put the Walt Disney Studio on the map as a viable Hollywood entity. No one can speculate exactly what would have happened had the Disney Studio chosen to continue producing cartoon "shorts" only. Mickey Mouse might have become old hat. The studio might have lost its creative edge. Fortunately for Disneyana collectors Walt chose to set his sights on a larger goal than simply the production of one popular Mickey Mouse cartoon after another. Historians have called Walt Disney a visionary. Animation film experts have called him a genius. And most Disneyana collectors look up to him with friendly admiration and a child-like awe and simply call him "Walt." Though we may not own his autograph, nor ever have been fortunate enough to shake his hand, he seems our friend. Almost family. And it was his creation of the countless Disney feature films that taught us the real spectacle of fairy tales. It is this sense of awe, this endearment, that drives today's Disneyana collectors through countless toy shows and flea markets searching for remembrances of those Saturday afternoon matinees filled with wicked witches, beautiful princesses, seven little dwarfs, a wooden puppet who dances without strings, and of course, Mickey Mouse.

Film animation underwent a unique evolution at the Walt Disney Studios in the 1930's. Walt knew that animation could make a greater impact on the movie world than simply filling the open time slots between feature films and the refreshment stand. But the Studio did not jump immediately from the Mickey Mouse short cartoons to the feature length animation films. There was a logical progression. The "Silly Symphonies" were short subject films which had no unifying character from one film to the next. Neither did they have any unifying theme. From "Flowers and Trees," the world's first color cartoon, to "Three Little Pigs," the "Silly Symphonies" allowed Walt and his studio to experiment with special effects, new animation techniques, color animation, and the relationship of animation to the other most important aspects of the film experience, music and sound. These "Symphonies," then, were stepping stones to the experimental full-length animation feature project, *Snow White and the Seven Dwarfs.*

One of the most popular of all the Disney short animation films was "Three Little Pigs," which appeared in 1933. Because America had only recently slipped into the grasp of the Great Depression, this little film with its unlikely heroes became something of a national symbol as the "little guy" attempted to hold off the "Big Bad Wolf." The famous song, "Who's Afraid of the Big Bad Wolf," made its debut in the film and was a hit not only because of its catchy tune and tie-in to the story, but also because it symbolized American triumph and bravery in hard times. Therefore, aside from Mickey and Minnie Mouse, Three Little Pigs collectibles are some of the earliest Walt Disney Enterprises pieces.

The THREE LITTLE PIGS CELLULOID WINDUP TRAPEZE TOY pictured in Plate #490 is a highly unusual item because it was designed with three celluloid characters. Normally, Japanese celluloid acrobatic windup toys featured one or two figures. The fact that this toy presents all three pigs on the mechanical swing makes it a very desirable Three Little Pigs collectible. Notice that all three of the pigs are dressed differently.

THE BIG BAD WOLF ALARM CLOCK shown in Plate #491 is a superior alarm clock collectible. Designed with a snarling Big Bad Wolf on the face and the Three Little Pigs spaced around the hour positions, it is a striking and beautiful timepiece. The words "Who's Afraid of the Big Bad Wolf" are written around the top of the clock face. This clock was manufactured by Ingersoll. The WHO'S AFRAID OF THE BIG BAD WOLF – THREE LITTLE PIGS BISQUE FIGURES SET shown with its original colorful box was made in Japan and distributed by George Borgfeldt. Although the figures themselves are not uncommon, it is rare to find such sets in their original boxes.

The THREE LITTLE PIGS TIN TEA SET manufactured by the Ohio Art Company of Bryan, Ohio, in the early 1930's is pictured in Plates #494 and #495. The enlargement of the tea tray in Plate #494 shows the wonderful colors and strong graphic design of the tin lithography on these pieces. The entire set is pictured in Plate #495. Several other fine examples of Ohio Art Three Little Pigs pieces are pictured in Plates #496 and #497. The THREE LITTLE PIGS WATERING CAN is one of the harder to find sprinkler versions manufactured by Ohio Art in the 1930's. The THREE LITTLE PIGS PAIL as pictured in Plate #497 is also an unusual design because of the addition of a neat "deluxe" platform base. This pail also pictures Disney's Little Red Riding Hood on the reverse side. The large THREE LITTLE PIGS SAND PAIL shown in Plates #498 and #499 shows the vibrant colors used by Ohio Art in its 1930's tin lithography. On this pail, the pigs are shown playing their musical instruments in front of the straw house while the wolf awaits them hungrily.

The two styles of THREE LITTLE PIGS TOOTHBRUSH

HOLDERS pictured in Plates #500 and #501 are interesting because of both their striking similarity and their subtle difference. The bisque toothbrush holder in Plate #500 shows the two musical pigs playing their instruments while the "Practical Pig" works on a stack of bricks with a trowel. The style shown in Plate #501 is identical to Plate #500 *except* for the substitution of a drum and cymbal where the bricks were. This is one of those oddities that occur when designs at the factory are changed slightly. It is believed that the style shown in Plate #500 is the earlier of the two designs. The small THREE LITTLE PIGS AND THE BIG BAD WOLF BISQUE SET pictured in Plate #503 is hard to find with an included wolf. The pig bisques are relatively common but the wolf is not. Collectors should jump at the chance to buy a complete set whenever one is offered.

Two very interesting Three Little Pigs sets are pictured in Plates #504 and #505. The first of these two plates shows a complete set of the THREE LITTLE PIGS SEIBERLING FIGURES manufactured by Seiberling Latex Products Company of Akron, Ohio, in the 1930's. Because these pigs are made of hollow rubber, they are often found in badly damaged condition. It is extremely rare to find a complete set in as good a condition as those pictured in Plate #504. It remains a puzzle to us all why the "Practical Pig" was molded with a darker shade of rubber, but he is painted with detailing very similar to the other two. All three pig figures have movable heads. The THREE LITTLE PIGS WOOD FIGURES pictured in Plate #505 are an extremely rare set of characters manufactured by Fun-E-Flex. Although this company must have turned out thousands upon thousands of the Mickey and Minnie figures in the 1930's, the Three Little Pigs figures are very hard to find today, especially as a complete set!

Several different styles of PATRIOT CHINA THREE LITTLE PIGS ceramic cups, plates and bowls manufactured by the Salem China Company are pictured in Plates #508, #509, #510, and #511. All of these ceramic pieces bear bright decal graphics on glazed china surfaces. WALT DISNEY'S OWN LITTLE RED RIDING HOOD GAME pictured in Plate #512 also features the Big Bad Wolf and the Three Little Pigs on the box lid and the game board. This game was manufactured by the Parker Brothers Company of Salem, Massachusetts. Another THREE LITTLE PIGS GAME BOARD is pictured in Plate #513. It is titled "WHO'S AFRAID OF THE BIG BAD WOLF – WALT DISNEY'S OWN GAME" and was manufactured by the Einson Freeman company in 1933.

One of the most beautiful areas of Disneyana collecting is Snow White and the Seven Dwarfs memorabilia. Since many of the Snow White items were geared toward purchase by little girls, this area of Disneyana collecting is popular among women, doll collectors, and those collectors who like adding a softer touch to their Disneyana collections. It is amazing that so many Snow White and the Seven Dwarfs items were manufactured in such a short time. Undoubtedly, the popularity of the film itself and its uniqueness as the first full-length animated feature helped to boost sales of toys related to the film. But it must also have been the film's broad appeal to all little girls that made merchandising and marketing of the items so successful.

The SNOW WHITE AND THE DWARFS PULL TOY manufactured by N.N. Hill Brass and pictured in Plate #522 is a wonderful example of a pull toy designed for a little girl. Although certainly many little boys must have owned this toy too, it definitely is designed with a more feminine touch. The blue birds circling the hub of the wheel are typical of the softer touches and borders often found on the Snow White toys. Pictured in Plate #523 is the Fisher Price DOPEY AND DOC PULL TOY. When pulled along, the interesting little wooden toy has fun action: Doc and Dopey alternately chop at the tree stump which rests in the center as the toy moves along. The exact same Dopey figure is used on a single dwarf pull toy also made by Fisher Price in the 1930's which is pictured in Plate #524. He strikes the stump "drum" with two alternating mallets when the toy is pulled along.

The DOPEY NIGHT LIGHT manufactured in 1938 by the Micro-Lite Company of New York is an interesting little Snow White character piece. A tin lithographed cylinder holds the battery inside and has a light bulb on top. The scene on the cylinder pictures the dwarfs finding Snow White in bed. Next to the cylinder stands a 3" die-cut Dopey figure who appears to be holding it up. The switch for this light is on the base. Similar Mickey Mouse and Donald Duck versions of this light were manufactured and are pictured elsewhere in this book.

The Knickerbocker Toy Company produced many different styles and lines of Snow White and the Seven Dwarfs character dolls in the late 1930's. Many fine examples of these can still be found today, some even with their original Knickerbocker wrist tags intact. These wrist tags picture the face of a Snow White doll in the middle surrounded by the faces of all of the dwarf dolls. Not only does the wrist tag help to identify the doll's maker, it also significantly increases the value of the doll itself. The DOPEY WOOD COMPOSITION DOLL manufactured by Knickerbocker is pictured in Plate #527. This doll is a perfect example of this line of composition dolls and it is pictured with its original Knickerbocker tag. Because the composition on all of these dolls is covered with a hard paint finish, many have survived in excellent condition. However, Disneyana collectors should be aware that fine composition dolls can seemingly self-destruct overnight. The problems? Moisture, temperature fluctuations, and direct sunlight. Whenever composition is exposed to extremes of temperature or humidity, it can crack or split immediately, scarring the toy forever. Collectors should take precautions to make sure their composition toys are protected from extremes.

Another character doll worthy of special note is the large HAPPY THE DWARF DOLL which was manufactured by Chad Valley of England in the 1930's. This doll bears an excellent keness to the movie character and is constructed completely cotton fabric, linen, and wool felt. His hair-like wool beard is l original. As pictured in Plate #528, this doll's facial atures are painted on molded cloth. The SNOW WHITE OLL pictured in Plate #530 has an oilcloth face and was anufactured by Ideal Toy and Novelty in the 1930's. Her tin and velvet dress is original and has silkscreened designs Snow White and the Seven Dwarfs around the bottom lthough these have faded from age). The DOPEY DOLL ctured in Plate #533 was also manufactured by Chad alley of England in the 1930's and is shown with his original g. This doll is substantially smaller than the Happy doll own in Plate #528. Obviously, several different sizes and ts of these dolls were manufactured in the late 1930's by e Chad Valley Company.

Additional dwarf dolls manufactured by the Knickerbocker y Company in the 1930's are pictured in Plates #534 and 536. All are completely wood composition and dressed in iginal velvet clothing. Plate #538 begins several hotographs of the rare MADAME ALEXANDER SNOW HITE AND THE SEVEN DWARFS MARIONETTES anufactured by the Alexander Doll Company in the 1930's. iese puppets are rarely found as a complete set and even ngle examples are hard to come by. All have wonderfully etailed wood composition heads, hands, and feet. The mainder of their wood jointed bodies are covered with cloth stumes appropriate to their character. Probably the hardest find of all the examples pictured is SNOW WHITE herself, ctured in Plate #538. Also shown in Plates #539 through 542 are BASHFUL, DOC, DOPEY, AND HAPPY. All have ack cords with a wooden marionette control at the top.

Two superior DWARF LAMP examples are pictured in lates #544 and #545. Both lamps pictured were anufactured by La Mode Studios of California in 1938 and re marked "copyright Walt Disney Enterprises." Although the mps appear to be wood composition, they are actually plaster overed with a rich and colorful glaze. Both are shown with riginal lamp shades. The DOPEY LAMP has a shade picturing opey with bubbles coming out of his ears. The DOC LAMP ictures Doc and all of the dwarfs dancing with Snow White. he inclusion of the original shade with one of these lamps can ouble or even triple the value of the item! La Mode Disney ems are particularly popular among California Disneyana ollectors. Five additional La Mode pieces are pictured in lates #546 through #549 and in Plate #551. Pictured in late #546 is a rare DOPEY NIGHT LIGHT by La Mode. This articular style is much harder to find than the standard OPEY LAMP pictured in Plate #547. The GRUMPY OOKEND pictured in Plate #549 is also worthy of notice. his piece would have originally been sold as one of a matched air of Grumpy figures.

Not all significant and collectible Snow White and the even Dwarfs collectibles came from American ianufacturers. The S. Maw and Sons Company of England manfactured several beautiful ceramic Disney pieces in the 1930's. All are marked with the words "Genuine Walt Disney Copyright – Foreign" stamped on the base. Pictured in Plates #552 and #553 are beautiful examples of detailing in glazed CERAMIC TOOTHPICK HOLDER FIGURES of Doc, Snow White, Bashful and Dopey. Aside from being hard to find and unusual English Disneyana collectibles, one of the things that is so satisfying to Disney collectors about these pieces is their true likeness to the film characters and their exquisite detailing. This is also true of the DOPEY AND HAPPY BOOKENDS (Plate #554) which are a beautiful example of still another type of item manufactured by S. Maw and Sons in the 1930's.

The complete set of SNOW WHITE AND THE SEVEN DWARFS CELLULOID FIGURES pictured in Plate #558 is an unusual Japanese-produced 1930's character set. Single examples of dwarfs from this set are not often found, and the complete set as pictured is extremely rare. The BISQUE SNOW WHITE AND THE SEVEN DWARFS SETS pictured in Plate #560 and #561 are more common than their celluloid counterpart, but they are still highly collectible among today's Disneyana enthusiasts. The bisque set pictured in Plate #560 is the largest of all 1930's Snow White bisque sets with Snow White measuring 6½" tall! The smaller versions of this set are more common, but are still very collectible because of their bright colors and the excellent likenesses to the Disney characters. The complete boxed set of SNOW WHITE AND THE SEVEN DWARFS BISQUE FIGURES pictured in Plate #563 is worthy of special attention. All of the dwarf figures pictured in this set are in absolute mint condition and the box itself is also near mint. The box lid to this set is one of the most beautiful and colorful of all the boxed Disney bisque sets.

The DOPEY WINDUP TIN WALKER manufactured by Louis Marx in 1938 is one of the very few windup toys associated with Snow White and the Seven Dwarfs manufactured in the 1930's. This may be due in part to the fact that Snow White was seen as a more marketable toy theme for girls, and toymakers may have generally regarded tin windups as "boy toys." This may account for the fact that there was never a Snow White character windup toy manufactured by Louis Marx. The Marx Dopey windup character is pictured in Plate #564. A mint condition MADAME ALEXANDER DOPEY COMPOSITION DOLL is pictured in his original box along with original wrist tag in Plate #565. The end of this shoebox-sized container has a blue on white graphic printed label from Snow White and the Seven Dwarfs.

The gorgeous TINS shown in Plates #566, #568, and #569 all present Snow White and the Seven Dwarfs as main characters in absolutely splendid color lithography. All of these examples were manufactured in Belgium in the 1930's, and consequently are quite rare. The first example shows Snow White with virtually all of the 1930's Disney characters playing in a meadow. The latter two examples recreate scenes from the movie itself. Because these tins are so exquisite and represent such superior color tin lithography, they are also often collected by advertising and tin collectors.

The Ohio Art Company of Bryan, Ohio, manufactured several interesting Snow White and the Seven Dwarfs tea sets and watering cans during the late 1930's. Two sizes of the SNOW WHITE WATERING CAN are pictured in Plate #570. The designs on both are identical, and the picture lithographed on the back sides of the cans is shown in Plate #571. These cans are relatively scarce compared to some of the other Disney tin pieces by Ohio Art. Plates #572 and #573 show two different beautiful SAND PAIL examples with Snow White character lithography. The giant pail pictured in Plate #573 is one of the largest sand pails ever produced by the Ohio Art Company. Pictured in Plates #574 and #575 are items from the 1938 SNOW WHITE TEA SET also manufactured by Ohio Art which are marked "c. Walt Disney Enterprises."

The complete set of SEIBERLING RUBBER DWARF FIGURES from *Snow White and the Seven Dwarfs* is pictured in Plate #577. These are relatively common as single items, but much harder to find as a complete set. The hollow rubber Snow White figure was much less durable and she is almost impossible to find unless a collector stumbles upon a boxed set! A complete set of these figures is permanently on display in the "Walt Disney Story" memorabilia exhibit just inside the Magic Kingdom at Walt Disney World. That display alone is probably responsible for showing more non-collectors how charming Disneyana can be than any other display in Walt Disney World. The SNOW WHITE CHARACTER GLASSES pictured in Plate #576 are extremely colorful and rather unusual. Each appears to have a durable 1930's character decal attached to the front of a juice glass.

The Halsam Company manufactured several different sizes of SNOW WHITE AND THE SEVEN DWARFS BLOC SETS during the 1930's. Two size variations of these sets a pictured in Plates #580 and #581. The larger boxed s contains 32 "safety" blocks and the smaller boxed s contains nine. Each block in the set is printed with letters a embossed pictures of all of the characters from the mov ranging from the dwarfs to Snow White and the Prince. T box lid illustrations are very colorful as are the paints on t blocks. Two contrasting SNOW WHITE GAMES we manufactured by rival game companies in the 1930's. T Parker Brothers game, SNOW WHITE AND THE SEVE DWARFS, WALT DISNEY'S OWN GAME, is pictured in Plat #582, #583, and #584. This is by far the game with t superior design. The game board, game box and playing piec are all beautifully graphic examples of scenes and characte from the Disney movie. Even collectors of games in gener anxiously seek out this version. It is absolutely exquisit Another fine game version simply titled THE GAME OF SNO WHITE AND THE SEVEN DWARFS was manufactured by t Milton Bradley Company in the 1930's. This game is pictur in Plate #590. Although the box lid for the game set is qui colorful, it lacks the super coloring of the Parker Brothe example and most collectors agree that the likenesses Snow White and the Dwarfs are just not as true to the Disn characters themselves on this design. However, despite th lack, it is still highly collectible because it is only one of ve few Snow White games ever produced.

The SNOW WHITE AND THE SEVEN DWARFS TARGE GAME pictured in Plates #586 and #587 is a fine examp of 1930's paper lithography. The game box is striking, and t gravity propelled target board shows wonderful design ar coloring. When one target is knocked off the slide, the othe slip down to take its place, with the object of the game bei to shoot down all targets. Considering the fact that most these sets were actually played with and the force of the dar knocking the targets off the board time after time must ha been terrific, it is fortunate that any of the sets survived *at a* When found in good condition, they are highly collectible.

The SNOW WHITE EMERSON RADIO pictured in Pla #591 is a rare and eagerly sought Snow White charact collectible. The figures appear to be hand carved into the rad cabinet. Actually, similar to the Mickey Mouse Emerson Radi the construction is a molded wood composition desig Examples of these are extremely hard to find, and the few th make it to antique shows can often be snatched up by vintag radio collectors. This is one Disney item to grab up quickl they usually don't sit around at shows very long!

Two larger collectibles worthy of special note are th SNOW WHITE TREASURE CHEST intended to be used as child's toy box and the SNOW WHITE AND PRINC CHARMING ROCKING TOY. These toys are pictured in Plate #600 and #601. The treasure chest toy boxes are relative rare today because they were constructed only of cardboar over wooden frames. Most of these were probably used for uple of years in the late 1930's and then discarded. though the SNOW WHITE ROCKER is also a relative rity, these were sturdily built, so those that did survive can ten be found in excellent condition. Both of these larger ms are hard to display along with smaller items or among llections displayed in cramped quarters. It takes a llector blessed with "room to grow" to accommodate such ge collectible items.

Many varieties of SNOW WHITE AND THE SEVEN VARFS MECHANICAL VALENTINES are pictured in Plates 602 through #604. The graphics on these designs are all high quality and the addition of moving parts makes them ry desirable items of Disney memorabilia. The SNOW HITE COLORING SET and the SNOW WHITE PICTURE JZZLES boxed sets in Plates #606 and #607 have vivid d attractive box graphics. A vast array of Snow White book les appears at the end of the Snow White and the Seven varfs section. Most of these examples have wonderful color ustrations as a tribute to the Disney artists. The most markable of the group is the SNOW WHITE AND THE EVEN DWARFS CUT-OUT BOOK which appears in Plate 616. Not only are all of the characters and the backgrounds perbly colorful and bright, they can also be punched out to rm ingenious 3-D buildings, trees, and backgrounds for the nch-out standup characters included. A dilemma most llectors face after purchasing a fine example of this book is punch or not to punch?" That is a question! Punching out figures grossly defaces the rest of the book and devalues but the scene created by the assembled set is almost worth e lost value! To each his own: it is a decision only the llector himself can make.

Ferdinand the Bull made his debut as an animated short in 38 just after Snow White and the Seven Dwarfs in 1937 and st before Pinocchio in 1940. Although the Snow White erchandising wave had not yet ebbed, the introduction of rdinand items related to the popular short film filled a void, pecially for animal lovers. There were no cute little animal aracter toys associated with Snow White since she and the arfs shared the bill. As a result, kind little Ferdinand with soft heart melted his way into the American toy marketing ainstream. Snow White was still going strong as a toy erchandising subject in 1938, but there was plenty of room r a cute little bull to be taken by the horns!

The FERDINAND THE BULL PULL TOY manufactured by N. Hill Brass and pictured in Plate #626B is an extremely re pull toy from the 1930's. When pulled along, Ferdinand's ad moves up and down as he "sniffs" a flower in the metal p and the action rings a bell. As mentioned earlier in this ok, toys manufactured by N.N. Hill Brass are much more arce than Fisher Price toys, and the fact that this toy is signed in the likeness of a more minor Disney character akes it even more unusual. The FERDINAND THE BULL OOD JOINTED DOLL manufactured by the Ideal Novelty d Toy Company is pictured in Plate #627 along with its original box. Although the Ideal doll is not uncommon, it is rarely found with its original box, and the graphics on the box are excellent.

The FERDINAND THE BULL TIN WINDUP TOY by Louis Marx is a rather common tin windup, but it is one of the few metal toy examples of this character. Dated 1938 and copyright Walt Disney Enterprises, the toy features vibrating, jumping action caused by a madly spinning tail. This toy is pictured in Plate #630. A much rarer tin Ferdinand toy is the FERDINAND AND THE MATADOR TIN WINDUP TOY pictured in Plate #629. This toy features unique "charging" action by Ferdinand brought about by the windup mechanism and the metal spring which joins the matador cart and the Ferdinand cart. The matador has jointed arms which allow the red cape to move up and down freely. Because of its rarity and its intricate design, this is an extremely important Ferdinand toy.

The Crown Toy and Novelty Company manufactured several different Disney wood composition banks with locking metal trap doors during the 1930's. The Crown Toy FERDINAND THE BULL BANK pictured in Plate #631 is one of the harder to find composition varieties manufactured by that company. The FERDINAND THE BULL CUT-OUTS BOOK pictured in Plate #633 features large cut-out figures of all the major characters in the film along with their accessories. This is one of the most colorful of the cut-out books of Disney characters marketed in the 1930's.

After *Snow White and the Seven Dwarfs* in 1937 and "Ferdinand the Bull" in 1938, the Walt Disney Studios brought forth what many Disneyana fans and animation film critics believe was Disney's most artistically perfect animated feature of all time, *Pinocchio.* Although *Snow White* may have been dearest in the hearts of Walt Disney and his original artists because it was their *first* feature, *Pinocchio* was by far their most beautiful work. The color, the spectacle, the smooth animation sequences including the human Geppetto, the absolutely miraculous animation backgrounds, the experimentation with interesting camera angles and zooming, and the dynamic strength of characterization all combined to make *Pinocchio* an animation history milestone that has never really been surpassed. And if ever there was a character who virtually cried out to be mass produced into toys, it was Walt Disney's Pinocchio! Consider this: Pinocchio was first a puppet, then half puppet and half boy. The combination of these qualities helped him to become one of the best loved of all the 1940's Disney characters. Toy designers under the authorization of the Walt Disney Studio had a heyday with Pinocchio. For the first time, they had an actual puppet character to adapt to puppet toys. And the results were nothing short of spectacular!

One of the cutest and most popular Pinocchio character toys manufactured was the IDEAL PINOCCHIO DOLL produced by the Ideal Novelty and Toy Company of Long Island City, New York. This great toy is pictured in Plate #638 along with its beautiful original box. This doll has multi-jointed arms and legs and a jointed neck which allows him lots of flexibility and interesting posing possibilities. The doll is made entirely of wood and wood composition and is finished in bright lacquers. The GIANT PINOCCHIO WOOD JOINTED DOLL, also manufactured by Ideal in 1939-1940, is pictured in Plate #639. One of the most attractive of all Pinocchio dolls because he appears closest to the actual animated character's design is the PINOCCHIO WOOD COMPOSITION DOLL manufactured by the Knickerbocker Toy and Doll Company. Pictured in Plate #640 with his original hat, clothes, felt shoes, and tag, he appears as if he had just stepped off the movie screen! The smaller KNICKERBOCKER PINOCCHIO DOLL pictured in Plate #642 is equally attractive and true to the film character's likeness.

The PINOCCHIO JOINTED ARM DOLL manufactured by Crown Toy and Novelty and pictured in Plate #641 is a colorful wood composition figure pictured with his original wrist tag. Plate #644 pictures two other examples of a Crown Toy product, the CROWN TOY PINOCCHIO HAND PUPPET. Two other Crown Toy Pinocchio character examples are the PINOCCHIO WOOD COMPOSITION BANK pictured in Plate #652 and the JIMINY CRICKET COMPOSITION BANK pictured in Plate #651. Each of these wood composition banks has a brightly painted surface and a locking metal trap door in the base.

Plate #646 pictures both the IDEAL PINOCCHIO WOOD COMPOSITION DOLL and the IDEAL JIMINY CRICKET WOOD COMPOSITION DOLL. The Jiminy Cricket doll is by far the rarest of the pair, but most collectors strive to acquire examples of both dolls because they complement one another so nicely in size, colors, and design. The JIMINY CRICKET DOLL is fully jointed with painted-on facial features while the Pinocchio doll has a sculptured face with finely detailed features. These dolls are also desired by general line doll collectors. One of the rarest of all the Pinocchio character dolls pictured in this book is the GEPPETTO DOLL BY CHAD VALLEY OF ENGLAND pictured in Plate #647. This doll is pictured with all original clothes and his original wrist tag. Most of the doll's construction is stuffed linen or felt with additional cloth and felt costuming. However, the construction of the doll's head is a genuine oddity. The head appears to be of a light composition or even celluloid coated with a thin layer of soft rubber which has been hand painted. The detailing and characterization of the doll is superb. This is an extremely rare and unusual doll!

The JIMINY CRICKET DOLL pictured in Plate #648 was manufactured by the Knickerbocker Toy Company. The doll shown has its original tag, but the hat is a replacement. Note how this doll's design makes him look much more like a real cricket, but a little less like the Disney character. Regardless of that fact, this is a highly collectible doll particularly because he is an excellent mate to the Knickerbocker Pinocchio dolls. Plate #650 pictures t smallest version of the IDEAL PINOCCHIO COMPOSITIC DOLL. Although his design is not identical to the much larg dolls also manufactured by Ideal, he is still very similar construction and coloring.

An interesting line of toys to be manufactured as sole Pinocchio-related is the wood composition figures market by Multi Products in the late 1930's. This compa manufactured a broad line of Pinocchio wood compositi figurines in at least three different sized sets. T PINOCCHIO MULTI PRODUCTS FIGURE pictured in Pla #653 is one of the largest of figures produced by th company. Plates #655 through #657 show the variety figures which were produced, including figures of Pinocch Geppetto, Jiminy Cricket, Gideon the Cat, Lampwick, a Figaro. Plate #658 shows the tiniest set of these figur marketed as miniature versions of the much larger figur One of the intrinsic appeals of the Pinocchio figur manufactured by Multi Products is their resemblance hand-carved European wood figures. The hand-carved lo was achieved by finely molded details in the compositi pressing process and an antique looking natural wood a color finish. They look similar to some of the finely carv artisan pieces which are imported from Italy and sell in so of the finest gift shops today. But what makes them appealing to Disney collectors is that the Multi Produc pieces *look* European and Old-World style, and they a actually pure 1939-1940 American Disneyana!

The Fisher Price Company produced several ve colorful Pinocchio pull toy designs in 1939 and 1940. T FISHER PRICE PINOCCHIO EXPRESS TOY pictured Plate #659 is a wonderfully colorful toy with excelle graphic designs all over it. When pulled along, Pinocchi legs "pedal" the unicycle with fun action. All around the c that he pulls are faces of familiar *Pinocchio* mov characters. This is a toy that is prized by Disneya collectors and Fisher Price collectors alike. Its rarity a its wonderful design make it a toy of genuine value. Al pictured in this chapter is the much more comm PINOCCHIO RIDING A DONKEY PULL TOY manufactur by Fisher Price. When this toy is pulled along, t Pinocchio figure rocks back and forth and strikes a b with his mallet.

Several sizes of PINOCCHIO BISQUES which were ma in Japan are pictured in Plate #665, and a "knock-o unauthorized GLAZED CERAMIC PLANTER looking ve much like a Brayton Laguna Pottery piece picturing Pinocc with Figaro is shown in Plate #666. An interesting set of Pinocchio character bisque figures is pictured in Plate #6 Notice the relative size of each figure and the fact that th were not produced in any relative scale. An almost identi set of green glazed ceramic figures manufactured by Natio Porcelain is pictured in Plate #668.

Two very fine Louis Marx Company tin windup t

examples devoted to Walt Disney's Pinocchio are pictured in Plates #669 and #670. The PINOCCHIO WALKER WINDUP TOY pictured in Plate #669 is not a rare toy, but because it is a Disney windup from the 1930's manufactured by Marx, it is valuable to both Disneyana collectors and general line toy collectors. The PINOCCHIO THE ACROBAT TOY pictured in Plate #670 is a tin windup toy with excellent action. When the windup platform rocks back and forth, the jointed Pinocchio figure on the trapeze swings back and forth and sometimes even flips. Pictured with its original box, the toy features colorful lithography on the Pinocchio figure and the multi-character decorated base.

A beautiful PINOCCHIO TEA SET AND TRAY by the Ohio Art Company from 1939 – 1940 is pictured in Plates #675 and #676. This gorgeous Ohio Art tea set has superb color lithography and intricate character designs on each piece. It is one of the rarest of all the Disney tea sets. Note the beauty and quality of the lithography in the enlargement of the tray in Plate #675. The PINOCCHIO THE MERRY PUPPET GAME manufactured by Milton Bradley is an attractive game set from 1939. Plates #679 and #680 picture this colorful game box, board, and inside box contents. The finest beauty of this game set is the box itself. Another colorful Pinocchio game set is the PITFALLS OF PINOCCHIO MARBLE GAME by Whitman pictured in Plate #681. One of the rarest of all the Pinocchio games in this book is the WALT DISNEY'S PIN THE NOSE ON PINOCCHIO GAME manufactured by Parker Brothers of Salem, Massachusetts, and pictured in Plates #683 and #684. The object of this game was very much like that of "Pin the Tail on the Donkey" except this one works by placing wooden noses with rubber suction cups on a suspended game board.

The boxed set of SIX PINOCCHIO BOOKS pictured in Plates #686 through #689 is an unusual set of the Pinocchio character story and paint books which are often found individually. Inclusion of the original gift box makes it a rare set. Additionally, the PINOCCHIO – A PUPPET SHOW cardboard storybook puppet theatre manufactured by Whitman is another unusual paper Disneyana collectible. This set includes a puppet theatre stage, backdrops, and all of the Disney Pinocchio characters designed as puppets on long paper handles. The colors used on this set are absolutely fantastic! Many other fine Pinocchio paper items and books help to round out this section, but the final four picture Plates, #709 through #713, illustrate a beautiful original set of 1939 PINOCCHIO LITHOGRAPHS in their original frames. The fine studio quality of these makes them particularly interesting to Disneyana collectors appreciative of original animation art.

Walt Disney's *Pinocchio* rounded out the 1930's for the Studio. *Pinocchio* was released in February 1940, but some of the merchandise has a 1939 copyright date because Disney wanted to get the merchandise on the shelves before the film was released. These items, and all items manufactured after late 1939 to 1940, are marked with the "new" copyright notice, "Walt Disney Productions." Toys after Pinocchio will never have the "Walt Disney Enterprises" copyright notice. With this final, significant film of a momentous Hollywood decade, the Walt Disney Studio began to "turn the corner" toward a new, modern era, the fabulous Forties. No one knew how soon the world would be at war, but the optimism and youthfulness that Walt Disney's film animation and toys had brought the nation would be cherished forever. As the song "When You Wish Upon A Star" surfaced as a symbol for not only the film *Pinocchio* but for the Disney Studio itself, Americans looked up to the heavens and into their hearts for the peace and dreams of their youth.

The peace of the moment was soon to end. But the childhood dreams of "When You Wish Upon A Star" would endure. Walt Disney would see to that.

PLATE 490: THREE LITTLE PIGS CELLULOID WINDUP, 1930's, c. Walt Disney Enterprises.

PLATE 491: WHO'S AFRAID OF THE BIG BAD WOLF ALARM CLOCK was made by the Ingersoll-Waterbury Company.

PLATE 492: THREE LITTLE PIGS BOXED BISQUE SET is handpainted. Each pig is 4½" tall.

PLATE 494: "WHO'S AFRAID OF THE BIG BAD WOLF" TEA TRAY, by Ohio Art and c. Walt Disney Enterprises. Extremely bright tin lithography.

PLATE 493: "WHO'S AFRAID OF THE BIG BAD WOLF" game board by Marks Brothers of Boston, Massachusetts, c. Walt Disney.

PLATE 495: THREE LITTLE PIGS TIN TEA SET, 1930's, Walt Disney Enterprises, including tray shown in Plate #494.

PLATE 496: THREE LITTLE PIGS TIN WATERING CAN manufactured by the Ohio Art Company of Bryan, Ohio, 1930's, c. Walt Disney Enterprises.

PLATE 497: ITEM A - THREE PIGS SAND PAIL by Ohio Art, 1930's. ITEM B - THREE PIGS TOY WASH TUB by Ohio Art, 1930's.

LATE 498: THREE LITTLE PIGS 8" SAND AIL by Ohio Art, 1930's. (Front view shown.)

PLATE 499: THREE LITTLE PIGS 8" SAND PAIL by Ohio Art, rear view.

PLATE 500: "THREE LITTLE PIGS" BISQUE TOOTHBRUSH HOLDER, c. Walt Disney, 1930's. Pictures practical pig with bricks and trowel.

PLATE 501: "THREE LITTLE PIGS" BISQUE TOOTHBRUSH HOLDER, 1930's, c. Walt Disney, picturing Practical Pig playing a drum.

PLATE 502: ITEM A – FIDDLER PIG, 5" bisque figure, c. Walt Disney, 1930's. ITEM - B FIFER PIG, 5" bisque figure, 1930's.

PLATE 503: BIG BAD WOLF AND THREE LITTLE PIGS BISQUE SE
1930's, Japan. Pigs are approximately 3" tall, Big Bad Wolf is 3½".

PLATE 504: SEIBERLING RUBBER THREE LITTLE PIGS are hollow and rarely found in excellent condition.

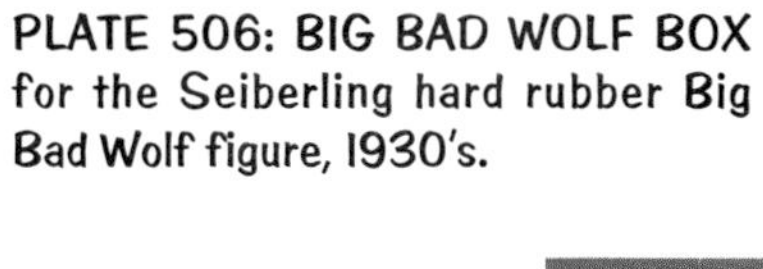

PLATE 506: BIG BAD WOLF BOX for the Seiberling hard rubber Big Bad Wolf figure, 1930's.

PLATE 507: FUN-E-FLE
DISNEY PIG FIGURE, c. W
Disney Enterprises, 1930's.

PLATE 505: WOODEN THREE LITTLE PIGS are Fun-E-Flex figures. They were made in Japan.

PLATE 508: PRACTICAL PIG CERAMIC CHILD'S CUP by Patriot China, 1930's, c. Walt Disney Enterprises.

PLATE 509: "WHO'S AFRAID OF THE BIG BAD WOLF" child's ceramic cup by Patriot China, 1930's and c. Walt Disney Enterprises.

PLATE 510: THREE LITTLE PIGS CHILD'S CEREAL BOWL, glazed china, 1930's, c. Walt Disney. Manufactured by Patriot China.

PLATE 511: CHILD'S CERAMIC PLATE picturing Three Little Pigs, Grandma, and Little Red Riding Hood, 1930's, c. Walt Disney. Manufactured by Patriot China.

PLATE 512: "WALT DISNEY'S OWN GAME RED RIDING HOOD with Big Bad Wolf and 3 Little Pigs" c. Walt Disney Enterprises. Manufactured by Parker Brothers, 1930's.

PLATE 513: "WALT DISNEY'S OWN GAME WHO'S AFRAID OF THE BIG BAD WOLF, c. 1933 Walt Disney Enterprises. Manufactured by Einson-Freeman Co.

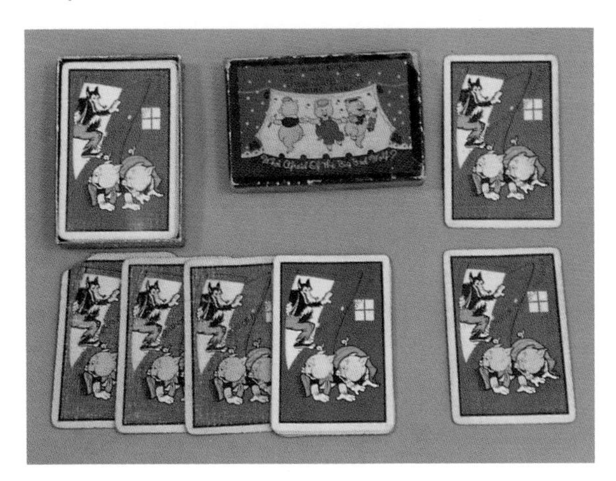

PLATE 514: WALT DISNEY SILLY SYMPHONY THREE LITTLE PIGS PLAYING CARDS, c. Walt Disney Enterprises in the 1930's. All cards in this boxed set have the same design on the back.

PLATE 515: THREE LITTLE PIGS SOAP from the 1930's showing three different colored individual pig soaps.

PLATE 516: THREE LITTLE PIGS BRIDGE SCORE SHEET was made by the Western P & L Company of Racine, Wisconsin, in 1932.

PLATE 517: WALT DISNEY'S THREE LITTLE PIGS GAME BOARD manufactured by Einson-Freeman in the 1930's.

PLATE 518: "THE BIG BAD WOLF AND LITTLE RED RIDING HOOD" ILLUSTRATED STORYBOOK, 1930's.

PLATE 519: "THREE LITTLE PIGS" ILLUSTRATED 1930'S STORYBOOK, from the Disney Silly Symphony.

PLATE 520: THREE PIGS PROHIBITION METAL TRAY. This tray was not a licensed piece but was obviously based on the Disney characters.

PLATE 521: THREE LITTLE PIGS ASHTRAYS are made of ceramic, circa 1930's.

PLATE 522: SNOW WHITE AND THE DWARFS PULL TOY 1938. Manufactured by N.N. Hill Brass and copyright Walt Disney Enterprises. N.N. Hill Brass Toys are generally quite hard to find on the market.

PLATE 524: DOPEY DRUMMER PULL TOY by Fisher Price, c. 1937 by Walt Disney Enterprises.

PLATE 523: DOC AND DOPEY PULL TOY manufactured by Fisher Price Toys and copyright 1937 Walt Disney Enterprises. When pulled along, the dwarfs strike the stump with their mallets.

PLATE 525: DOPEY TIN LITHOGRAPH AND CARDBOARD NIGHT LIGHT by Micro-Lite Company of New York, c. Walt Disney Enterprises, and manufactured in 1938. Light bulb is battery powered.

PLATE 526: SNOW WHITE COMPOSITION DOLL in original dress manufactured by the Knickerbocker Toy Company in the late 1930's.

PLATE 527: DOPEY DOLL was made by the Knickerbocker Toy Company. He is 9" tall and made of composition.

PLATE 528: HAPPY THE DWARF DOLL, 12" tall, manufactured by Chad Valley of England in the 1930's. The doll is constructed of cloth and felt.

PLATE 529: DOPEY THE DWARF COMPOSTION DOLL by Knickerbocker. Similar doll to one pictured in Plate #527, but slightly different costuming.

PLATE 530: SNOW WHITE CLOTH-FACED DOLL manufactured by Ideal Toy and Novelty in the 1930's.

PLATE 531: BASHFUL THE DWARF CLOTH AND LINEN DOLL, manufactured by Knickerbocker Toy in 1938. (Beard shown is a replacement.)

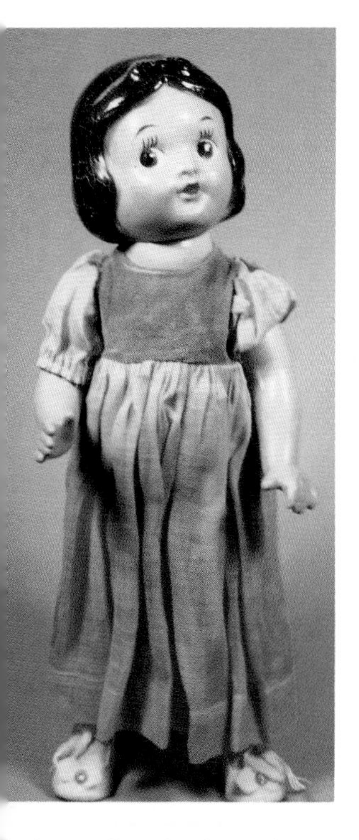

LATE 532: SMALL WOOD OMPOSITION SNOW WHITE OLL manufactured by nickerbocker in the late 930's.

PLATE 533: DOPEY CLOTH AND FELT CHARACTER DOLL by Chad Valley of England, 1930's, by Walt Disney, shown with original clothes, hat, and tag.

PLATE 534: ITEM A – DOC COMPOSITION DOLL by Knickerbocker Toy Company. ITEM B – BASHFUL COMPOSITION DOLL by Knickerbocker Toy Company.

PLATE 535: DOPEY LINEN-FACED DOLL manufactured by the Knickerbocker Toy Company in 1938.

PLATE 536: ITEM A – SLEEPY COMPOSITION DOLL by Knickerbocker, 1930's. ITEM B – GRUMPY COMPOSITION DOLL by Knickerbocker, 1930's.

PLATE 537: ITEMS A THROUGH D - CLOTH FACE DWARF DOLLS with velvet and oilcloth clothes, probably by the Richard G. Krueger Company of New York.

PLATE 538: SNOW WHITE MARIONETTE wood composition doll manufactured by the Alexander Doll Company of New York in 1938.

PLATE 539: BASHFUL THE DWARF MARIONETTE manufactured in 1938 by the Alexander Doll Company of New York.

PLATE 540: DOC THE DWARF MARIONETTE by the Alexander Doll Company of New York, 1930's.

PLATE 541: DOPEY THE DWARF MARIONETTE by the Alexander Doll Company, 1938.

PLATE 542: HAPPY THE DWARF MARIONETTE manufactured by the Alexander Doll Company in the 1930's. Wood composition.

PLATE 543: DOPEY COMPOSITION BANK with metal trap door on base manufactured by Crown Toy and Novelty. 1930's Walt Disney Enterprises.

PLATE 544: DOPEY LAMP was manufactured by LaMode Studios. It is made of Modeware, a type of plaster.

PLATE 545: DOC LAMP manufactured by LaMode Studios in the 1930's. This plaster lamp has a colorful finish and is shown with its original shade.

PLATE 546: DOPEY NIGHT LIGHT manufactured by LaMode Studios in the 1930's. This colorful lamp is marked "Dopey" and "Walt Disney Enterprises."

PLATE 547: DOPEY LAMP manufactured by LaMode Studios in the 1930's, c. Walt Disney Enterprises. Marked "Dopey" on front.

PLATE 548: SNOW WHITE PLASTER COMPOSITION LAMP by LaMode Studios in the 1930's. Marked clearly c. "Walt Disney Enterprises" with a label on the base.

PLATE 549: GRUMPY THE DWARF PLASTER BOOKEND manufactured by LaMode, 1930's.

PLATE 550: GLAZED CERAMIC DOPEY FIGURE by American Pottery, circa 1938. This company's figures are painted in exquisite detail.

PLATE 551: SNOW WHITE PLASTER COMPOSITION NIGHT LIGHT manufactured by LaMode Studios, 1930's.

LATE 552: TWO SNOW WHITE CHARACTER CERAMIC TOOTHPICK OLDER FIGURES made in England by S. Maw and Sons 1930's. ITEM – DOC CERAMIC TOOTHPICK HOLDER. ITEM B – SNOW WHITE ERAMIC TOOTHPICK HOLDER.

'LATE 554: DOPEY AND HAPPY BOOKENDS are made of a glazed eramic by S. Maw, and Sons of England.

PLATE 553: CERAMIC DWARF TOOTHPICK HOLDERS by S. Maw and Sons of England. ITEM A – BASHFUL CERAMIC TOOTHPICK HOLDER. ITEM B – DOPEY CERAMIC TOOTHPICK HOLDER.

PLATE 555: SNOW WHITE AND DOC THE DWARF glazed ceramic dish, 6" in diameter, circa 1938.

PLATE 556: HAPPY THE DWARF GLAZED CERAMIC CUP AND SAUCER SET, 1930's, manufactured in England.

PLATE 557: SNOW WHITE AND THE DWARFS DECORATIVE WOODEN PLAQUE, circa 1930's. This is a copyrighted piece since each dwarf has his name on the front of his hat.

PLATE 558: CELLULOID SNOW WHITE AND THE SEVEN DWARFS were made in Japan.

PLATE 559: LARGE CELLULOID DWARF figures from Snow White, circa 1930's.

PLATE 560: SNOW WHITE AND THE DWARFS BISQUE FIGURES, SET. Pictured here are the largest bisque figures made: Dwarfs 5" tall and Snow White 6½" tall, 1930's, Japan. Also shown is a Bakelite napkin ring to show relative size of dwarfs.

PLATE 561: SNOW WHITE AND SEVEN DWARFS BISQUE SET. Each dwarf measures 3½" and Snow White is 5" tall.

PLATE 562: SNOW WHITE AND THE SEVEN DWARFS boxed bisque set showing colorful box inside and graphic cover. This set was distributed by George Borgfeldt in the 1930's.

PLATE 563: SNOW WHITE AND SEVEN DWARFS Seiberling figures set, circa 1938.

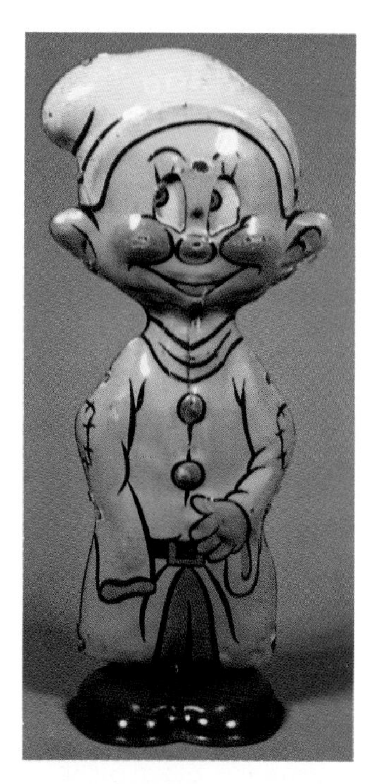

LEFT – PLATE 564: DOPEY WINDUP TIN WALKER manufactured by Louis Marx in the 1930's, c. Walt Disney Enterprises. When toy rocks back and forth, his eyes move.

RIGHT – PLATE 565: DOPEY COMPOSITION DOLL manufactured by Alexander Doll Company, 1930's. Shown in original box and packaging.

ATE 566: EARLY LITHOGRAPHED DISNEY TIN picturing nearly ery 1930's Disney character prior to Pinocchio. This is an extremely e and desirable tin done in bright colors. Circa 1938.

PLATE 567: SNOW WHITE TEA SET was made by the Aluminum Goods Company in the 1930's.

PLATE 568: SNOW WHITE AND THE SEVEN DWARFS TIN, from Belgium, 1930's, covered with intricate, beautiful lithography.

PLATE 570: ITEM A - OHIO ART SNOW WHITE WATERING CA 1930's, Walt Disney Enterprises, 6" tall. ITEM B - OHIO ART SNC WHITE WATERING CAN, 1930's, 8" tall.

PLATE 569: SNOW WHITE AND THE SEVEN DWARFS tin from Belgium, 1930's. This is another example of the exquisite Belgian tins. This one shows the dwarfs kneeling around Snow White as the Prince arrives.

PLATE 572: SNOW WHITE SAND PAIL by Ohio Art of Bryan, Ohio, 1938, Walt Disney Enterprises. This pail measures 5" tall.

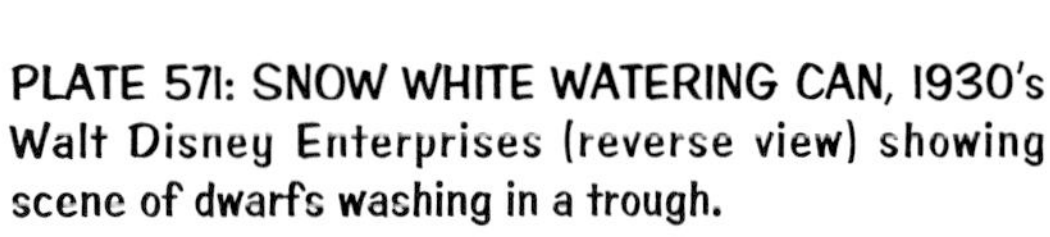

PLATE 571: SNOW WHITE WATERING CAN, 1930's Walt Disney Enterprises (reverse view) showing scene of dwarfs washing in a trough.

PLATE 573: SNOW WHITE GIANT SAND PAIL by Ohio Art in the 1930's. This is the largest of all Snow White pails, measuring 10" tall.

PLATE 574: SNOW WHITE TRAY from a 1930's Ohio Art Tea Set picturing Doc playing the piano while Snow White sings.

PLATE 575: SNOW WHITE TEA SET by Ohio Art, 1938, Walt Disney Enterprises. Shown here are various pieces included with a set.

PLATE 576: SNOW WHITE AND THE SEVEN DWARFS character glasses, 1930's. Each glass features a decal of a different character.

PLATE 577: SEVEN DWARFS CHARACTER FIGURES manufactured by Seiberling Latex products of Akron, Ohio, in the 1930's. All of the dwarfs are made of solid rubber and are excellent likenesses of the film characters.

PLATE 578: SNOW WHITE CHARACTER SOAP in a storybook box, circa 1938 Walt Disney Enterprises.

PLATE 579: SNOW WHITE AND THE SEVEN DWARFS boxed soap figures, circa 1938 Walt Disney Enterprises.

PLATE 580: SNOW WHITE AND THE SEVEN DWARFS SAFETY BLOCKS set by Halsam, 1938 c. Walt Disney Enterprises. This set contains 9 wooden blocks.

PLATE 582: DETAIL OF GAME LABEL FOR PARKER BROTHERS SNOW WHITE AND THE SEVEN DWARFS GAME, 1930's.

PLATE 581: SNOW WHITE AND THE SEVEN DWARFS SAFETY BLOCKS deluxe large set manufactured by Halsam and c. Walt Disney Enterprises. This set contains 32 character blocks.

PLATE 583: GAME BOARD AND PLAYING PIECES FOR PARKER BROTHERS SNOW WHITE GAME manufactured in the 1930's.

PLATE 584: WALT DISNEY'S OWN GAME SNOW WHITE AND THE SEVEN DWARFS manufactured by Parker Brothers of Salem, Massachusetts, in 1938. This is the most beautiful of all Snow White games.

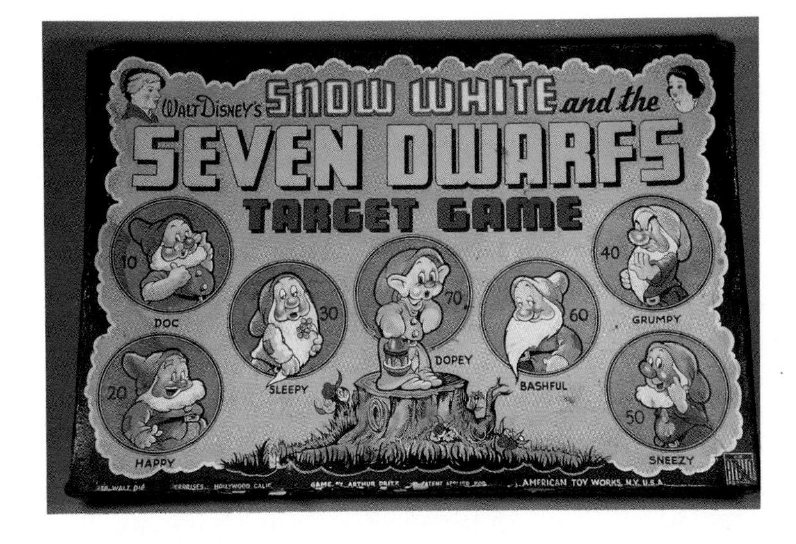

PLATE 586: WALT DISNEY'S SNOW WHITE AND THE SEVEN DWARFS TARGET GAME manufactured by American Toy Works of New York in the 1930's.

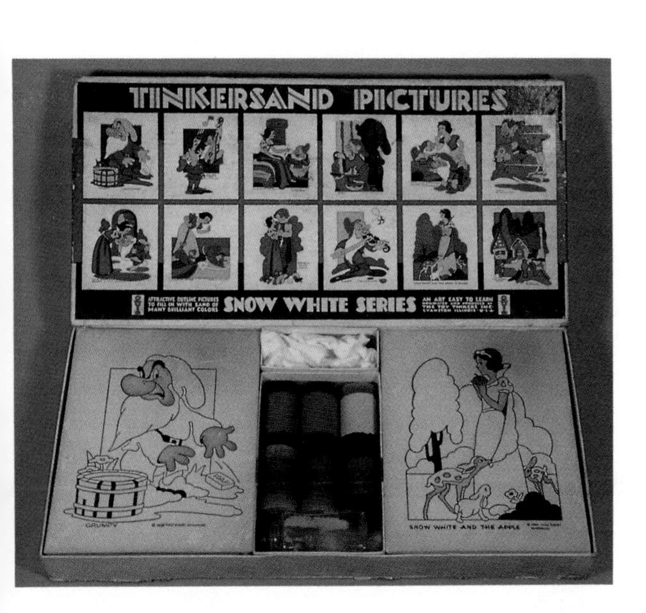

PLATE 585: SNOW WHITE TINKERSAND PICTURES manufactured by Toy Tinkers Inc. in 1938, c. Walt Disney Enterprises.

PLATE 587: TARGET GAME FOUND INSIDE BOXED SET pictured in Plate #586 manufactured by American Toy Works and c. Walt Disney Enterprises.

PLATE 588: SNOW WHITE AND THE SEVEN DWARFS CARD GAME manufactured by Pepys of England in the 1930's.

PLATE 589: SNOW WHITE AND THE SEVEN DWARFS CARD GAME "British Manufacture" by Pepys Games of London in the 1930's. The cards are extremely colorful.

PLATE 590: THE GAME OF SNOW WHITE AND THE SEVEN DWARFS manufactured by Milton Bradley in the 1930's, c. Walt Disney Enterprises.

PLATE 591: SNOW WHITE RADIO was made by the Emerson Company. The knobs are referred to as "acorn" knobs.

PLATE 592: SNOW WHITE AND THE SEVEN DWARFS BAKELITE CHARACTER NAPKIN RINGS, circa 1930's and copyright Walt Disney Enterprises.

PLATE 593: SNOW WHITE AND PINOCCHIO CHARACTER BAKELITE PENCIL SHARPENERS from the 1930's marked "copyright Walt Disney Enterprises."

PLATE 594: SNOW WHITE AND THE SEVEN DWARFS AND DOPEY DIME REGISTER BANKS, c. 1938 Walt Disney Enterprises. Each holds $5.00 worth of dimes.

PLATE 595: SNOW WHITE AND THE SEVEN DWARFS CHARMS, celluloid made in Japan, 1930's.

PLATE 596: SNOW WHITE AND THE SEVEN DWARFS DECALS, circa 1930's, to be used on children's furniture, woodwork, etc.

PLATE 597: DOPEY PLAYING CARDS boxed set with a standard deck, c. 1938 Walt Disney Enterprises.

PLATE 598: SNOW WHITE AND THE SEVEN DWARFS CHARACTER PURSE, late 1930's, c. Walt Disney Enterprises.

PLATE 599: SNOW WHITE AND THE SEVEN DWARFS MOVIE PICTURE MACHINE. Flip card viewer used as a 1930's Pepsodent toothpaste premium, c. Walt Disney Enterprises.

PLATE 600: SNOW WHITE AND THE SEVEN DWARFS TREASURE CHEST, dated 1938 and c. Walt Disney Enterprises. These cardboard and wood framed boxes were designed to be used as toy boxes.

PLATE 601: WALT DISNEY'S SNOW WHITE ROCKING TOY picturing the Prince and Snow White in a boat. This rocking toy will seat two small children and is marked c. Walt Disney Enterprises.

PLATE 602: SNOW WHITE AND THE SEVEN DWARFS MECHANICAL VALENTINES dated 1938 and c. Walt Disney Enterprises.

**'LATE 603: SNOW WHITE AND THE SEVEN DWARFS 1930's
1ECHANICAL VALENTINES** marked "c. Walt Disney Enterprises."

**'LATE 604: COMPLETE SET OF SNOW WHITE AND THE SEVEN
'WARFS FIGURAL, MECHANICAL VALENTINES** from 1938, marked c.
/alt Disney Enterprises.

PLATE 605: SNOW WHITE AND GRUMPY FRAMED PICTURES,
1938, with each marked "c. Walt Disney Enterprises" in original fancy
frames.

**PLATE 606: WALT DISNEY'S SNOW WHITE AND THE
SEVEN DWARFS COLORING SET** published by Whitman
in 1938 and c. Walt Disney Enterprises.

**PLATE 607: WALT DISNEY'S SNOW WHITE AND THE
SEVEN DWARFS PICTURE PUZZLES** manufactured by
Whitman Publishing and c. Walt Disney Enterprises.

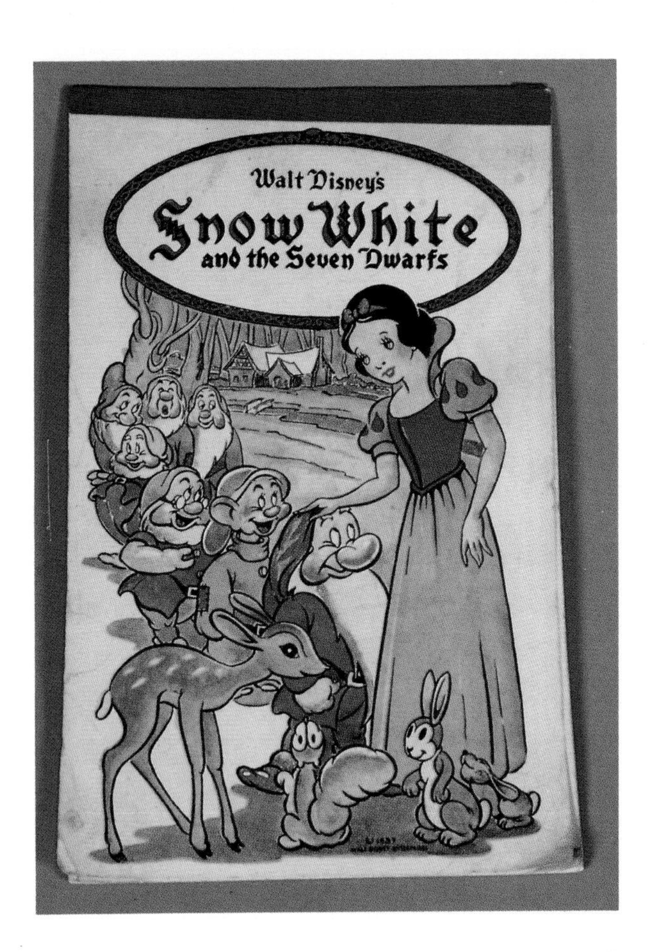

PLATE 608: SNOW WHITE AND THE SEVEN DWARFS PENCIL TABLET, 1937 Walt Disney Enterprises.

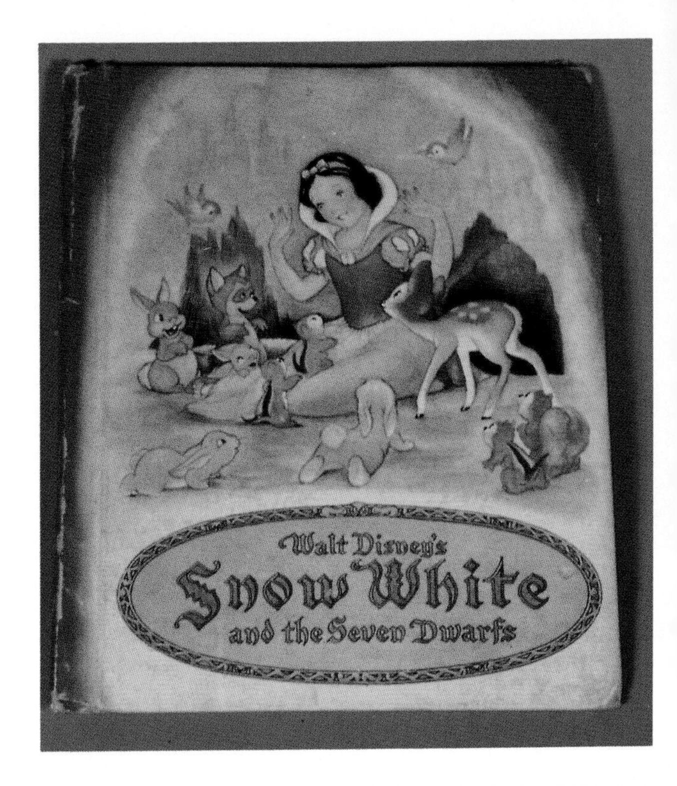

PLATE 609A: WALT DISNEY'S SNOW WHITE AND THE SEVEN DWARFS small storybook, c. 1937 Walt Disney Enterprises.

PLATE 609B: WALT DISNEY'S SNOW WHITE AND THE SEVEN DWARFS JINGLE BOOK c. 1938 Walt Disney Enterprises and given as a premium for buying "Deitzens Vitamin D Bread."

PLATE 609C: SNOW WHITE AND THE SEVEN DWARFS PAINT BOOK, c. Walt Disney Enterprises, copyright 1938. This large format coloring book features a full color artist's palette design on the cover.

PLATE 610: COMPLETE STORY OF WALT DISNEY'S SNOW WHITE AND THE SEVEN DWARFS, published by Grosset & Dunlap and c. 1937 Walt Disney Enterprises.

PLATE 611: WALT DISNEY'S SNOW WHITE AND THE SEVEN DWARFS A WALT DISNEY AUTHORIZED EDITION, c. 1938 Walt Disney Enterprises. Linen-like story book.

PLATE 612: SNOW WHITE AND THE SEVEN DWARFS MIRROR from a vanity set, c. Walt Disney.

PLATE 613: SNOW WHITE AND THE PRINCE English post card, 1938, picturing the Prince carrying Snow White home to his castle.

PLATE 614: WALT DISNEY SNOW WHITE AND THE SEVEN DWARFS PAINT BOOK C. 1938 by Walt Disney Enterprises.

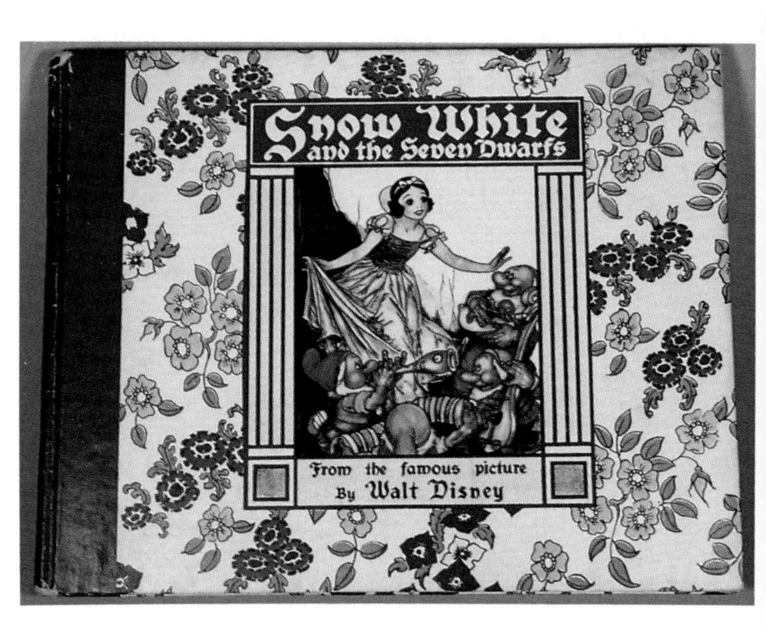

PLATE 615: SNOW WHITE AND THE SEVEN DWARFS FROM THE FAMOUS PICTURE BY WALT DISNEY, c. 1938 Walt Disney Enterprises. This is a storybook with colorful illustrations inside.

PLATE 616: SNOW WHITE AND THE SEVEN DWARFS CUT-OUT BOOK, c. Walt Disney Enterprises. This set includes punch-out figures, characters, animals, trees, and a cottage. This example is completely uncut.

PLATE 617: Inside detail of one page of the Snow White cut-out book pictured in Plate #616.

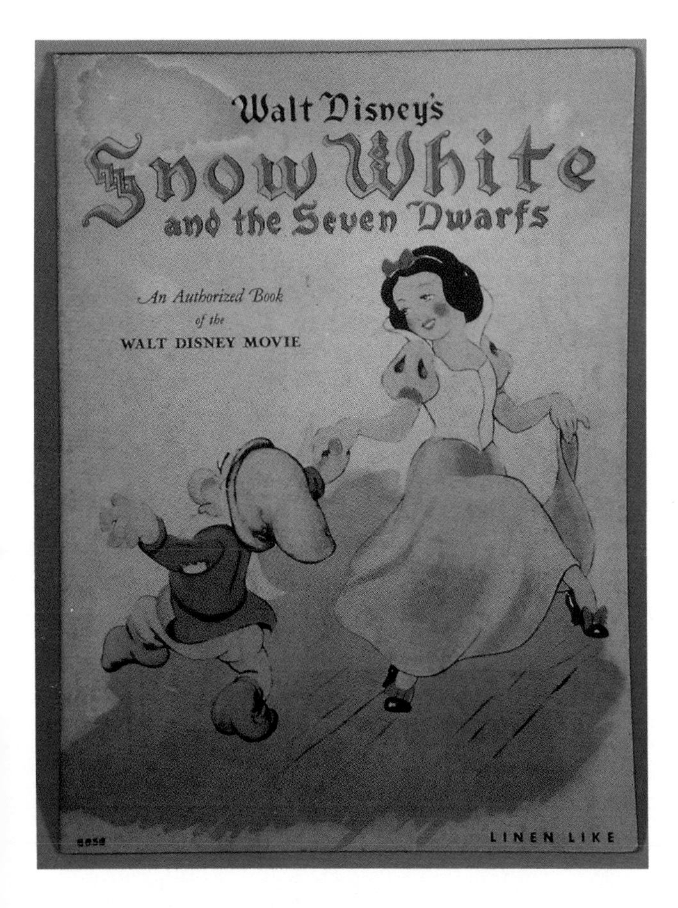

PLATE 618: WALT DISNEY'S SNOW WHITE AND THE SEVEN DWARFS authorized book, linen-like, c. Walt Disney Enterprises.

PLATE 619: WALT DISNEY'S SNOW WHITE AND THE SEVEN DWARFS scrapbook, c. Walt Disney Enterprises.

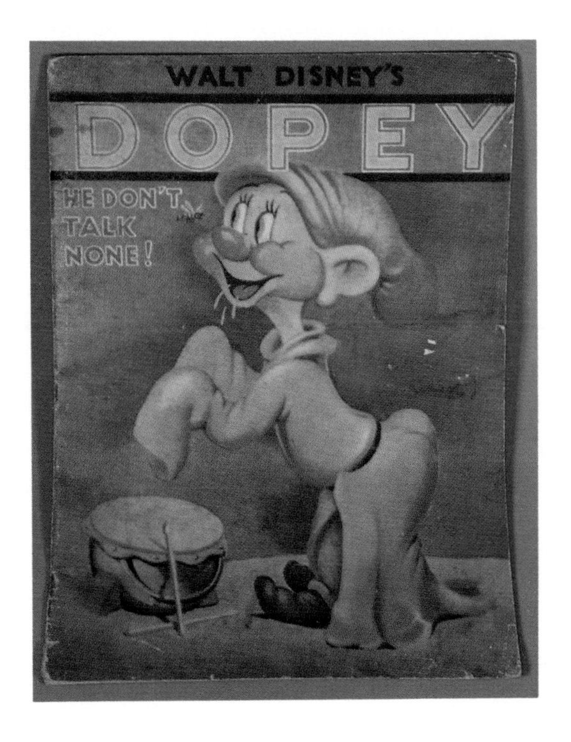

PLATE 620: WALT DISNEY'S DOPEY: HE DON'T TALK NONE c. 1937 Walt Disney Enterprises.

PLATE 621: SNOW WHITE FRAMED CALENDAR PRINT c. 1938 Walt Disney Enterprises.

PLATE 622: *WALT DISNEY'S SNOW WHITE AND THE SEVEN DWARFS* – THE BIG LITTLE BOOK, c. Walt Disney Enterprises.

PLATE 623: WALT DISNEY'S SNOW WHITE AND THE SEVEN DWARFS movie theater lobby card, original 1951 re-release design.

PLATE 624: SNOW WHITE MOVIE THEATER LOBBY CARD showing Snow White with the animals in the woods.

PLATE 625: SNOW WHITE LOBBY CARD from a movie theat showing Snow White kissing Dopey.

PLATE 626: SNOW WHITE LOBBY CARD from a movie theater showing the dwarfs at the end of the bed.

PLATE 626B: FERDINAND THE BULL PULL TOY by N.N. Hill Brass Company, c. 1938 Walt Disney Enterprises.

PLATE 627: FERDINAND THE BULL DOLL MANUFACTURED BY IDEAL TOY AND NOVELTY, c. 1938 Walt Disney Enterprises. Pictured with original box.

PLATE 628: FERDINAND'S CHINESE CHECKERS WITH THE BEE manufactured by Parker Brothers and copyright 1938 by Walt Disney Enterprises.

PLATE 629: FERDINAND THE BULL AND THE MATADOR tin windup toy c. 1938 Walt Disney Enterprises, manufactured by Louis Marx & Company.

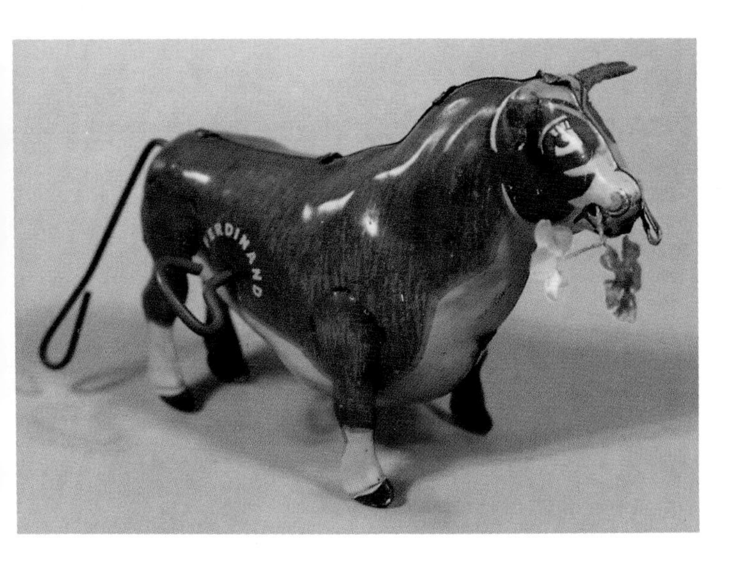

PLATE 630: FERDINAND THE BULL WINDUP TOY by Marx c. 1938 Walt Disney Enterprises.

PLATE 631: FERDINAND THE BULL COMPOSITION BANK manufactured by Crown Toy and Novelty, 1938 c. Walt Disney Enterprises.

PLATE 632: FERDINAND THE BULL CHALKWARE COMPOSITION FIGURE, 1930's.

PLATE 633: FERDINAND THE BULL CUT-OUTS BOOK FROM THE WALT DISNEY PRODUCTION, c. Walt Disney Enterprises.

PLATE 634: WALT DISNEY'S FERDINAND THE BULL linen-like story book c. 1938 Walt Disney Enterprises.

PLATE 635: PIN THE TAIL ON FERDINAND THE BULL A WALT DISNEY PARTY GAME c. 1938 Walt Disney Enterprises. Manufactured by Whitman Publishing.

PLATE 636: BRAYTON LAGUNA POTTERY FIGURE OF FERDINAND THE BULL. This figure presents Ferdinand as a young calf.

PLATE 637: FERDINAND THE BULL FIGURE by Seiberling Latex of Akron, Ohio c. Walt Disney Enterprises.

PLATE 638: WOODEN PINOCCHIO DOLL was made by the Ideal Toy Company in 1939, c. Walt Disney Productions.

PLATE 639: WOODEN PINOCCHIO was made by Ideal Toy and Novelty Company. He is 19" tall.

PLATE 640: PINOCCHIO DOLL MANUFACTURED by Knickerbocker, 1939, c. Walt Disney with composition head and body and jointed arms and legs.

PLATE 641: WOODEN PINOCCHIO was made by the Crown Toy Company, c. Walt Disney Enterprises.

PLATE 642: COMPOSITION PINOCCHIO was made by the Knickerbocker Toy Company. He is 10" tall and the clothes are made of cloth and felt.

PLATE 643: PINOCCHIO WOOD COMPOSITION DOLL manufactured in 1939 by Crown Toy and Novelty.

PLATE 644: PINOCCHIO HAND PUPPETS manufactured by Crown Toy and Novelty Company in 1939-1940, c. Walt Disney Productions.

PLATE 645: PINOCCHIO WINDUP was distributed by George Borgfeldt. He is made of composition and is 10½" tall.

PLATE 646: PINOCCHIO AND JIMINY CRICKET wood composition jointed dolls manufactured by Ideal Novelty and Toy Company, 1939.

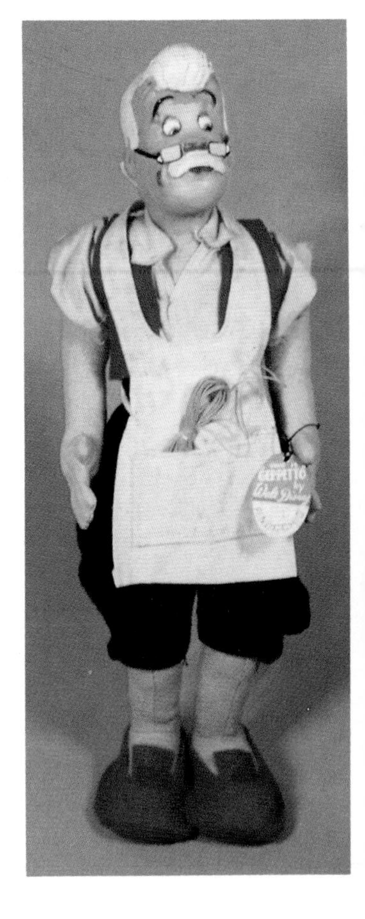

PLATE 647: CLOTH AND WOODEN GEPPETTO was produced by the Chad Valley Company. The head is covered with a thin layer of rubber.

PLATE 648: JIMINY CRICKET WOOD COMPOSITION DOLL by Knickerbocker, 1939 c. Walt Disney Porductions.

PLATE 649: FUN-E-FLEX PINOCCHIO FIGURE, circa 1939 and copyright Walt Disney Productions.

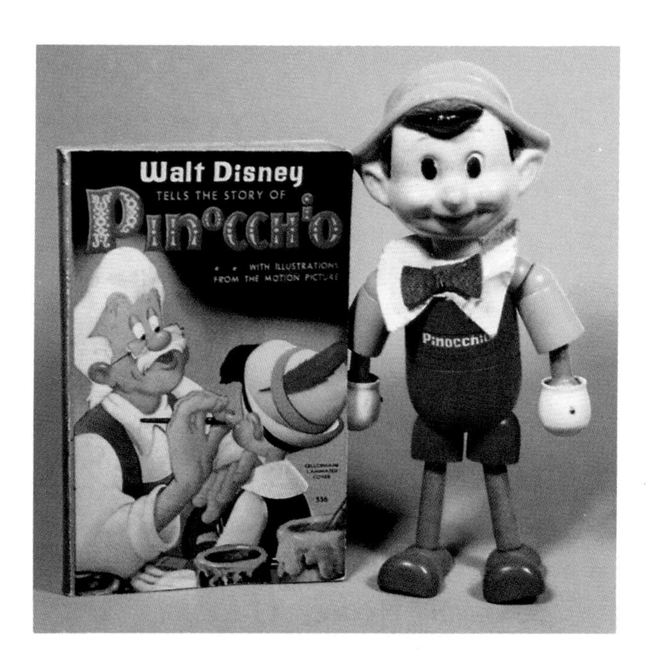

PLATE 650: ITEM A - PINOCCHIO SMALL PAPERBACK BOOK, 1939. c. Walt Disney Productions. ITEM B - PINOCCHIO WOOD COMPOSITION JOINTED DOLL by Ideal, c. 1930-1940.

PLATE 651: JIMINY CRICKET WOOD COMPOSITION BANK by Crown Toy and Novelty Company c. Walt Disney Enterprises.

PLATE 652: PINOCCHIO WOOD COMPOSITION BANK by Crown Toy and Novelty Company, c. Walt Disney Enterprises.

PLATE 653: GIANT WOOD COMPOSITION PINOCCHIO FIGURE manufactured by Multi Products of Chicago, 1940.

PLATE 654: PINOCCHIO RUBBER FIGURE c. 1939 by Walt Disney Productions and manufactured by Seiberling Latex.

PLATE 655: GEPPETTO, PINOCCHIO AND JIMINY CRICKET WOOD COMPOSITION FIGURES by Multi Products of Chicago.

PLATE 656: GIDDY, GEPPETTO, AND LAMPWICK WOOD COMPOSITION CHARACTER FIGURES by Multi Products of Chicago, Illinois.

PLATE 657: FIGARO THE CAT AND PINOCCHIO WOOD COMPOSITION FIGURES by Multi Products of Chicago. All figures by this company look hand carved.

PLATE 658: GEPPETTO, PINOCCHIO AND LAMPWICK miniature 1½" wood composition figures by Multi Products of Chicago.

PLATE 659: PINOCCHIO EXPRESS PULL TOY manufactured by Fisher Price in 1939, c. Walt Disney Productions.

PLATE 662: ITEMS A THROUGH C - PINOCCHIO CHARACTER MECHANICAL VALENTINES manufactured in 1939 and copyright Walt Disney Productions.

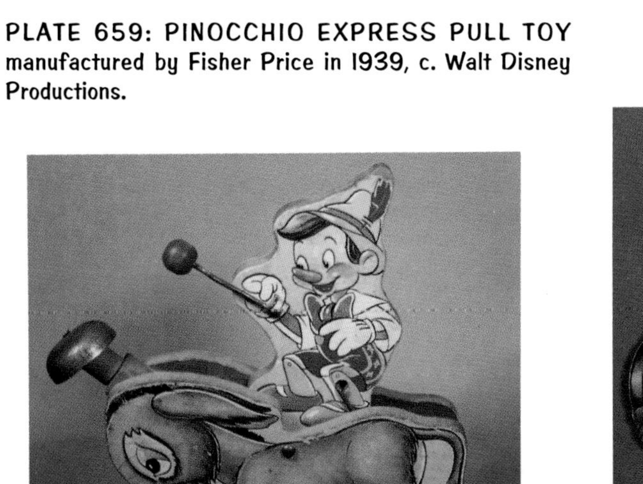

PLATE 660: WALT DISNEY'S PINOCCHIO RIDING THE DONKEY PULL TOY manufactured by Fisher Price Toys, circa 1939-1940.

PLATE 663: PINOCCHIO OVERSIZE GIANT MECHANICAL VALENTINES produced in 1939 and copyright Walt Disney Productions.

PLATE 661: ITEMS A THROUGH D - PINOCCHIO MECHANICAL VALENTINES with moving parts are each marked "c. 1939 W.D.P."

PLATE 664: THE PINOCCHIO BETTER LITTLE BOOK published by Whitman in 1939 and 1940. This is one of the less common Better Little Book titles.

PLATE 665: ITEM A THROUGH C - Three different varieties of Pinocchio bisque figures made in Japan in the 1930's. The largest version is 5" tall and is the rarest.

PLATE 666: PINOCCHIO SMALL CERAMIC PLANTER with Figaro the Cat by his side. As the piece is unmarked, it is probably an unauthorized piece.

PLATE 667: ITEMS A THROUGH F - pictured here is a set of 3½" JAPANESE BISQUE PINOCCHIO CHARACTER FIGURES marketed in 1939 and 1940. The Pinocchio figure is the most common.

PLATE 668: ITEMS A THROUGH G - WALT DISNEY'S PINOCCHIO CHARACTER GLAZED CERAMIC FIGURES manufactured by the National Porcelain Company. Pictured here is a complete set.

PLATE 669: PINOCCHIO TIN WINDUP WALKER TOY manufactured by the Louis Marx Company in 1939. Not only does his body rock back and forth, his eyes also move from side to side.

PLATE 670: PINOCCHIO THE ACROBAT WINDUP is tin and made by the Marx Company in 1939.

PLATE 671: CLEO THE GOLDFISH CHARACTER JUICE GLASS, circa 1940, marked "W.D.P."

PLATE 672: WALT DISNEY'S JIMINY CRICKET character soap shown with original treasure chest box.

PLATE 673: WALT DISNEY'S PINOCCHIO COLOR BOX, circa 1940's, contains watercolor paints. This set was manufactured by the Transogram Company of New York.

PLATE 674: FIGARO TIN WINDUP CAT FROM WALT DISNEY'S PINOCCHIO, c. 1939. This toy, shown with its original box, was manufactured by the Louis Marx Company of New York City. The ears are missing off this example.

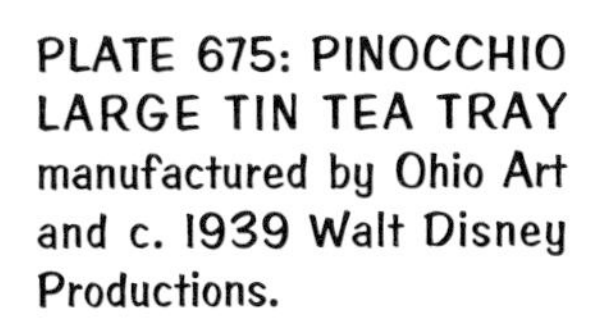

PLATE 675: PINOCCHIO LARGE TIN TEA TRAY manufactured by Ohio Art and c. 1939 Walt Disney Productions.

PLATE 676: PINOCCHIO CHARACTER TEA SET c. 1939 was manufactured by the Ohio Art Company. This is one of the rarest of all 1930's Disney tea sets.

PLATE 677: PINOCCHIO CARDBOARD DISPLAY FIGURE, circa 1939 featuring a perky walking Pinocchio figure.

PLATE 678: PINOCCHIO LUNCH PAIL picturing all of the major characters from the film lithographed around the container, circa 1940.

PLATE 679: PINOCCHIO THE MERRY PUPPET GAME manufactured by Milton Bradley and c. 1939 Walt Disney Productions.

PLATE 680: PINOCCHIO THE MERRY PUPPET GAME board and contents of box pictured in Plate #679. This game was manufactured by the Milton Bradley Company of Springfield, Massachusetts.

PLATE 681: WALT DISNEY'S PITFALLS OF PINOCCHIO GAME manufactured by Whitman Publishing in 1940. The game action is a simple marble and dice journey game.

PLATE 682: WALT DISNEY'S PINOCCHIO CIRCUS 1939 premium punch-out set which could be assembled into a circus set with standup accessories.

PLATE 683: PIN THE NOSE ON WALT DISNEY'S PINOCCHIO BOXED PARTY GAME copyright 1939 by the Parker Brothers Company.

PLATE 684: GAME BOARD and wooden noses with soft rubber suction cups attached to make them adhere to the game board. c. 1939 Walt Disney Productions.

PLATE 685A: LIBERTY MAGAZINE of March 2, 1940 picturing Pinocchio, Jiminy Cricket, Figaro, and Cleo the Goldfish on the cover.

PLATE 685B: WALT DISNEY'S PINOCCHIO ring game from 1939 with the object to "ring" Pinocchio's nose. Construction is of wood with a paper lithographed Pinocchio label on both sides.

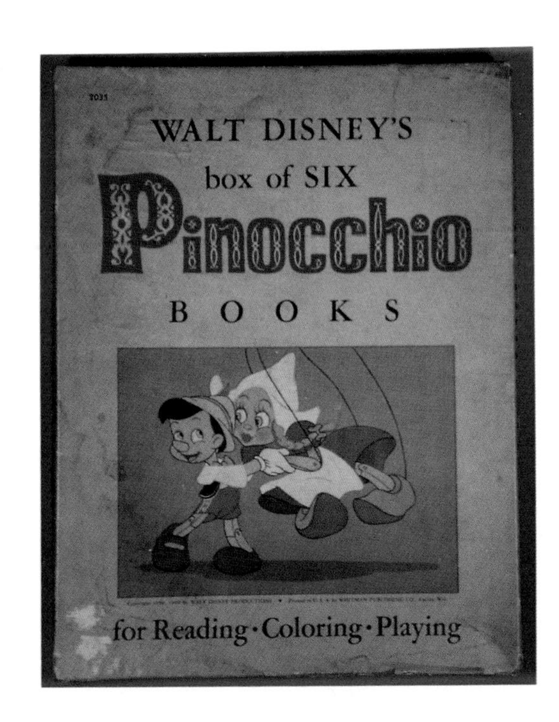

PLATE 686: WALT DISNEY'S BOX OF SIX PINOCCHIO BOOKS. Published by Whitman Publishing and copyright 1939, 1940 Walt Disney Productions. Pictured here is the box for the complete set.

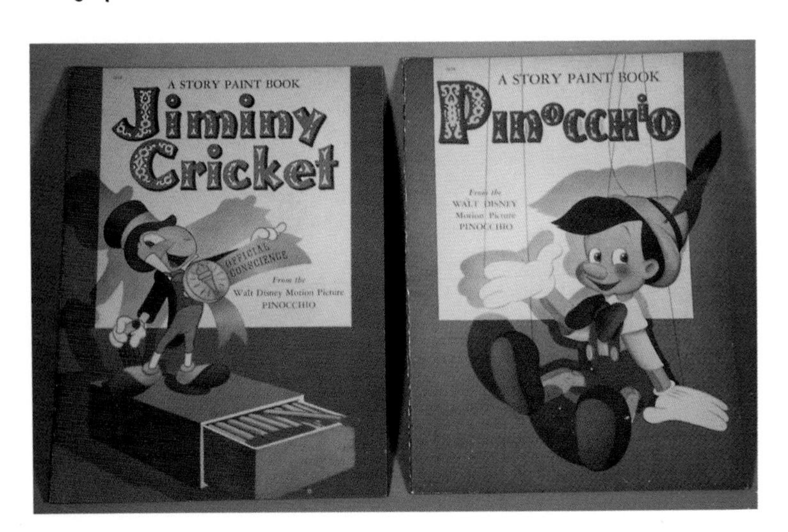

PLATE 687: ITEM A – JIMINY CRICKET STORY PAINT BOOK. Published by Whitman and c. 1939 Walt Disney Productions. ITEM B – PINOCCHIO STORY PAINT BOOK. Published by Whitman and copyright 1939.

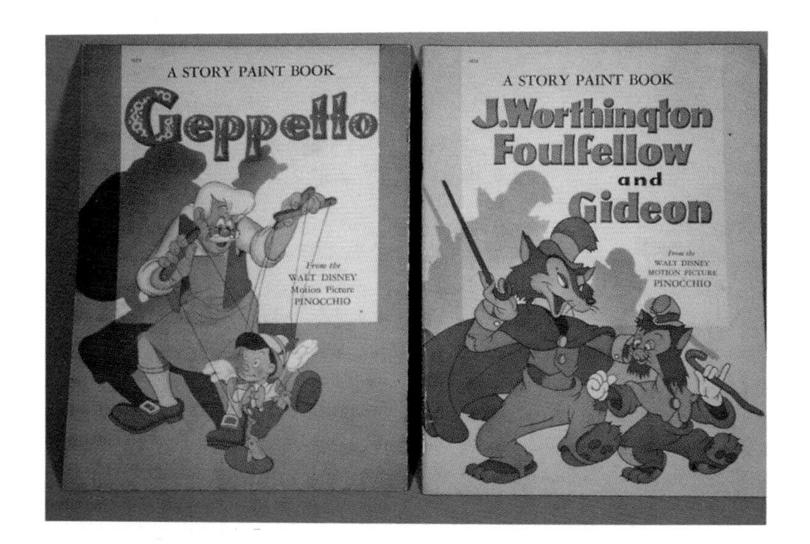

PLATE 688: ITEM A – GEPPETTO STORY PAINT BOOK published by Whitman 1939 and c. Walt Disney Productions. ITEM B – J. WORTHINGTON FOULFELLOW AND GIDEON STORY PAINT BOOK, 1939, by Whitman.

PLATE 690: PINOCCHIO STORYBOOK "WALT DISNEY'S PINOCCHIO," c. 1939, 1940 by Walt Disney Productions. This large book contains beautiful full color illustration taken directly from the animated film.

PLATE 689: ITEM A – THE BLUE FAIRY STORY PAINT BOOK, 1939 by Whitman Publishing ITEM B – FIGARO AND CLEO STORY PAINT BOOK, 1939 c. Walt Disney Productions.

PLATE 691: WALT DISNEY'S PINOCCHIO, A PUPPET SHOW with stage and 8 characters manufactured by Whitman. This boxed set assembles to a beautiful 3-D puppet theatre!

PLATE 692: WALT DISNEY'S PINOCCHIO SCHOOL TABLET c. 1939 by Walt Disney Productions. Because such tablets were normally used up and thrown away, these are relatively rare.

PLATE 693: WALT DISNEY'S PINOCCHIO SCHOOL TABLET, c. 1939 Walt Disney Productions.

PLATE 694: WALT DISNEY'S PINOCCHIO PICTURE BOOK, by Whitman publishing, and copyright 1939-1940 by Walt Disney Productions. Note the unusual die-cut figural top edge of the book.

PLATE 695: ILLUSTRATIONS inside of book pictured in Plate #694. c. 1939-1940 Walt Disney Productions.

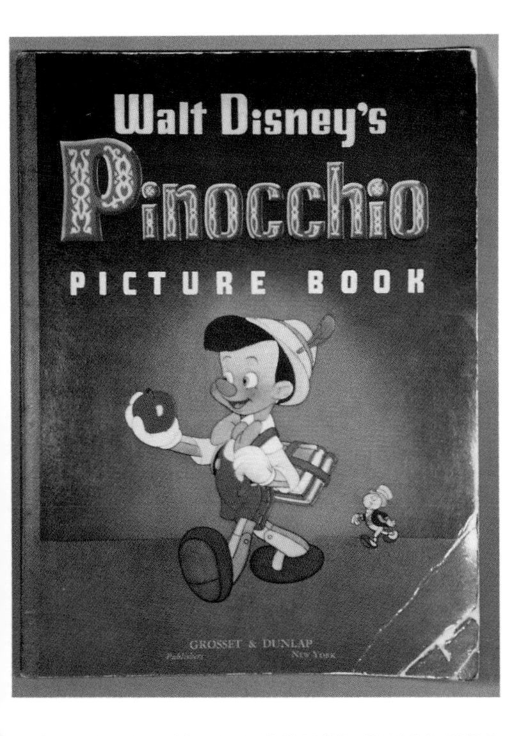

PLATE 696: WALT DISNEY'S PINOCCHIO PICTURE BOOK published by Grosset and Dunlap in 1939-1940, c. Walt Disney Productions.

PLATE 697: INSIDE ILLUSTRATIONS of Grosset and Dunlap Pinocchio Book pictured in Plate #696. This book contains some of the most beautiful color illustrations of all the Disney Pinocchio Books.

PLATE 698: WALT DISNEY'S PINOCCHIO STORYBOOK, c. 1939 Walt Disney Productions.

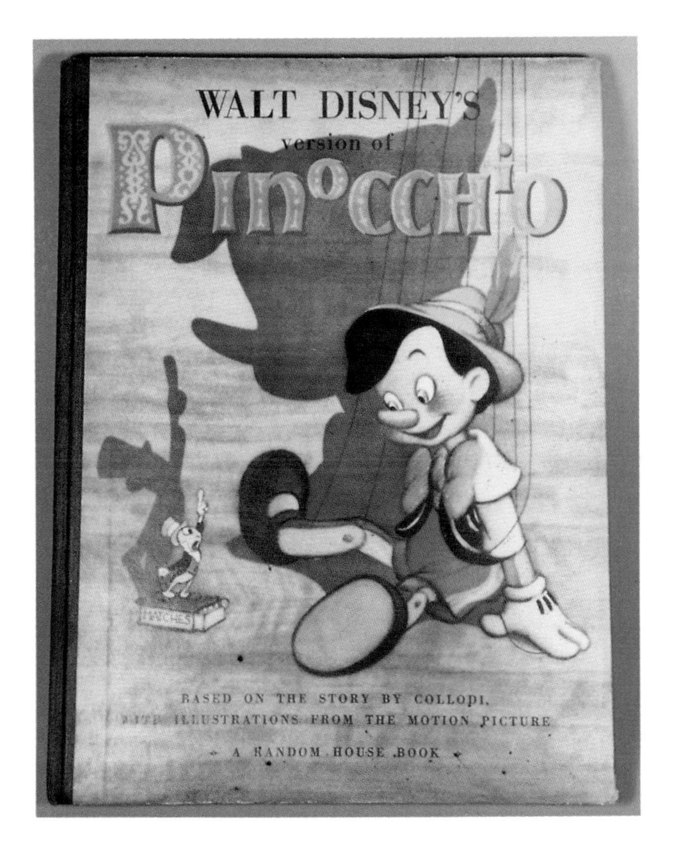

PLATE 699: WALT DISNEY'S VERSION OF PINOCCHIO published by Random House in 1939 and c. Walt Disney Productions.

PLATE 700: WALT DISNEY'S VERSION OF PINOCCHIO book published by Grosset and Dunlap in 1939–1940. This small format book with color illustrations originally sold for 10¢.

PLATE 701: WALT DISNEY'S PINOCCHIO small linen-like soft cover book, c. 1939 Walt Disney Productions.

PLATE 702A: WALT DISNEY'S PINOCCHIO PICTURE PUZZLES c. 1939 Walt Disney Productions and published by Whitman Publishing Company of Racine, Wisconsin.

PLATE 702B: Puzzles contained inside boxed **PINOCCHIO PICTURE PUZZLES** shown in plate #702A.

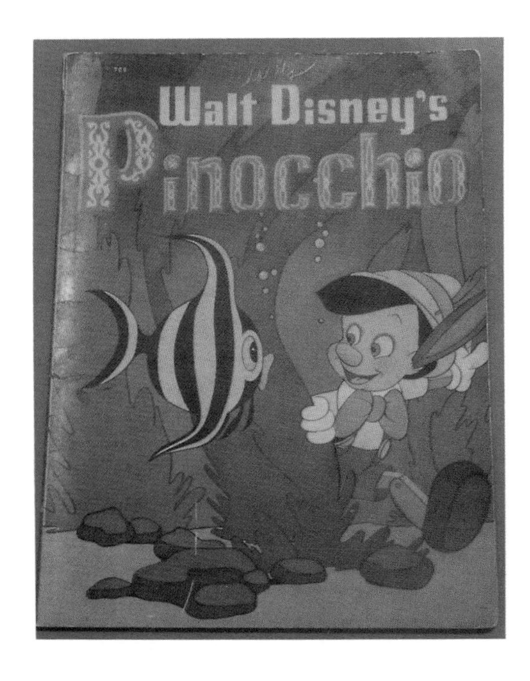

PLATE 703: WALT DISNEY'S PINOCCHIO STORYBOOK, c. 1939 Walt Disney Productions picturing Pinocchio on the cover with his donkey ears in an underwater scene.

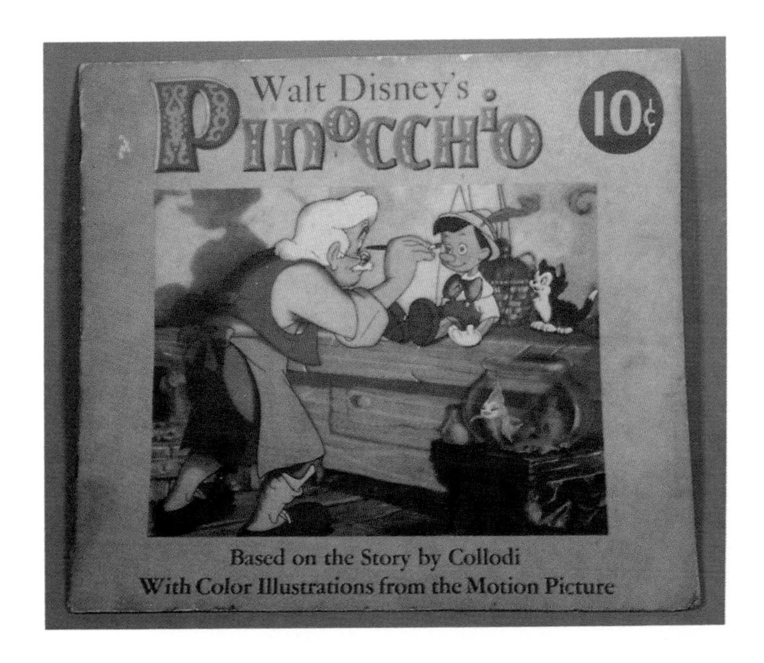

PLATE 704: WALT DISNEY'S PINOCCHIO SMALL SOFTCOVER STORYBOOK, c. 1939 Walt Disney Productions. This storybook features full color illustrations from the motion picture.

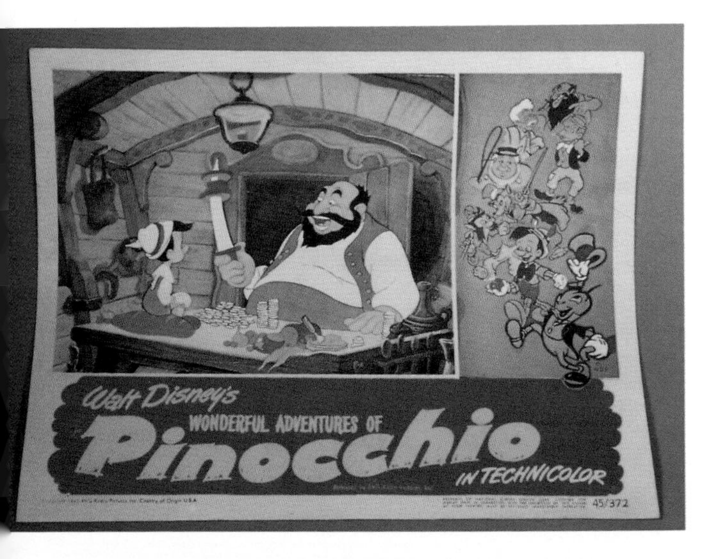

PLATE 705: ORIGINAL PINOCCHIO MOVIE THEATER LOBBY CARD from the 1945 re-release of Pinocchio.

PLATE 707: PINOCCHIO CHARACTER TARGETS from a dart gun target set manuyfactured by American Toy Works. This is the complete set of 8 targets.

PLATE 706: ITEMS A & B – PINOCCHIO SHEET MUSIC TITLES "Give A Little Whistle" and "Little Wooden Head." Sheet music examples with Disney character covers are highly collectible.

PLATE 708: PINOCCHIO PAPER MASK, c. 1939 by Walt Disney Productions and manufactured by Einson-Freeman. A set of the Pinocchio character masks including Geppetto, Figaro, Jiminy Cricket, and Cleo the Goldfish was given away as a Gillette Razor Blades premium.

PLATE 709: ORIGINAL 1939 PINOCCHIO PRINT, c. 1939 Walt Disney Productions, still in its original 1930's frame.

PLATE 711: ORIGINAL 1939 PINOCCHIO PRINT. Part of a complete set of four pictured here.

PLATE 710: ORIGINAL 1939 PINOCCHIO framed print, c. Walt Disney Productions.

PLATE 712: ORIGINAL 1939 PINOCCHIO PRINT, c. Walt Disne Productions.

CHAPTER FOUR

DISNEYANA OF THE 1940'S, 1950'S AND 1960'S

Although most collectors of Disneyana today would agree that the true "Golden Age" of Disney character toy production was the 1930's, most would also agree that the 1940's, 1950's and 1960's also saw the production of many unique, interesting, and valuable Disney toys. From the rare and unusual Occupied Japanese celluloid windup toys pictured at the beginning of this chapter to the more common dime store toys pictured throughout this section, the supply and variety of items produced under the authorization of the Walt Disney Studios during these three decades seems almost endless. And although many collectors like to focus on Disneyana collectibles from the 1930's, it is the collectibles from the 1940's, 1950's, and 1960's that are increasing in value sometimes at almost astronomical rates!

The decade of the 1940's brought an admiring public *Pinocchio, Fantasia, Bambi, Dumbo, The Three Caballeros, Song of The South* and a host of short Mickey Mouse and Donald Duck cartoons. The 1950's saw the production of *Cinderella, Alice in Wonderland, Peter Pan, Lady And The Tramp,* and *Sleeping Beauty.* The 1950's also represent a very significant period of branching out for the Walt Disney Studio, with the opening of the world-famous Disneyland. The advent of Disneyland and America's love affair with the new electronic medium of television are both unique milestones in the popular and cultural history of the 1950's in this country. *The Mickey Mouse Club* also appeared as a now classic early television production during this decade. All across America on school day afternoons, youngsters sat in front of the small oval black and white picture tubes mesmerized by early Mickey cartoons, Mouseketeers, and of course, Annette. Days of such sheer simplicity, splendor, and fun are not soon to be forgotten. That is why the Disneyana collectibles from the 1950's are treasured so dearly by a whole generation of Mouseketeers – to keep the *Mickey Mouse Club* alive!

The 1960's brought with them the flourishing of Disneyland, *Walt Disney's Wonderful World of Color* as a spectacular Sunday evening television show brought out just when color TV was becoming popular, and a host of new animated features. *One Hundred And One Dalmatians, The Jungle Book, The Sword In The Stone,* and, of course, the live action hit *Mary Poppins* all appeared during this decade. Plans for a new super Disney theme park in central Florida began to take shape, and, before it could be complete, the world would lose the Maker of the Mouse.

It is ironic that with the death of Walt Disney in 1966, the Pop-Art revolution of the mid-1960's began to thrust comic art and character watches once again into the limelight. Walt Disney never really got to see how crazy people could get over collecting the early Disney memorabilia. As with any great artist, it is almost as if the memorabilia wasn't really collectible until we lost Walt. After his death, we all scrambled for some tangible way to hang on to those earlier, carefree, childhood Disney days. And scramble we did, for many of the nation's leading Disneyana collectors have now been at it for almost 30 years! Although these "old guys" who have amassed absolutely phenomenal collections got in when the going was good and even rare pieces didn't cost them an arm and a leg, there is still plenty of good Disney memorabilia available on the market to satisfy even the novice collector. And collecting Disneyana from the 1940's, 1950's and 1960's is a logical place to start.

The MICKEY MOUSE ON A HORSE CELLULOID WIND-UP pictured in Plate #713 is a cute 1940's Occupied Japan piece. When wound, the horse bounces with lively action and Mickey sort of rattles about from all the jumping. Because the intense action of these brittle and fragile celluloid toys caused many of them to absolutely self-destruct, near mint condition examples of these toys are hard to find. An even rarer Occupied Japanese celluloid toy is the MICKEY MOUSE ON PLUTO CELLULOID TOY pictured in Plate #714. The front axle is off center so that when Pluto rolls along he bobbles up and down in front producing a pleasing riding action. The windup mechanism is hidden inside the front wheel itself. Two sizes of MICKEY MOUSE CELLULOID FIGURES are pictured in Plate #715. Usually, jointed celluloid figures that have strings with rings attached to them were intended to be hanging crib toys. The larger of the two DONALD DUCK 1940's CELLULOID FIGURES pictured in Plate #716 also has a ring attached. The DONALD DUCK BOXERS pictured in Plate #717 have no Disney markings whatsoever and are probably unlicensed, but they are unmistakably designed after Donald Duck. Note their similarity to the celluloid figures pictured in Plate #716. Except for the boxing glove arms, the two sets of figures are nearly identical.

An interesting 1940's DONALD DUCK CELLULOID WINDUP TOY is pictured in Plate #719. When this toy is wound, Donald scoots across the floor on his belly as his head moves freely from side to side. Because of the extreme fragility of Donald's long neck on this toy, examples in mint condition are very hard to find. The MICKEY MOUSE

CELLULOID FIGURE ON A RED BALL pictured in Plate #720 is a vibrantly colorful crib toy. It is not hard to imagine the twinkle in a very young child's eye as he stared up at both the familiar Mickey Mouse figure and the bright red ball!

The Sun Rubber Company of Barberton, Ohio, manufactured a durable line of hard rubber vehicle toys in the 1940's. This grouping includes a MICKEY MOUSE IN THE FIRE ENGINE, DONALD DUCK IN A CONVERTIBLE SEDAN, DONALD DUCK TRACTOR, MICKEY MOUSE TRACTOR, and the MICKEY MOUSE AIRPLANE. All of these toys are pictured in Plates #721 and #722. Eight different styles of 1940's Disney character FISHER PRICE PULL TOYS are pictured in Plates #723 through #730. The DONALD DUCK PULL TOY CART and the DONALD DUCK ENGINEER LOCOMOTIVE PULL TOY pictured in Plate #723 and #724 respectively are relatively common later Fisher Price toy examples. The DONALD DUCK DOUGHBOY PULL TOY pictured in Plate #725 is highly unusual and a wonderful WWII era Fisher Price piece, especially for those who specialize in pull toys. A lively looking Pluto pulls a Donald figure dressed in an Army uniform and hat who rides in an artillery wagon. It is very hard to find. The DONALD DUCK XYLOPHONE PLAYER PULL TOY by Fisher Price that is pictured in Plate #727 is also worthy of attention because of its wonderful design, colorful graphics, and very large size.

The mint and absolutely complete MICKEY MOUSE VIEWER FILMS STORE DISPLAY is a rare point-of-sale toy collectible. Although smaller complete sets including the plastic viewer are not uncommon, such a large and complete store stock item containing an assortment of 66 films in total is a real rarity. The set pictured in Plate #731 was never used or played with. It is a real wonder how such an item has survived in mint condition over the past 50 years. The DONALD DUCK JACK IN THE BOX manufactured by Spear in the 1940's shown in Plate #734 is yet another interesting Donald item with its composition character figure and wooden box.

Two ceramic character items from the 1940's Disney film "The Three Caballeros" are pictured in Plates #735 and #736. Plate #735 pictures a PANCHITO LAMP manufactured by the Railley Corporation of Cleveland, Ohio, in 1947. Although the lamps were manufactured by Railley, they utilized figures or molds identical to the American Pottery Company figurine styles of the same period. Ceramic character lamps with their original lamp shades are rare and highly desired by today's Disneyana collectors. The JOE CARIOCA CERAMIC FIGURE shown in Plate #736 is an American Pottery piece which shows this company's high quality and fine detail on character designs which are very true to their animated counterparts.

The Leeds China Company was responsible for an almost endless array of glazed ceramic Disney character planters, banks, figurines, cookie jars, and salt and pepper shakers brought to the market in the 1940's and 1950's. Although these were easily found in abundant supply less than ten years ago, their increasing popularity and skyrocketing value has made them one of the most economically volatile collectible items o the past two years. The depth of this line of Disney characte memorabilia seems almost mind-boggling. Although man novice collectors assume that the SNOW WHITE CERAMIC PLANTER and SNOW WHITE BANK pictured in Plate #737 ar from the 1930's original release of the film, that assumption i incorrect since the company mainly manufactured glaze ceramic Disney items from the late 1940's and on into th 1950's. Also pictured in this section are a DOPEY CERAMIC PLANTER and a DOPEY CERAMIC STILL FIGURE (Plat #738) manufactured by Leeds. Because Leeds China wa based in Chicago, Illinois, many examples of ceramic Disne items by this company have surfaced in the upper Midwes The quality of items manufactured by Leeds is alway consistent, with the glazed figures having colorful soft past highlights painted under the glossy glaze. Only a few of th styles have painted-on accents applied over the glaze, and thi is especially true of the several planters which can be foun with gold highlighting. A Leeds DONALD DUCK STILL FIGUR is pictured in Plate #741 and a colorful DONALD DUC PITCHER by the same company is pictured in Plate #74 Still figurines which are not banks or planters are among th rarest of the Leeds designs and often command the highes prices. Two giant cookie jars manufactured by Leeds in th 1940's are the MICKEY MOUSE TURNABOUT COOKIE JA pictured in Plate #743 (which has Minnie Mouse on th reverse) and the DONALD DUCK TURNABOUT COOKIE JA (which has Minnie on the reverse).

The JOE CARIOCA WINDUP COMPOSITION FIGUR pictured in Plate #750 is an interesting 1940's windup to Character toys from the popular 1940's film *The Thre Caballeros* are few and far between. *The Three Caballer* utilized Donald Duck as its star and featured the characters Panchito the Rooster and Joe Carioca the Parrot. These tw characters never got the marketing exposure that oth characters received. As a result, toy examples of the characters are quite hard to find.

Walt Disney's *Bambi* inspired a wonderful line character figurines manufactured by the American Potte Company of Los Angeles in the 1940's. A grouping of fo SMALL ANIMAL FIGURINES along with a large 8" BAM CERAMIC FIGURE is pictured in Plate #751. A much small series of figures by the same company is pictured in Pla #752 showing THUMPER, FLOWER AND BAMBI FIGURE The American Pottery oval sticker originally placed on figurines when found today increases the value of the figuri itself. Unfortunately, since many original purchasers in t 1940's viewed these stickers as no more desirable than a pri tag, many were removed. Leeds China BAMBI CHARACTE PLANTERS are pictured in Plates #757 and 758, picturi Thumper and Flower. Two other Bambi items worthy of spec note are the AMERICAN POTTERY BAMBI PITCHER shown Plate #759 and the rare THUMPER PULL TOY manufactur by Fisher Price in the 1940's. Both items present wonder graphic treatments of the Disney Bambi characters. Finally, the two standard sizes of STEIFF BAMBI FIGURES shown in Plate #761 are highly collectible examples for both Disneyana collectors and general line doll collectors alike.

The appearance of *Dumbo* as a feature film in 1941 managed to bring about only a lukewarm marketing of the character. The fact that the U.S. was quickly heading into a major World War and world-wide tensions were mounting certainly must have affected the marketing of toys in general. As a result, toys manufactured in Dumbo's likeness from the original 1941 release of the film are almost non-existent. The DUMBO PITCHER and the DUMBO SALT AND PEPPER SHAKERS manufactured by Leeds and pictured in Plates #766 and #767 appeared in the late 1940's. The BABY DUMBO CERAMIC FIGURE by American Pottery as pictured in Plate #770 is also a later 1940's piece.

The MOUSEKETEER TELEVISION pictured in Plate #774 is an interesting 1950's item which was obviously a tie-in to the popular afternoon *Mickey Mouse Club* television program. Pictures on a long paper scroll travel past the screen to show stories and scenes in a moving sequence. Part of this toy's splendid appeal are its bright graphics of a 1950's Mickey and Minnie Mouse along with two children wearing Mouseketeer hats pictured on the top. The MICKEY MOUSE CLUB NEWSREEL PROJECTOR pictured in Plate #779 is another fine Mickey Mouse Club 1950's vintage item. Along with the film and the projector was a record which could be played on any standard phonograph. Pictured on the original box front are Jimmie and an unidentified young Mouseketeer.

The DISNEYLAND MONORAIL GAME pictured in Plate #780 is an example of an item marketed in conjunction with the early operating days of Disneyland. Collectors should be aware that items marked "Disneyland" were not necessarily a tie-in to the theme park. Even as early as the late 1940's, examples of Disney character toy sets can be found bearing the name "Disneyland" though the park itself was not even thought of. An example is the DISNEYLAND AMERICAN SAFETY BLOCKS SET pictured in Plate #771 showing Snow White as its latest character on the box illustration. Marked clearly as a "Walt Disney Enterprises" item by Halsam, this shows clear proof that the Disney Studios were using the term "Disneyland" on their authorized toys even in the late 1930's. Therefore, "Disneyland" on a toy's title does not always mean that the toy was from the 1950's or was a tie-in to the California theme park.

The much later SCHUCO DONALD DUCK pictured in Plate #794 was manufactured in the 1960's. Shown with its original box, it is much different from the early long-billed DONALD SCHUCO WINDUP pictured in the 1930's Donald Duck section. The giant LARS DOLL pictured in Plate #795 is also a 1960's item, yet even though this is a much more recent doll, the scarcity of the number of these imported into the U.S. and the top-notch quality of the dolls themselves make it a highly desirable and collectible Disneyana piece!

The MECHANICAL DISNEY PARADE ROADSTER pictured in Plates #798 and #799 is a fine example of a 1950's Louis Marx Company Disney tin windup piece. Notice the bright colors and graphics on the crisp original box and the vivid designs on the car itself. Also note the different "passengers" in the two versions shown. Evidently, there was not much discretion applied to exactly which character figures would be stuck into the car at the factory.

Two toys that are interesting to contrast are pictured in Plates #800 and #801. For nearly twenty years, the Louis Marx Company had been a household word in America when it came to good quality, fun windup toys. Once post-war wounds were healed and Japan began producing its own fine quality tin windup toys in the late 1950's and early 1960's, it was virtually impossible for the American-made Marx toys to compete. So rather than compete, they imported! Although the Louis Marx line continued on into the 1960's, toys imported by Marx from Japan bore their own distinct marking, "Line Mar Toys." There is relatively little difference in the quality or design of the Line Mar toys as compared to regular Marx toys. Notice as an example the MICKEY THE DRIVER BY MARX pictured in Plate #800 and shown with its original box. The MICKEY THE DRIVER BY LINE MAR pictured in Plate #801 has a different box design and a metal head on the Mickey figure as opposed to the plastic head on the Marx example. But, the cars themselves are identical. There is NO difference. In truth, the Japanese Line Mar car is the better toy because of the all-metal Mickey figure. Contrary to what "Made in Japan" may have meant to some in the 1960's, the quality of the Line Mar toys is at least equal and sometimes surpasses the Marx toys of the same period.

The Chein DISNEYLAND ROLLERCOASTER and DISNEYLAND FERRIS WHEEL pictured in Plates #802 and #803 are extremely colorful tin Disney items. The rollercoaster utilizes a windup lift mechanism and the Ferris wheel is powered by a large windup coil spring wrapped around the center axle of the wheel. The Marx DISNEY DIPSY CAR featuring Donald in this crazy tin windup car's driver seat is pictured with its original box in Plate #804. A more standard DONALD THE DRIVER BY MARX is pictured in Plate #805.

The WALT DISNEY'S TELEVISION CAR manufactured by Marx and shown with its original colorful box is pictured in Plate #806. This is an interesting toy because of the addition of a "television screen" on top of the car which appears to light up when the friction car's mechanism makes sparks from within. A MICKEY MOUSE DIPSY CAR manufactured by Line Mar is pictured in Plate #807. Note, once again, the use of a full metal Mickey figure on a Line Mar toy. One of the most common metal windup toys of the 1950's and early 1960's is the CASEY JUNIOR DISNEYLAND EXPRESS pictured in Plate #808. Although the toy itself is more common than most windups, mint-in-box examples as pictured are much rarer. The GOOFY THE WALKING GARDENER appears to be a Louis Marx toy, but according to our collector source is an imported

Spanish toy. What makes this toy interesting is that it utilizes the identical jointed tin Goofy figure found on the Walt Disney's DONALD DUCK DUET TIN WINDUP TOY manufactured by Marx and pictured in Plate #817.

Two MICKEY MOUSE ON THE SCOOTER WINDUPS are pictured in Plates #810 and #811. The tin windup Mickey pictured in Plate #810 is extremely rare and features color enamel finishes combined with vibrant lithography. The plastic MICKEY MOUSE SCOOTER JOCKEY pictured in Plate #811 is more common than the rare tin version, but is unusual because of its original box. Two colorful Donald Duck windups are pictured in Plates #818 and #819. The MECHANICAL DONALD DUCK DRUMMER by Line Mar and pictured in Plate #818 features beautiful design on both the box and the toy. When wound, the DONALD DUCK DRUMMER features excellent drumming action. The MECHANICAL WHIRLING TAIL DONALD DUCK pictured in Plate #819 is shown with its wonderful box and original umbrella in Donald's hand. Collectors should note that the umbrella on this toy is often missing, so before purchasing such an example a close inspection should be made. The MINNIE MOUSE IN THE ROCKING CHAIR is a fine Line Mar tin windup piece. Not only does the metal chair rock back and forth when wound, the Minnie figure also quickly "knits" with her knitting needles in cute action.

Plate #822 pictures a very rare LINE MAR MICKEY MOUSE RIDING PLUTO WINDUP TOY. This is one of the most beautiful and colorful of all the Line Mar toys and is intriguing because of its rarity and the interesting small scale of Mickey as compared to a much larger Pluto. Mickey is much larger than Pluto on most standard 1960's toy designs. This is one of the best of all Disney Line Mar toys and should never be passed up at a reasonable price. Plate #823 pictures a wonderful musical trio that any collector would be happy to welcome into his home. The MUSICAL PLUTO, MICKEY THE XYLOPHONE PLAYER, and DONALD THE DRUMMER were windup toys all manufactured by Line Mar in the 1960's and were designed in exact scale to be utilized as a set if desired. Side by side, the three pieces make an absolutely superb display! What a great little band!

The MICKEY MOUSE ON A UNICYCLE and the MICKEY MOUSE ON ROLLERSKATES pictured in Plates #826 and #827 are two very rare Line Mar windup toys. Both toys have tin bodies for the Mickey characters with the addition of cloth pants, and both show excellent windup action. The WALT DISNEY'S ROCKING CHAIR WINDUP TOY by Line Mar pictured with its original box in Plate #829 is another rare Disney Line Mar item utilizing a hard celluloid or plastic Donald figure and a tin windup rocking "chair" designed as Dumbo. Here, the collector gets three major characters in one toy: Donald Duck, Pluto, and Dumbo. The JIMINY CRICKET LINE MAR WINDUP and the GOOFY TIN WINDUP LINE MAR TOY are pictured in Plates #830 and #831. Both show examples of very bright and colorful tin lithography.

The PLUTO WINDUP TOY pictured in Plate #832 is an unusual Line Mar style from the 1960's and the PLUTC PULLING THE CART FRICTION TOY is an example of anothe quality Line Mar toy. The PLUTO ON A UNICYCLE pictured i Plate #834 is yet another highly desirable 1960's Line Ma windup. When wound, the interesting balancing action on all o the unicycle toys by Line Mar is superb. An extremely rar Pluto Line Mar toy is the MICKEY'S DELIVERY pictured i Plate #837 showing Pluto driving a delivery wagon wit lithographed faces of Mickey and Pluto on the wagon sides. Thi is a friction toy. The Line Mar DISNEY CHARACTEF CAROUSEL featuring small figures of Mickey, Goofy, Donald and Pluto on a merry-go-round pictured in Plate #838 i another rare Line Mar toy.

The MICKEY THE MAGICIAN LINE MAR TOY is wonderfully colorful tin lithographed toy pictured in Plate #839 Because this toy uses all of the bright primary colors in strongl graphic patterns, it is one of the most strikingly colorful of a the Line Mar toys. The DISNEYLAND FIRE DEPARTMEN BATTERY OPERATED FIRE TRUCK is one of the rarest of a Disney 1960's Line Mar designs. Because it contains colorfu figures of Pluto, Mickey, and Donald Duck all worked into th functional design of a big, red fire truck it is an absolutel remarkable Line Mar toy example. It is also one of the ver largest Disney Line Mar toys ever manufactured. The LINE MAI GYM TOYS ACROBATS pictured in Plates #842 and #84 show how the same multi-character box was used to packag different character versions of the same toy. The DONALI DUCK LINE MAR ACROBAT is pictured in Plate #842 and th PLUTO LINE MAR ACROBAT is pictured in Plate #843. A PINOCCHIO CHARACTER WINDUP manufactured by Line Ma in the 1960's is pictured in Plate #847.

Rounding out this chapter are three fine examples of th French BAYARD DISNEY CHARACTER CLOCKS. Th MICKEY MOUSE BAYARD CLOCK is probably the mos sought-after because of its wonderful 1930's Mickey graphi figure. However, collectors should note that although this cloc appears to be of the best of the 1930's designs, it was actuall manufactured in the 1960's. This clock is pictured in Plat #858. The PLUTO BAYARD CLOCK and the PINOCCHI BAYARD CLOCK are pictured in Plates #859 and #86C Even though these clocks are only about 30 years old, thei designs are unique and they are highly collectible items eve among collectors of 1930's vintage Disneyana because of the tie-in to the earlier characters.

Although we have concluded our "tour" of forty years o Disney character memorabilia with toys from the 1960's, th show still goes on. Disney merchandise continues to b manufactured at a feverish pace today, and with the addition o each new film and each new character, the prized Disneyan collectibles of the future are born. Undoubtedly, with th success of the Walt Disney Studio's *The Little Mermaid* an *Beauty and the Beast*, many great items of Disneyan collectibles for the twenty-first century are hitting the to market today.

And as each new child is born, and each new Disney toy is purchased, yet another lover of the Walt Disney characters and the fun they represent is created. Walt Disney would be very happy to know that his imaginative dream and his company's financial prosperity live on.

So as each of us continues to feel the goose bumps when we hear "When You Wish Upon a Star" played while old Geppetto gazes out into the chilling and starry night sky, the Disney dream lives on. And as each of us daily, or weekly, or monthly acquires yet another much loved addition to our Disneyana collections, the dream lives on. Whenever Mickey Mouse's happy grin still cheers up adults who turn to their collections for a little escape at the end of a hard day, the dream lives on.

Yes, the Disney dream is alive and well and walking about on the face of the earth today. And every Disneyana collector, young or old, novice or advanced, shares the dream of youth that keeps the dream alive. We are the dream keepers.

May our Disney toys keep us forever young.

PLATE 713: MICKEY MOUSE ON HORSE. Wind-up is celluloid made in Occupied Japan.

PLATE 714: MICKEY ON PLUTO is celluloid and was manufactured in Occupied Japan.

PLATE 715: MICKEY MOUSE Occupied Japan celluloids.

PLATE 716: **DONALD DUCK** celluloids from Occupied Japan.

PLATE 717: **DONALD DUCK BOXERS** is a celluloid windup from Occupied Japan.

PLATE 718: **CELLULOIDS** from Occupied Japan.

PLATE 719: **CRAWLER DONALD DUCK** celluloid windup toy was made in Japan in the 1940's. The head of the duck actually scoots along the ground.

PLATE 720: **MICKEY MOUSE CELLULOID SQUEEZE TOY** was made in Japan in the 1940's. This toy was designed as a crib toy.

PLATE 721: **MICKEY MOUSE AND DONALD DUCK VEHICLES MANUFACTURED** by the Sun Rubber Company of Barberton, Ohio, in the 1940's.

PLATE 722: DONALD DUCK AND MICKEY MOUSE VEHICLES manufactured by the Sun Rubber Company of Barberton, Ohio, in the 1940's, c. Walt Disney Productions.

PLATE 723: DONALD DUCK FISHER PRICE PULL TOY with cart and swinging baton, c. Walt Disney Productions.

PLATE 724 DONALD DUCK FISHER PRICE PULL TOY #450, circa 1940's. When pulled along, the wooden clanger strikes the locomotive bell.

PLATE 726: MICKEY MOUSE DRUMMER PULL TOY manufactured by Fisher Price circa 1940's.

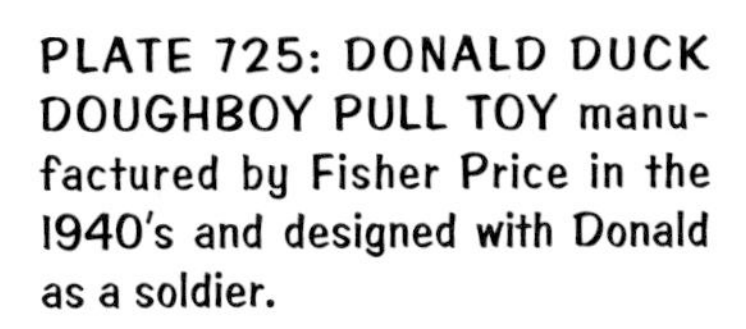

PLATE 725: DONALD DUCK DOUGHBOY PULL TOY manufactured by Fisher Price in the 1940's and designed with Donald as a soldier.

PLATE 727: DONALD DUCK XYLOPHONE PLAYER PULL TOY, c. 1940's by Walt Disney Productions and manufactured by Fisher Price.

PLATE 728: DONALD DUCK DRUM MAJOR PULL TOY #400 manufactured by Fisher Price toys.

PLATE 729: MICKEY MOUSE CHOO-CHOO #485 PULL TOY manufactured by Fisher Price toys. This is one of the more common Mickey pull toys.

PLATE 730: DONALD DUCK WITH BATON AND PULLING CART pull toy #400-500 and manufactured by Fisher Price. When pulled along, the action moves Donald's arm and the baton spins.

PLATE 731: ORIGINAL POINT-OF-SALE STORE DISPLAY FOR MICKEY MOUSE VIEWER FILMS from the 1940's. Absolutely unused and untouched, this display holds 66 films! c. Walt Disney Productions.

PLATE 732: DONALD DUCK CARPET SWEEPER dated 1940 c. Walt Disney Productions. This sweeper will actually sweep up objects on the floor!

PLATE 733: INGERSOLL MICKEY MOUSE ALARM CLOCK, 1940's, c. Walt Disney Productions.

PLATE 734: DONALD DUCK JACK-IN-THE BOX, circa 1940, and copyright Walt Disney Productions. This wood composition head figure with a cloth body in a soft wood box was manufactured by Spear.

PLATE 735: PANCHITO THE ROOSTER CERAMIC CHARACTER LAMP manufactured by the Railley Corporation in the 1940's.

PLATE 736: JOE CARIOCA GLAZED CERAMIC FIGURE manufactured by the American Pottery Company in the 1940's.

PLATE 737: ITEM A - SNOW WHITE PLANTER manufactured by Leeds China in the 1940's. ITEM B - SNOW WHITE BANK manufactured by Leeds China in the 1940's.

PLATE 739: DOPEY CERAMIC LAMP manufactured by the Railley Corporation in the 1940's.

PLATE 738: ITEM A - DOPEY CERAMIC PLANTER by Leeds. ITEM B - DOPEY STILL CHARACTER FIGURINE by Leeds in the 1940's.

PLATE 740: DONALD DUCK GLAZED CERAMIC LAMP, c. Walt Disney Productions and circa 1940's.

PLATE 741: DONALD DUCK GLAZED CERAMIC FIGURE manufactured by the Leeds China Company of Chicago in the 1940's.

PLATE 742: DONALD DUCK PITCHER, circa 1940's, c. Walt Disney Productions and manufactured by Leeds China.

PLATE 743: MICKEY MOUSE LEEDS CHINA TURNABOUT COOKIE JAR with Minnie Mouse on the reverse.

PLATE 744: DONALD DUCK TURNABOUT COOKIE JAR with Joe Carioca on the reverse manufactured by Leeds China in the 1940's.

PLATE 745: PINOCCHIO CHALKWARE CARNIVAL FIGURE circa 1940's.

PLATE 746: DONALD DUCK CARNIVAL FIGURE of chalkware, circa 1940's.

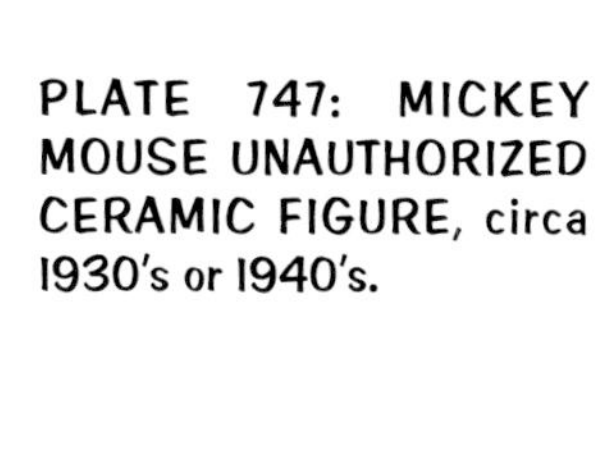

PLATE 747: MICKEY MOUSE UNAUTHORIZED CERAMIC FIGURE, circa 1930's or 1940's.

PLATE 748: DONALD DUCK CHARACTER MOLDING AND COLORING SET, manufactured by Model-Craft of Chicago.

PLATE 749: GIDEON THE CAT COLORFUL CERAMIC FIGURE manufactured by Goebel.

PLATE 750: JOE CARIOCA WOOD COMPOSITION DISNEY WINDUP FIGURE, circa 1940's.

PLATE 751: ITEMS A THROUGH E - BAMBI, FLOWER, THUMPER (grey version), **THUMPER'S GIRLFRIEND, AND THUMPER** (brown version) by American Pottery of Los Angeles in the 1940's.

PLATE 752: ITEMS A THROUGH C - BABY THUMPER, BABY BAMBI, AND BABY FLOWER small American Pottery glazed ceramic figures c. Walt Disney Productions, 1940's.

PLATE 753: WALT DISNEY'S BAMBI HANKIES BOOK, c. 1941, 1942 Walt Disney Productions.

PLATE 754: WALT DISNEY'S BAMBI PAINT BOOK, circa 1941 and c. Walt Disney Productions.

PLATE 755: INTERIOR OF BAMBI HANKY BOOK PICTURED IN PLATE #753 showing two Bambi hankies.

PLATE 756: ITEMS A AND B - WALT DISNEY'S THUMPER and WALT DISNEY'S BAMBI ILLUSTRATED STORY BOOKS, c. 1942 Walt Disney productions.

PLATE 758: FLOWER THE SKUNK CERAMIC PLANTER manufactured by Leeds China, circa 1940's. c. Walt Disney Productions.

PLATE 757: THUMPER PLANTER manufactured by Leeds China in the 1940's.

PLATE 759: ITEM A - BAMBI AND FLOWER glazed ceramic planter, probably an unauthorized piece. ITEM B - BAMBI GLAZED CERAMIC PITCHER manufactured in the 1940's by the American Pottery Company.

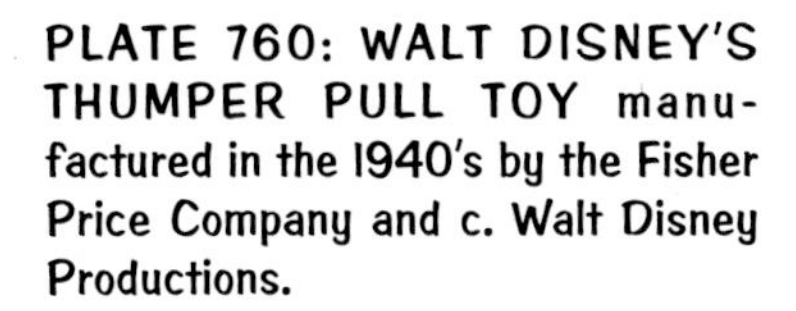

PLATE 760: WALT DISNEY'S THUMPER PULL TOY manufactured in the 1940's by the Fisher Price Company and c. Walt Disney Productions.

PLATE 761: ITEM A - 5" STEIFF BAMBI DOLL with original tag, button, and label. ITEM B - 9" STEIFF VELVET BAMBI DOLL with original button and tag.

PLATE 762: MINNIE MOUSE SCHUCO MASCOTT DOLL, cloth and plastic windup by Schuco of Germany, c. Walt Disney Productions.

PLATE 763: MICKEY MOUSE SCHUCO WINDUP FIGURE made in Germany and c. Walt Disney Productions.

PLATE 764: INGERSOLL MICKEY MOUSE WRIST WATCH BOX (only). From the 1940's.

PLATE 765: DISNEY MUSICAL SWEEPER by Fisher Price plays "Whistle While You Work," c. Walt Disney Productions.

PLATE 766: DUMBO THE ELEPHANT GIANT CERAMIC PITCHER marked c. Walt Disney Productions and manufactured by Leeds China.

PLATE 767: DUMBO SALT AND PEPPER SHAKERS by Leeds China in the 1940's, c. Walt Disney Productions.

PLATE 768: DISNEY CHARACTER PARTY HATS from a 1940's birthday party kit, c. Walt Disney Productions.

PLATE 769: DONALD DUCK AND MICKEY MOUSE CRAYONS SET c. 1946 Walt Disney Productions and manufactured by Transogram.

PLATE 770: BABY DUMBO GLAZED CERAMIC FIGURE by American Pottery, c. Walt Disney Productions, 1940's.

PLATE 771: DISNEYLAND AMERICAN SAFETY BLOCKS by Halsam, c. Walt Disney Enterprises.

PLATE 772: DONALD DUCK DOCTOR KIT, c. 1940's. Walt Disney Productions.

PLATE 773: MICKEY MOUSE LIBRARY OF GAMES, c. Walt Disney Productions and circa 1940's.

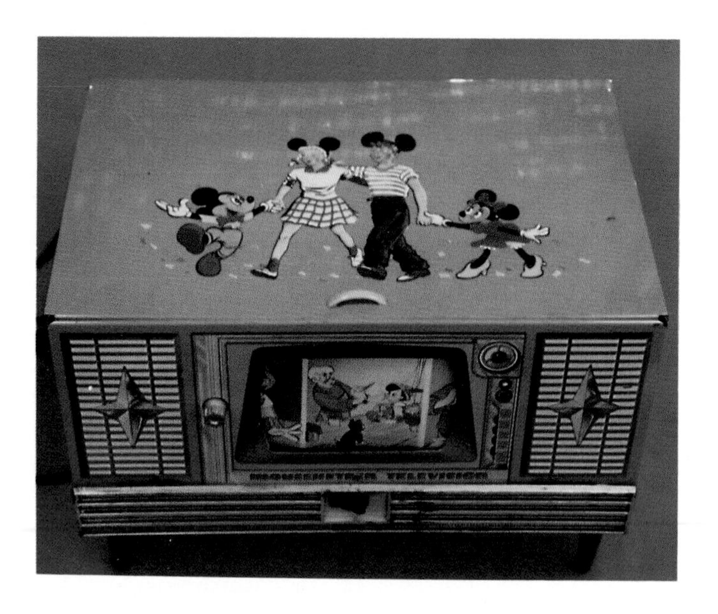

PLATE 774: MOUSEKETEER TELEVISION 1950's paper scroll picture toy with a tin lithographed television cabinet.

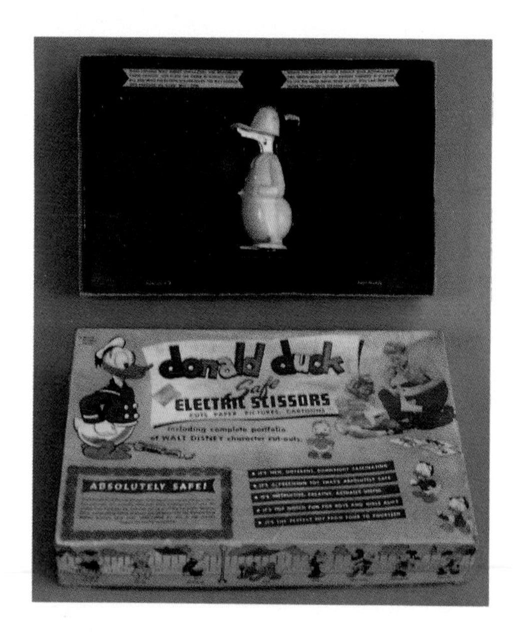

PLATE 775: DONALD DUCK SAFE ELECTRIC SCISSORS, circa 1950's and shown with original box.

PLATE 776: SCUFFY SHOE POLISH with Disney Mickey Mouse character box, circa 1950.

PLATE 777: DONALD DUCK PLASTIC HANDLE UMBRELLA circa 1940's. The umbrella is plaid with a wooden handle.

LATE 778: WALT DISNEY CHARACTER MAGIC ERASABLE ICTURES art set from the 1950's which includes 24 erasable picture lates.

PLATE 779: MICKEY MOUSE CLUB NEWSREEL WITH SOUND manufactured by Mattel in the 1950's. The set included a record, projector, screen, and slides.

LATE 780: DISNEYLAND MONORAIL GAME, circa 1950's and anufactured by Parker Brothers, Inc.

PLATE 782: DONALD DUCK'S TIDDLEY WINX GAME manufactured by Jay Mar and c. Walt Disney Productions.

PLATE 781: DISNEYLAND MUSICAL ORGAN GRINDER tin crank toy, 1950's c. Walt Disney Productions.

PLATE 783: MICKEY MOUSE WEATHER HOUSE all plastic novelty barometer. This toy barometer actually works.

PLATE 784: DONALD DUCK OHIO ART SAND PAIL manufactured in the 1950's by the Ohio Art Company of Bryan, Ohio.

PLATE 785: SMALL 3" DONALD DUCK SAND PAIL was manufactured by Happynak of England.

PLATE 786: DONALD DUCK TEA TRAY manufactured by Ohio Art and c. Walt Disney Productions.

PLATE 787: ITEM A – DONALD DUCK 3" SAND PAIL by Ohio Art. **ITEM B – MICKEY MOUSE 4" PAIL** manufactured by Happynak of England.

PLATE 788: DONALD DUCK TIN LITHOGRAPHED REGISTER BANK, circa 1950's and c. Walt Disney Productions.

PLATE 789: 2ND NATIONAL DUCK BANK TIN SAVINGS BANK, circa 1950's and c. Walt Disney Productions. When a coin is placed on Donald's tongue and a window is pulled he "swallows" the coin.

PLATE 790: MICKEY MOUSE TIN TOP from the 1950's manufactured by Chein and c. Walt Disney Productions.

PLATE 791: WALT DISNEY'S DUMBO tin windup toy manufactured by Louis Marx in the 1940's.

PLATE 792: ITEMS A AND B - DONALD DUCK WALKER TOYS manufactured by Marx in the 1960's.

PLATE 793: ITEMS A AND B - JIMINY CRICKET CHARACTER MUGS with moving eyes, from the 1960's, c. Walt Disney Productions.

PLATE 794: DONALD DUCK WINDUP TOY manufactured by Schuco of W. Germany in the 1960's. This toy is made of metal, cloth, and plastic.

PLATE 795: GIANT DONALD DUCK CHARACTER DOLL manufactured by Lars of Italy in the 1960's.

PLATE 796: DONALD DUCK AND HIS NEPHEWS plastic windup toy by Marx, c. Walt Disney Productions.

PLATE 797: DONALD THE SKIER action toy manufactured by Louis Marx in the 1960's, c. Walt Disney Productions.

PLATE 798: This **MECHANICAL DISNEY PARADE ROADSTER** was manufactured by Louis Marx and Sons. It is a "Spring Motor Windup" shown with its original box.

PLATE 799: MECHANICAL DISNEY PARADE CAR manufactured by Marx toys and copyright Walt Disney Productions.

PLATE 800: MICKEY THE DRIVER tin and plastic windup car manufactured by Marx and Company and shown with its original box. The Mickey head and body are hard plastic.

PLATE 801: MECHANICAL MICKEY THE DRIVER tin windup car manufactured by Line Mar toys of Japan. Note that the car in #800 and #801 is the same, but the Mickey figure in this version is all tin, not plastic.

LATE 802: DISNEYLAND ROLLERCOASTER tin windup toy anufactured by Chein and c. Walt Disney Productions.

PLATE 803: DISNEYLAND FERRIS WHEEL manufactured by Chein in the 1950's, c. Walt Disney Productions. The color lithography on this toy makes it extremely bright and attractive.

PLATE 804: DONALD DUCK DISNEY DIPSY CAR manufactured by Marx and pictured with its original box, c. Walt Disney Productions.

PLATE 805: DONALD THE DRIVER manufactured by Louis Marx and Company. The waving Donald figure is hard plastic, c. Walt Disney Productions.

PLATE 807: MICKEY MOUSE ALL TIN WINDUP DIPSY CAR by Line Mar Toys of Japan. This is similar to the Marx Disney Dipsy cars except for the metal rather than plastic Mickey Mouse figure.

PLATE 806: WALT DISNEY'S TELEVISION CAR manufactured by Louis Marx and Company and c. Walt Disney Productions. Pictured with its colorful original box.

PLATE 808: CASEY JUNIOR THE DISNEYLAND EXPRESS tin and plastic windup train by Louis Marx and Company, late 1940's and c. Walt Disney Productions.

PLATE 809: GOOFY THE WALKING GARDENER tin windup toy 1940's, probably of foreign manufacture but this toy does utilize the Marx Goofy figure.

PLATE 810: MICKEY MOUSE ON THE SCOOTER lithographed tin windup toy. Mickey's head has an unusual shape.

PLATE 811: WALT DISNEY'S MICKEY MOUSE SCOOTER JOCKEY, manufactured by Mavco, has an all plastic windup mechanism.

PLATE 812: MICKEY MOUSE EXPRESS TIN WINDUP TRAIN TOY manufactured by Louis Marx, c. Walt Disney Productions.

PLATE 813: DISNEYLAND WINDUP TRAIN SET manufactured by Marx. The windup plastic engine pulls three tin cars around the colorful track and through two tunnels.

PLATE 814: WALT DISNEY'S MECHANICAL TRICYCLE WITH REVOLVING BELL tin and celluloid windup toy by Louis Marx and Company, c. Walt Disney Productions.

PLATE 815: MICKEY MOUSE WINDUP CAR manufactured by Marx in the 1950's and copyright Walt Disney Productions.

PLATE 816: DONALD DUCK WINDUP CAR BY MARX, 1950's, c. Walt Disney Productions.

PLATE 817: WALT DISNEY'S DONALD DUCK DUET tin windup dancers toy manufactured by Louis Marx in the 1940's, c. Walt Disney Productions.

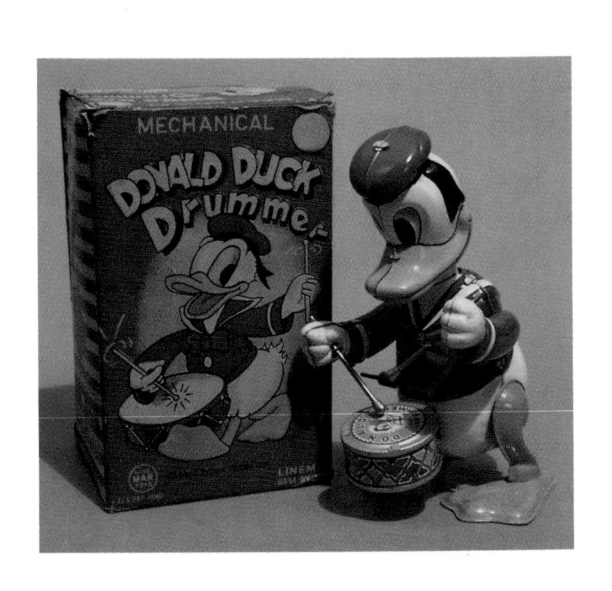

PLATE 818: MECHANICAL DONALD DRUMMER windup toy manufactured by Line Mar Toys in the 1950's, c. Walt Disney Productions. This toy is pictured with its original box.

PLATE 819: MECHANICAL WHIRLING TAIL DONALD DUCK made by Line Mar Toys in the 1960's and pictured with its original box.

PLATE 820: MINNIE MOUSE IN THE ROCKING CHAIR tin windup by Line Mar toys in the 1950's, c. Walt Disney Productions.

PLATE 821: MICKEY MOUSE WIND-UP FIGURE BY LINE MAR TOYS, Japan. This tin litho windup has whirling tail action and is c. Walt Disney Productions.

PLATE 822: This MICKEY MOUSE RIDING PLUTO ROCKING HORSE is one of the rarest and most desirable of Line Mar Toys; c. Walt Disney Productions.

PLATE 823: ITEM A – MUSICAL PLUTO tin windup manufactured by Line Mar, Japan. ITEM B – MICKEY MOUSE XYLOPHONE PLAYER by Line Mar Toys, tin windup. ITEM C – DONALD DUCK DRUMMER tin windup by Line Mar Toys, Japan.

PLATE 824: WALT DISNEY'S MICKEY MOUSE METEOR TRAIN manufactured by Marx and c. Walt Disney Productions.

PLATE 826: MICKEY MOUSE RIDING A UNICYCLE WINDUP manufactured by Line Mar Toys, Japan, c. Walt Disney Productions.

PLATE 825: MICKEY MOUSE AND DISNEY CHARACTER MINIATURE TIN TRAIN, c. Walt Disney Productions.

PLATE 827: MICKEY MOUSE ON ROLLERSKATES WINDUP TOY by Line Mar Toys of Japan and c. Walt Disney Productions.

PLATE 828: ITEM A - MICKEY MOUSE PLASTIC WINDUP TOY by Marx. ITEM B - MICKEY MOUSE XYLOPHONE PLAYER TIN WINDUP (small version) by Line Mar.

PLATE 829: WALT DISNEY'S ROCKING CHAIR tin and celluloid windup toy manufactured by Line Mar, c. Walt Disney Productions and shown with its original box.

PLATE 830: JIMINY CRICKET WINDUP TOY by Line Mar, 1960's, c. Walt Disney Productions.

PLATE 832: PLUTO WINDUP CHARACTER TOY manufactured by Line Mar in the 1960's, c. Walt Disney Productions.

PLATE 831: GOOFY TIN WINDUP FIGURE manufactured in the 1960's by Line Mar, c. Walt Disney Productions.

PLATE 833: PLUTO PULLING A CART tin friction toy manufactured by Line Mar Toys, Japan, 1960's, c. Walt Disney Productions.

PLATE 834: PLUTO RIDING A UNICYCLE TIN WINDUP TOY manufactured by Line Mar Toys and c. Walt Disney Productions.

PLATE 835: PLUTO BATTERY OPERATED LANTERN shown with its original box and manufactured by Line Mar, c. Walt Disney Productions.

PLATE 836: PLUTO TIN WINDUP TOY WITH WHIRLING TAIL ACTION manufactured by Line Mar Toys and c. Walt Disney Productions.

PLATE 837: PLUTO ON MICKEY'S DELIVERY CART metal and celluloid friction toy by Line Mar and c. Walt Disney Productions.

PLATE 838: DISNEY CHARACTER CAROUSEL tin windup toy by Line Mar, 1960's c. Walt Disney Production.

PLATE 841: WALT DISNEY FIRE DEPARTMENT FIRE ENGINE battery operated toy by Line Mar toys, 1960's, c. Walt Disney Productions.

PLATE 839: THE GREAT MICKEY THE MAGICIAN windup toy by Line Mar, c. Walt Disney Productions.

PLATE 840: ITEMS A AND B - PLUTO AND DONALD DUCK ON MOTORCYCLES manufactured by Line Mar, 1960's. These small friction toys are only 3" long.

PLATE 842: DONALD DUCK GYM TOY WINDUP ACROBAT by Line Mar in the 1960's. Shown with original box.

PLATE 843: PLUTO GYM-TOY ACROBAT windup action toy manufactured by Line Mar Toys, 1960's, c. Walt Disney Productions.

PLATE 844: ITEM A – LUDWIG VON DRAKE TIN WINDUP WALKER, 1960's, Line Mar Toys. ITEM B – LUDWIG VON DRAKE GO CART ACTION TOY, 1960's manufactured by Line Mar.

PLATE 845: DONALD DUCK'S GASOLINE COMPANY FRICTION TRUCK is all tin and bears Disney characters on both sides of the tanker, circa late 1950's.

PLATE 846: PECOS BILL WINDUP COWBOY c. Walt Disney Productions, plastic windup by Louis Marx.

PLATE 847: PINOCCHIO TIN WINDUP WALKING TOY manufactured by Line Mar Toys in the 1960's.

PLATE 848: ITEMS A AND B - SNOW WHITE AND CINDERELLA PLASTIC FIGURES used as watch stands in the 1960's, c. Walt Disney Productions.

PLATE 849: CINDERELLA WORK SONG, Golden Record, 1950's, c. Walt Disney Productions.

PLATE 850: WALT DISNEY'S DANCING CINDERELLA AND THE PRINCE plastic windup figures manufactured by Irwin and c. Walt Disney Productions.

PLATE 851: WALT DISNEY CINDERELLA APRON, c. 1950's Walt Disney Productions. This is a fold-up pattern which was a give-away promotion by J.C. Penney.

PLATE 852: TWEEDLE DUM AND TWEEDLE DEE SALT AND PEPPER SHAKERS of glazed ceramic in the 1950's, c. Walt Disney Productions.

PLATE 853: KING OF HEARTS CERAMIC PITCHER, with glazed finish, from 1950's and marked "c. Walt Disney Productions King of Hearts."

PLATE 854: WALT DISNEY SLEEPING BEAUTY PAINT BY NUMBER manufactured by Transogram, c. 1959 Walt Disney Productions.

PLATE 855: WALT DISNEY'S LADY FROM LADY AND THE TRAMP PLATFORM TOY, c. 1955 Walt Disney Productions.

PLATE 856: WALT DISNEY'S WHIRLING MARY POPPINS TOY plastic windup character by Marx, 1960's.

PLATE 857: LUDWIG VON DRAKE VINYL SQUEEZE TOY, 1960's, c. Walt Disney Productions.

PLATE 858: MICKEY MOUSE ALARM CLOCK by Bayard of France, 1960's. This clock looks like a 1930's design but is actually a more modern item.

PLATE 859: PLUTO ALARM CLOCK c. 1964 Walt Disney Productions, manufactured by Bayard of France.

PLATE 860: PINOCCHIO ALARM CLOCK c. 1967 Walt Disney Productions. Manufactured by Bayard of France.

AUTHOR AND COLLECTOR PROFILES

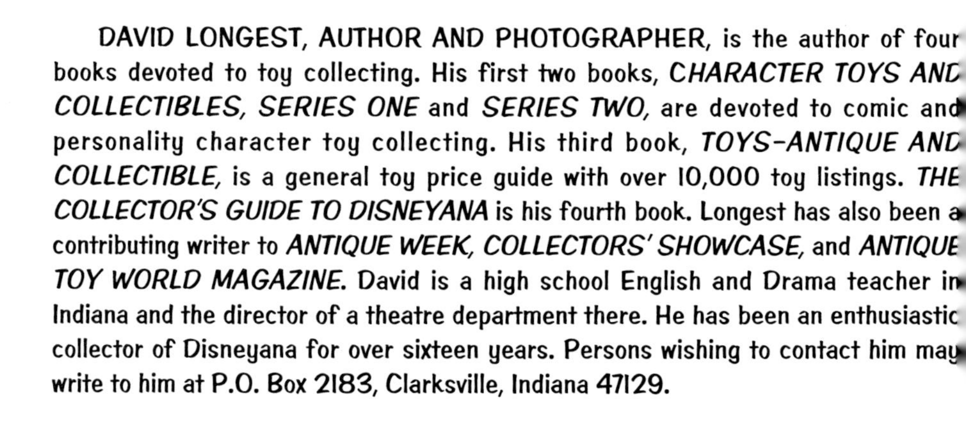

DAVID LONGEST, AUTHOR AND PHOTOGRAPHER, is the author of four books devoted to toy collecting. His first two books, *CHARACTER TOYS AND COLLECTIBLES, SERIES ONE* and *SERIES TWO*, are devoted to comic and personality character toy collecting. His third book, *TOYS–ANTIQUE AND COLLECTIBLE*, is a general toy price guide with over 10,000 toy listings. *THE COLLECTOR'S GUIDE TO DISNEYANA* is his fourth book. Longest has also been a contributing writer to *ANTIQUE WEEK, COLLECTORS' SHOWCASE*, and *ANTIQUE TOY WORLD MAGAZINE*. David is a high school English and Drama teacher in Indiana and the director of a theatre department there. He has been an enthusiastic collector of Disneyana for over sixteen years. Persons wishing to contact him may write to him at P.O. Box 2183, Clarksville, Indiana 47129.

MICHAEL STERN, AUTHOR, is an advanced collector of Disneyana who is the author of two price guides on Disney toys, *STERN'S GUIDE TO DISNEY COLLECTIBLES, First* and *Second Series*, both published by Collector Books. Although Michael is an avid collector of all Disney characters, he is particularly fond of 1930's Mickey Mouse toys in the form of wooden, bisque and celluloid figures. He is a financial adviser with Lamon and Stern and runs a stock hedge fund called Zenith along with his partner, Hollis M. Lamon. Michael resides in Atlanta, Georgia, with his wife, Merrill, and twin daughters, Jenny and Lisa. Persons wishing to contact him may write to him at: 1950 North Park Place, Suite 100, Atlanta, Georgia 30339.

GEORGE HATTERSLEY, who resides in eastern Pennsylvania, has been collecting toys for seventeen years starting with cast iron and construction toys.

In 1976, a friend brought over three tin Disney toys, of which one was a Disney Ferris wheel. He thought it was unique because none of the Disney theme parks had one. From that moment on, it was only Disney for Hattersley. The more he learned, the more his collection expanded, from tin lithographs to early watches and currently to include pre-war and post-war celluloid.

His ultimate dream is to find that rare celluloid windup in its original box.

ELMER REYNOLDS, and his wife Viola, of central Indiana, have been avid toy collectors for nearly 18 years. They collect all areas of character items, ranging from early Disneyana to old time radio, television, and Rose O'Neill Kewpies.

They began collecting tin windup toys. But as the disease of collecting Disneyana spread, Viola developed a passion for early celluloid figures, while Elmer contracted a fever for Fisher Price toys. Although the Reynolds love Mickey Mouse, Elmer and Viola grew up in the 1940's when Donald Duck was quite the rage, which explains their greater love for Donald.

With the Reynolds, it is more than just a hobby. It's a love affair with Walt Disney. As Elmer explains it, "With us, it is a genuine admiration for Walt Disney and everything he stood for. Thus, as we collect Disneyana, we help perpetuate the great legacy he left all of us."

COLLECTOR RESOURCES

The field of Disneyana collectors is growing and the intensity of these Disney enthusiasts is overwhelming. Many publications and auction catalogs are available for those wishing to acquire Disney memorabilia through the mail. The following are publications that contain valuable information on a variety of Disneyana topics.

THE INSIDE COLLECTOR
P.O. Box 98
Elmont, New York 11003

COLLECTORS SHOWCASE
P.O. Box 837
Tulsa, OK 74101

ANTIQUE TOY WORLD
P.O. Box 34509
Chicago, Ill 60634

The following are reputable mail and phone bid auction houses that deal in Disneyana.

HAKE'S AMERICANA & COLLECTIBLES
P.O. Box 1444
York, PA 17405
(717)848-1333

SMITH HOUSE TOY SALES
P.O. Box 336
Eliot, ME 03903
(207)439-4614

ROBERT COUP
P.O. Box 348
Leola, PA
717-656-7780

A MOUSE IN THE HOUSE
VINTAGE DISNEYANA
P.O. Box 2183
Clarksville, IN 47129

NEW ENGLAND AUCTION GALLERY
P.O. Box 2273
W. Peabody, MA 01960-7273
(503)535-3140

Two national Disneyana collector clubs hold conventions annually and publish collector newsletters. Further information may be obtained by writing to:

THE MOUSE CLUB
2056 Cirone Way
San Jose, California 95124

THE NATIONAL FANTASY FAN CLUB
FOR DISNEYANA COLLECTORS
P.O. Box 19212
Irvine, California 92713

Also, the following dealer puts out a regular bi-monthly sales list containing hundreds of Disneyana collectibles for sale by mail:

ROBERT CROOKER
THE MOUSE MAN INK
P.O. Box 3195
Wakefield, MA 01880

THE DISNEYANA VALUE GUIDE

The value guide for Disneyana collectibles is to be used as a point of reference before buying or selling an item. Any value guide tends to be subjective in nature, and we've used the sources available to us to arrive at what we think are accurate price points in today's marketplace. The Disney toy market can change dramatically in a very short span of time.

We have determined the values for each item based on a number of factors and sources:

1. What we have paid for each item.
2. Auction catalogs.
3. Mail auction price realized lists.
4. Toy and doll show prices.
5. Antique Trader ads.

We feel the values suggested are excellent estimates of what each item is actually worth. The basic law of economics – supply and demand – can shoot holes through any value guide. The adage that the worth of a toy is what someone will pay for it is still prevalent for today's collectors.

The following descriptions relate to the condition of the toy and how they are priced accordingly.

GOOD CONDITION

A toy in good condition is in working order, has been used, shows general wear and tear. The toy must look fairly clean with little or no rust.

EXCELLENT, MINT CONDITION

Excellent means the toy is clean and looks as if it has never been used. It is complete and all functions are operative. *Mint* applies to mint in the box (MIB) and means the toy is in its original package. In many cases, the box is worth more than the item itself.

Each toy has been priced as it appears in the picture (with box, with tag, with label).

Plate	Description	Good	Excellent/ Mint
1	Mickey Mouse Hurdy Gurdy	$10,000	$12,500
2	Mickey Mouse Drummer	$5,500	$6,500
3-4	Mickey & Minnie Playland	$11,500	$13,000
5	Mickey & Minnie Motorcycle	$22,000	$25,000
6	Mickey Mouse Sparkler	$1,100	$1,300
7	Nifty Mickey Mouse Drummer	$1,300	$1,500
8	Mickey Mouse Lamp	$1,800	$2,000
9	Rambling Mickey Mouse	$8,500	$10,000
10	Hobby Horse Mickey Mouse	$1,000	$1,200
11	Cowboy Mickey On Pluto	$4,000	$5,500
12	Cowboy Mickey Mouse Celluloid	$3,500	$4,500
13	Mickey or Minnie Nursery Doll ea.	$350	$500
14	Mickey Mouse on Tricycle	$3,800	$4,000
15	Donald & Minnie on Trapeze	$1,500	$2,500
16	Mickey & Pluto Windup	$5,500	$6,000
17	Mickey & Minnie Acrobats	$600	$850
18	Mickey & Pluto Celluloid Windup Cart	$3,500	$4,000
19	Mickey Mouse Balancing Whirlygig	$3,000	$3,300
20	Minnie Mouse Celluloid Whirlygig on Cart	$2,200	$2,500
21	Mickey Drummer Celluloid	$10,000	$12,000
22	Mickey Mouse Ingersoll Watch & Store Display	$800	$1,200
23	Mickey Mouse Walker	$8,500	$10,000

Plate	Description	Good	Excellent/ Mint
24A	Mickey Celluloid Nodder	$1,400	$1,600
B	Mickey Pencil Sharpener	$150	$200
25	Hobby Horse Minnie Mouse	$1,500	$1,800
26	Rocking Horse Mickey	$3,500	$5,000
27	Mickey & Pluto Windup	$1,900	2,200
28	Mickey & Minnie Go Motoring	$3,200	$3,500
29	Minnie Mouse Celluloid	$350	$450
30	Minnie Mouse Celluloid	$350	$450
31	Swinging Exhibition Flights	$1,000	$1,300
32	Mickey On Wooden Scooter	$1,700	$1,800
33	Minnie Mouse Acrobat	$600	$700
34	Minnie Mouse Acrobat	$600	$700
35	Mickey & Minnie On Elephant	$7,200	$7,500
36	Mickey Mouse Cowboy Celluloid	$3,500	$4,500
37	Mickey Mouse Holding a Ball	$2,700	$3,000
38	Minnie Mouse Hula Dancer	$800	$950
39-40	Mickey & Minnie Acrobats	$1,200	$1,400
41	Mickey Celluloid Cart	$3,000	$3,500
42	Mickey Celluloid Cart	$3,000	$3,500
43	Mickey Mouse Nursery Doll	$350	$500
44	Rollover Schuco Mickey	$750	$800
45	Celluloid Minnie On Ball	$1,000	$1,150
46	Mickey Thermometer	$700	$750
47	Mickey Celluloid Boxers pr.	$1,200	$1,500
48	Mickey & Donald Rowboat	$4,200	$4,500
49	Celluloid Egg Timer ea.	$425	$450
50	Mickey Celluloid Band Set	$900	$1,000
51	Mickey Mouse Crib Toy	$125	$175
52	Mickey Mouse Rattle	$150	$200
53	Fun-E-Flex Mickey	$600	$750
54	Mickey Mouse Wooden Toy	$1,500	$1,750
55	Fun-E-Flex Mickey or Minnie ea.	$500	$650
56	Balancing Mickey Mouse	$1,000	$1,300
57	Mickey Mouse in Rowboat	$2,500	$3,200
58	Fun-E-Flex Figures ea.	$125	$165
59	Fun-E-Flex Mickey or Minnie ea.	$275	$350
60	Fun-E-Flex Mickey or Minnie ea.	$300	$425
61	Mickey Mouse Cane ea.	$200	$250
62	Mickey Mouse Baton	$500	$575
63	Mickey Mouse Springboard	$1,000	$1,200
64	Fun-E-Flex Minnie	$125	$165
65	Fun-E-Flex Minnie ea.	$175	$200
66	Fun-E-Flex Mickey ea.	$175	$200
67-77	Lionel Circus Train	$8,500	$10,000
78-79	Mickey Hand Car	$1,300	$1,600
80	Mickey Band Leader Doll	$2,000	$2,500
81	Mickey Mouse Knickerbocker Doll	$2,000	$2,500
82	Mickey or Minnie Knickerbocker Doll ea.	$1,500	$1,700
83	Small Cowboy Mickey	$350	$500
84	Large Cowboy Mickey	$2,500	$3,000
85	Large Cowgirl Minnie	$2,500	$3,000
86	Mickey 7" Steiff Doll	$2,200	$2,500
87	Mickey 9" Steiff Doll	$2,500	$2,800
88	Mickey 11" Steiff Doll	$2,700	$3,000
89	Mickey Steiff Hand Puppet	$1,500	$1,800
90	Mickey Mouse 9¼" Fun-E-Flex	$1,000	$1,200
91	Mickey Mouse French Aluminum Bank	$1,300	$1,500
92	Mickey Mouse 14" Cloth Knickerbocker Doll	$500	$800
93	Mickey Mouse 12" Cloth Knickerbocker Doll	$350	$600
94	Dean's Rag Book 5" Mickey	$500	$750
95	Dean's Rag Book 8" Mickey	$500	$750
96	Dixon Mickey Mouse Pen Holder	$450	$500
97	Dean's Rag Book Mickey	$500	$750
98	Knickerbocker Composition Mickey Doll	$800	$1,600
99	Mickey Mouse 7" Steiff Doll	$2,200	$2,500
100	Mickey Mouse Bisque	$4,500	$5,000
101	Musician Boxed Bisque Set	$1,200	$1,500
102-103	Two Pals Boxed Set	$1,200	$1,500
104	Three Pals Boxed Set	$1,500	$2,000
105	Minnie Mouse Toothbrush Holder	$400	$425
106 A	Minnie Toothbrush Holder	$400	$425
B	Toothbrush	$75	$125
107	Mickey & Minnie Toothbrush Holder	$300	$325
108	Mickey, Minnie and Pluto Toothbrush Holder	$300	$325

Plate	Description	Good	Excellent/ Mint
109	Mickey or Minnie Toothbrush Holder ea.	$400	$425
110	Mickey Toothbrush Holder ea.	$400	$425
111	Mickey Mouse German Sugar Bowl Set	$2,000	$2,500
112	Mickey or Minnie Bulbous Head Toothbrush Holder ea.	$400	$425
113	Mickey, Minnie & Donald Toothbrush Holder	$400	$425
114A	Mickey Bisque Toothbrush Holder	$300	$325
B	Mickey Musician Bisque	$200	$250
115	Mickey Bisque In Canoe	$3,500	$4,200
116A	Mickey With Cane Bisque	$100	$125
B	Mickey Ashtray	$500	$625
117	Mickey Mouse Cream Pitcher	$200	$225
118	Mickey 5½" Musician Bisque	$500	$550
119A	Mickey Catcher Bisque		
B	Mickey On Pluto Bisque	$100	$125
120	Mickey Musician Bisque		
121	Mickey & Minnie in Nightshirts Bisque	$225	$275
122	Musician Bisque Set	$425	$500
123	Mickey and Minnie China Salt and Pepper Shakers	$500	$550
124	Mickey Mouse Spring-Armed Celluloid Figure	$400	$600
125	Minnie Mouse Pincushion	$400	$500
126	Mickey Mouse Ashtray	$225	$275
127	Minnie Mouse Ashtray	$250	$300
128	Mickey & Pluto Ashtray	$275	$300
129	Mickey Musician Bisques Set	$500	$550
130	Mickey Baseball Bisque Set	$850	$900
131	Mickey Egg Timer	$400	$425
132	Mickey Ashtray	$100	$150
133	Minnie Mouse Plate	$125	$135
134	Mickey Bavarian Bowl	$300	$325
135	Minnie Mouse Plate	$100	$125
136	Minnie Mouse Cup & Saucer	$150	$250
137	Minnie Patriot Mug	$100	$125
138	Mickey Mouse Bowl	$120	$140
139	Mickey Mouse Patriot China Mug	$150	$200
140	Mickey Fireman Mug and Bowl	$200	$400

Plate	Description	Good	Excellent/ Mint
141	Minnie Mouse Patriot Cup & Saucer	$150	$250
142	Mickey Patriot Divided Dish	$135	$140
143	Mickey & Pluto Plate	$100	$110
144	Mickey Boxed Tea Set	$550	$625
145-146	Mickey Mouse Large French Pitcher	$400	$700
147	Mickey Krueger Cup	$200	250
148	Mickey & Betty Bowl	$350	$400
149	Mickey Mouse Lusterware Plate and Teapot pr.	$75	$125
150	Mickey Mouse Lusterware Doll Dish	$50	$100
151	Mickey Small Lusterware Creamer and Sugar Bowl	$75	$125
152	Mickey Mouse Lusterware Cup and Saucer	$50	$100
153	Libbey Mickey & Minnie Glasses	$170	$180
154	Mickey Bavarian Ashtray	$150	$160
155	Mickey Mouse French Creamer	$250	$500
156	Mickey Mouse Marks Brothers Bead Game	$125	$225
157	Mickey Hoop-La Game	$300	$500
158	Mickey Mouse Bagatelle	$300	$500
159	Mickey Mouse Piano	$1,500	$2,300
160	Mickey Roll 'em Game	$450	$500
161	Mickey Foundry Set	$350	$500
162	Mickey Soldier Set	$475	$525
163A,B	Mickey Mouse Circus Game, complete	$600	$900
164	Mickey Mouse Pop Game	$400	$650
165-166	Scatter Ball Game	$300	$475
167-170	Mickey Picture Puzzles Set	$350	$550
171-172	Mickey Mouse Target Game	$450	$525
173-174	Mickey Mouse Playing Cards each deck	$110	$125
175	Mickey Mouse Bow & Arrow Set	$125	$250
176	Coming Home Game complete	$150	$300
177	Old Maid Cards	$75	$95
178	Snap Cards	$125	$175
179	Mickey Mouse Dominoes	$125	$150
180	Mickey Safety Blocks	$225	$250

Plate	Description	Good	Excellent/ Mint
181-182	Mickey Mouse Marks Puzzles ea.	$65	$110
183	Old Maid Cards	$75	$95
184	Mickey Mouse Marks Puzzle	$65	$110
185	"Shuffled Symphonies" Cards	$85	$100
186	Mickey & Minnie Pillow Cover	$100	$115
187	Mickey Pull Toy	$350	$400
188	Mickey Mouse Xylophone Player	$300	$350
189	Mickey & Pluto Fisher Price	$400	$425
190	Mickey Rolling Toy	$225	$300
191	Mickey Mouse Target	$125	$200
192	Mickey Pull Toy	$300	$350
193	Mickey & Minnie Sand Pail	$200	$325
194	Mickey Washer w/Wringer	$500	$750
195	Mickey Mouse Washer	$325	$425
196A	Mickey Mouse Sand Pail	$200	$275
B	Mickey Mouse French Tin	$300	$425
197	Mickey Mouse English Tin	$350	$500
198	Mickey Mouse Sweeper	$200	$225
199	Mickey Band Sand Pail	$125	$225
200	Mickey Sand Pail	$125	$225
201-202	Minnie, Pluto & Mickey Sand Pail	$225	$300
203	Mickey Sand Pail	$100	$200
204	Mickey Watering Can	$75	$150
205	Mickey Ohio Art Tin Tray	$75	$150
206	Mickey Ohio Art Tin Tray	$100	$150
207	Mickey Mouse Watering Can	$100	$200
208	Mickey Mouse Watering Can	$125	$225
209	Mickey Sand Pail	$125	$250
210	Mickey Sand Pail	$75	$150
211-213	Mickey Sand Sifter ea.	$100	$200
214	Mickey Mouse Sand Pail	$75	$150
215	Mickey Mouse Wash Tub	$125	$175
216	Mickey Mouse Wash Tub	$125	$175
217	Mickey Mouse Sand Pail	$125	$225
218	Mickey Mouse Shovel	$75	$125
219-220	Mickey Mouse Tin Drum	$300	$500
221	Mickey Mouse Drum	$275	$300
222	Mickey Mouse Drum	$225	$250
223	Mickey Mouse Drum	$550	$600
224	Mickey Mouse Drum	$550	$600
225	Mickey Mouse Drum	$225	$250
226-230	Mickey Mouse Tops ea.	$300	$325
231	Mickey Sand Pail	$150	$225
232	Mickey Sand Pail	$150	$225
233	Mickey Sand Pail	$100	$200
234	Mickey Mouse Shovel	$75	$150
235	Mickey Tin Tea Set	$400	$450
236	Mickey Boxed China Tea Set	$350	$425
237	Mickey Mouse Wastebasket	$200	$400
238	Mickey Mouse Lunch Box	$2,500	$3,500
239	Mickey Watering Can	$200	$300
240	Mickey Mouse Sand Pail	$100	$225
241	French Sand Pail	$150	$300
242	Mickey Sand Pail	$125	$225
243	Mickey Sand Pail	$125	$250
244	Mickey Sand Pail	$150	$250
245	Mickey Mouse Tool Chest	$375	$400
246	Mickey Tool Chest	$250	$270
247-248	Mickey Mouse Potty	$300	$350
249	Mickey Telephone Bank	$325	$375
250	Mickey Mouse Telephone	$325	$375
251-252	Mickey Figural Pencil Boxes ea.	$225	$250
253	Mickey Printing Set	$175	$200
254	Mickey Pencil Box	$115	$120
255	Mickey Pencil Box	$115	$120
256	Mickey Mouse Dixon Map	$75	$150
257	Mickey Pencil Box ea.	$115	$120
258	Mickey Pencil Box	$130	$135
259-260	Mickey Pencil Box ea.	$115	$120
261	Mickey Mouse Pencil Box	$135	$150
262-263	Mickey Mouse Waddle Book	$3,200	$3,500
264-269	King Arthur's Pop-Up Book	$300	$500
270-271	Mickey Mouse Pop-Up Book	$225	$250
272-273	Minnie Mouse Pop-Up Book	$225	$250
274	Mickey Mouse Coloring Book	$100	$150
275	Mickey Composition Book	$95	$120
276	Story Of Mickey Mouse	$75	$150
277	Mickey Mouse Movie Stories	$100	$175
278	Mickey Mouse Alphabet Book	$75	$125
279	Walt Disney Paint Book	$75	$110
280	Mickey Mouse Coloring Book	$75	$120
281	Mickey Mouse Crusoe	$75	$100
282	Mickey Wee Little Books Set	$125	$200

Plate	Description	Good	Excellent/ Mint
283	Mickey Mouse Cookies Hat	$75	$110
284	Mickey Mouse ABC Story	$60	$100
285	Mickey Mouse Fire Brigade	$75	$100
286	Mickey Mouse Book 4	$100	$140
287A	Mickey Mouse Coming Home Game Tokens Box	$70	$125
B	Mickey Mouse In Ye Olden Days Pop-Up Book	$125	$200
288	40 Big Pages Of Mickey Mouse	$75	$120
289	Adventures Of Mickey Mouse	$50	$110
290	Mickey Mouse Stories	$60	$90
291	Adventures Of Mickey Mouse Book I	$70	$110
292	Mickey Mouse Has A Busy Day	$45	$75
293	Walt Disney Silly Symphony	$50	$85
294	Mickey Mouse and Pluto The Pup	$80	125
295	Mickey Mouse In Giantland	$60	$95
296A	Mickey Mouse and The Magic Carpet	$40	$75
B	Mickey Cine Art Film	$20	$35
297	Story Of Mickey Mouse	$25	$40
298	Mickey Mouse Print Shop	$140	$160
299 A-C	Mickey Mouse Recipe Cards ea.	$15	$25
300A	Mickey Mouse To Draw & Color	$75	$150
B	Mickey Mouse Recipe Scrap Book	$90	$135
301	Mickey Mouse Party Game	$95	$110
302	Walt Disney's Clock Cleaners	$75	$150
303	Walt Disney Annual	$50	$100
304	Mickey Mouse Valentine Card	$25	$35
305A	Mickey and Minnie Valentine	$25	$40
B	Minnie Mechanical Valentine	$20	$35
306	Minnie Mouse Valentine	$30	$45
307	Mickey Mouse Christmas Card	$35	$50
308	Mickey Mouse Sheet Music	$95	$150
309	Mickey Mouse Birthday Party Sheet Music	$75	$125
310	Mickey Mouse Lamp	$1,400	$2,000

Plate	Description	Good	Excellent/ Mint
311	Mickey Mouse Lamp With Filament	$450	$550
312	Mickey Mouse Lamp	$1,400	$2,000
313	Mickey Mouse Baby Rattle	$300	$325
314	Mickey Mouse Tambourine	$350	$375
315A	Left: Mickey Noisemaker	$90	$140
	Right: Mickey Party Horn	$80	$90
315B	Tall Mickey Party Horn	$125	$175
316	Noma Silly Symphony Lights	$225	$250
317	Mickey Mouse Noma Bells	$200	$225
318	Mickey Mazda Lights	$400	$425
319	Mickey Mouse Blackboard	$300	$320
320	Mickey Mouse Electric Alarm Clock	$1,350	$1,600
321	Mickey Ensign Music Box	$110	$115
322	Seiberling Mickey Mouse	$150	$175
323	Mickey Rolatoy	$400	$425
324	Jam Jar Bank	$150	$175
325	Mickey Post Office Bank	$125	$135
326	Crown Mickey Mouse Bank	$350	$400
327	Mickey Treasure Chest Bank	$350	$400
328	Mickey Mechanical Car With Box	$700	$725
329	Mickey Mechanical Car	$300	$350
330	Mickey Mouse Soap w/box	$300	$315
331	Mickey Mouse Soap w/box	$300	$325
332-333	Mickey Mouse Toilet Soap	$200	$225
334	Mickey Mouse Night Light	$550	$600
335	Mickey Mouse Flashlight	$1,000	$1,200
336	Mickey Mouse Talkie Jector	$1,000	$1,100
337	Movie Jector Film Display	$400	$425
338	Cine Art Film Display	$300	$325
339	Mickey Mouse Watch Box	$120	$125
340	Mickey Mouse Sled	$400	$450
341	Mickey Mouse Emerson Radio	$3,000	$3,500
342-343	Mickey Mouse Shortwave Radio	$2,500	$3,000
344	Mickey Mouse 1930's Soaps	$250	$400
345	Mickey Mouse Toy Chest	$225	$270
346	Mickey Mouse Print Shop	$140	$160
347	Baby Mickey Mouse Fork & Spoon with Holder	$450	$500
348	Mickey Mouse Seiberling	$200	$225
349	Mickey Mouse Seiberling	$200	$225

Plate	Description	Good	Excellent/ Mint
350A	Small Mickey Seiberling	$150	$175
B	Large Mickey Seiberling	$200	$225
351	Disney Beetleware Dishes ea.	$35	$50
352-353	Mickey Mouse Fork & Spoon	$275	$300
354	Mickey Mouse Brush Set	$300	$325
355	Mickey Mouse Brush ea.	$95	$105
356-357	Mickey Mouse Brush ea.	$75	$80
358	Mickey Mouse Birthday Candle Holders	$175	$185
359	Boxed Mickey Mouse Brush	$170	$185
360	Mickey Mouse Saxophone	$250	$275
361	Mickey Mouse Banjo	$350	$400
362	Mickey Mouse Bubble Buster	$150	$175
363	Mickey Mouse Trapeze	$50	$75
364	Mickey Mouse Porringer	$350	$375
365	Mickey Mouse Telephone	$275	$300
366	Mickey Mouse Tunnel	$400	$450
367	Mickey Mouse Cap	$125	$150
368	Mickey Mouse Ashtray	$400	$450
369	German Mickey Mouse	$300	$325
370A	Mickey Mouse Magic Slate	$60	$90
B	Minnie Mouse Bakelite Pencil Sharpener	$35	$60
C	Mickey Mouse Bakelite Pencil Sharpener	$50	$75
371	Mickey Mouse Pencil Sharpeners ea.	$35	$65
372	Mickey Mouse Rug	$275	$300
373	Mickey Mouse Rug	$150	$225
374	Mickey Mouse Transfer-o-s Display	$375	$420
375	Mickey Mouse Transfer-o-s	$60	$65
376	Mickey Scrap Book Set	$275	$300
377A	Mickey Mouse Lapel Watch	$600	$625
B	Mickey Mouse Book Bank	$125	$130
378	Mickey Mouse Small Bread Labels ea.	$15	$30
379	Mickey Mouse Dime Register Bank	$275	$300
380	Mickey Mouse Candy Bar Wrapper	$65	$90
381	Mickey Mouse Slide Pictures	$50	$55
382	Mickey Mouse Safety Film	$80	$85
383	Mickey Cine Art Film	$80	$85
384	Mickey Mouse Ingersoll Wrist Watch	$900	$1,000
385	Mickey Mouse Ingersoll Pocket Watch	$3,500	$4,000
386	Mickey Mouse Pocket Watch	$900	$950
387	Mickey Mouse Watch	$800	$900
388-389	Mickey Mouse Lapel Watch	$600	$625
390	Mickey Mouse Compact	$470	$500
391A	Mickey Mouse Pocket Knife	$250	$275
B	Mickey Mouse Scissors	$275	$300
392	Mickey & Minnie Celluloid Figures ea.	$110	$120
393	Mickey Celluloid Figures ea.	$110	$120
394	Mickey Mouse On Bridge	$375	$400
395	Mickey On Bridge	$350	$375
396	Mickey Mouse Celluloid Containers ea.	$100	$200
397	Mickey With Little Mickeys	$375	$400
398	Mickey Mouse Rattle	$200	$220
399	Mickey Mouse Celluloid Figure	$200	$300
400	Mickey Mouse Metal Figure	$100	$125
401	Mickey Mouse Celluloid Toy	$250	$275
402	Minnie Mouse Purse	$300	$325
403	Mickey Mouse Ring In Original Box	$200	$400
404	Donald Duck Celluloid Windup	$5,000	$5,500
405	Donald Duck Trapeze	$2,000	$2,200
406	Donald Duck Waddler	$1,500	$1,800
407	Donald Duck Windup	$350	$400
408	Donald Duck Nodder	$2,200	$2,500
409	Donald Duck Acrobat	$550	$600
410	Donald Duck Windup	$8,500	$9,000
411	Celluloid Donald Duck	$300	$325
412	Donald Duck and Pluto Windup	$2,200	$2,500
413A	Donald Duck Pencil Sharpener	$225	$250
B	Donald Duck Tape Measure	$250	$275
C	Celluloid Donald Duck	$150	$175
D	Celluloid Donald Duck	$100	$125
414	Donald Duck Drum Major	$1,200	$1,500

Plate	Description	Good	Excellent/ Mint
415	Donald Duck Composition Doll	$1,200	$1,500
416-417	Donald Duck Cloth Doll ea.	$450	$550
418	Donald Duck Bisque ea.	$130	$160
419A	Donald Duck On Tricycle Bisque	$225	$250
B	Donald Duck On Scooter Bisque	$225	$250
420	Donald Duck By Pillar Toothbrush Holder	$2,000	$2,200
421	Donald Duck Musician Bisque	$300	$350
422	Donald Duck Musician Bisque	$300	$350
423	Donald Duck Hands On Hips Bisque	$400	$425
424	Donald Siamese Toothbrush Holder	$400	$425
425	Donald Ceramic Ashtray	$375	$400
426	Donald Duck Fisher Price	$400	$425
427	Donald Duck Pull Toy	$275	$325
428	Donald Duck Fisher Price	$300	$325
429	Donald Duck Small Fisher Price	$250	$275
430	Donald Duck Toothbrush Holder	$300	$325
431	Donald Ceramic Planter	$500	$550
432	Donald Duck Crown Bank	$375	$400
433	Donald Duck Crown Bank ea.	$400	$450
434	Donald Duck Crown Bank	$375	$400
435	Donald Duck Pop Up Paddle	$500	$550
436	Donald Duck Cream Pitcher	$450	$550
437	Donald Duck Patriot Plate	$150	$160
438	Donald Duck Seiberling Figure ea.	$275	$350
439	Fisher Price Easter Parade	$800	$950
440	Donald Schuco Windup	$2,000	$3,000
441	Donald and Pluto Hand Car	$2,000	$2,200
442	Donald Duck Tin Tray	$125	$150
443	Donald Duck Tin Pail	$175	$185
444	Donald Duck Watering Can	$75	$150
445	Donald Duck Watering Can	$90	$175
446	Donald Duck Night Light	$350	$425
447	Donald Duck Telephone Bank	$450	$500
448	Donald Duck Tin Drum	$300	$350
449	Donald Duck Carpet Sweeper	$200	$225
450	Donald Duck Soap	$250	$275
451	Donald Duck Rowboat	$750	$850
452A	Donald Duck Pencil Sharpener	$225	$250
B	Donald Duck Tape Measure	$300	$350
453A	Donald Duck Brush	$85	$95
B	Donald Duck Celluloid Figure	$125	$150
454	Donald Duck Snow Shovel	$125	$250
455	Fun-E-Flex Donald Duck On Sled	$1,700	$2,000
456	Donald Duck Sand Shovel (large)	$100	$200
457	Donald Duck French Windup	$400	$450
458	Donald Duck Hair Brush ea.	$85	$95
459	Donald Duck Paint Box	$50	$75
460	Donald Duck Picture Storybook	$50	$75
461	Mickey Mouse & Donald Ski Jump Target	$140	$175
462	Donald Duck Linen Book	$150	$200
463	Donald Duck Umbrella	$275	$300
464	Mickey Mouse Magazine	$80	$125
465	Horace Horsecollar Fun-E-Flex	$2,500	$3,000
466A	Goofy Bisque	$90	$100
B	Horace Horsecollar Bisque	$90	$100
467	Clarabelle Cow Book	$30	$40
468	Fisher Price Pluto	$300	$350
469	Pluto Tin Windup ea.	$200	$250
470	Fun-E-Flex Pluto In His House	$400	$450
471A	Large Fun-E-Flex Pluto	$300	$325
B	Small Fun-E-Flex Pluto	$175	$200
472	Pluto Soap	$150	$175
473	Large Fun-E-Flex Pluto	$300	$325
474	Pop-Up Pluto	$75	$100
475	Large Stuffed Pluto	$225	$350
476	Pluto Patriot Mug	$85	$95
477	Donald, Mickey, & Elmer Elephant Tea Set	$225	$300

Plate	Description	Good	Excellent/ Mint
478	Elmer Elephant Bisque	$400	$450
479	Elmer The Elephant Book	$50	$85
480	Elmer Elephant Stuffed Musical Toy	$100	$150
481	Elmer The Elephant Soap	$250	$275
482	Pluto The Pup Picture Storybook	$75	$125
483	Mickey, Donald, Minnie Small Storybooks ea.	$30	$40
484	Mickey Mouse Movie Studio Color Set	$150	$200
485	Celluloid Charms ea.	$30	$35
486	Noma Silly Symphony Lights	$175	$250
487	Silly Symphony Fan	$75	$125
488	Disney Figural Bakelite Pencil Sharpeners ea.	$40	$75
489A	Pinocchio Pencil Sharpener	$300	$325
B	Pluto Pencil Sharpener	$350	$400
C	Mickey Mouse Pencil Sharpener	$300	$325
490	Three Little Pigs Trapeze	$1,200	$1,400
491	Big Bad Wolf Alarm Clock	$900	$950
492	Three Little Pigs Boxed Bisque Set	$450	$500
493	Big Bad Wolf Game Board (only)	$50	$75
494	Three Little Pigs Tin Tray	$50	$75
495	Three Little Pigs Tin Tea Set	$225	$300
496	Three Little Pigs Watering Can	$125	$150
497A	Three Little Pigs Sand Pail	$150	$200
B	Three Little Pigs Wash Tub	$125	$150
498-499	Three Little Pigs Sand Pail	$150	$200
500-501	Three Little Pigs Toothbrush Holder	$175	$200
502	Three Little Pigs Bisque ea.	$70	$75
503	Three Little Pigs & Wolf Bisque Set	$250	$300
504	Seiberling Three Little Pigs Set	$1,800	$2,000
505	Fun-E-Flex Three Little Pigs Set	$450	$500
506	Seiberling Big Bad Wolf figure w/box	$1,000	$1,200
507	Fun-E-Flex Pig	$150	$175
508	Practical Pig Cup, Patriot China	$75	$95
509	Three Little Pigs Patriot Mug	$75	$95
510	Three Little Pigs Bowl	$75	$80
511	Three Little Pigs Plate	$85	$100
512	Red Riding Hood Game	$125	$175
513	Who's Afraid Of The Big Bad Wolf Game	$75	$110
514	Three Little Pigs Cards	$100	$110
515	Three Little Pigs Soap	$200	$225
516	Three Little Pigs Score Sheet	$75	$80
517	Three Pigs Game Board	$65	$90
518	Big Bad Wolf Book	$75	$100
519	Three Little Pigs Book	$60	$85
520	Three Pigs Prohibition Tray	$125	$175
521	Three Little Pigs Ashtray ea.	$100	$125
522	Snow White Pull Toy	$375	$400
523	Fisher Price Dopey & Doc Pull Toy	$350	$375
524	Dopey Fisher Price Pull Toy	$250	$325
525	Dopey Night Light	$200	$225
526	Snow White Composition Doll	$200	$300
527	Dopey Knickerbocker Doll	$175	$200
528	Happy Doll By Chad Valley	$225	$300
529	Dopey Knickerbocker Doll	$175	$200
530	Snow White Cloth Doll By Ideal	$175	$250
531	Bashful Knickerbocker Cloth Doll	$150	$200
532	Snow White Small Composition Doll	$150	$200
533	Dopey Cloth Doll By Chad Valley	$150	$225
534	Doc and Bashful Knickerbocker Dolls ea.	$175	$200
535	Dopey Cloth Doll	$150	$200
536	Sleepy and Grumpy Knickerbocker Dolls ea.	$175	$200
537	Oilcloth Face Dwarf Dolls ea.	$125	$175
538	Snow White Madame Alexander Marionette	$200	$300

Plate	Description	Good	Excellent/ Mint
539	Bashful Madame Alexander Marionette	$175	$250
540	Doc Madame Alexander Marionette	$175	$250
541	Dopey Madame Alexander Marionette	$175	$250
542	Happy Madame Alexander Marionette	$175	$250
543	Dopey Crown Bank	$200	$225
544	Dopey Lamp With Shade	$550	$600
545	Doc Lamp With Shade	$550	$600
546	Dopey Night Light by LaMode	$150	$225
547	Dopey Lamp	$150	$175
548	Snow White Lamp	$200	$225
549	Grumpy Book End	$150	$175
550	Dopey American Pottery Figure	$150	$225
551	Snow White La Mode Night Light	$150	$250
552	Doc and Snow White Toothpick Holders ea.	$225	$275
553A	Bashful Toothpick Holder	$225	$275
B	Dopey Toothpick Holder	$225	$275
554	Dopey and Happy Book Ends pr.	$250	$275
555	Snow White and Doc China Plate	$60	$95
556	Happy Cup and Saucer, English	$75	$100
557	Snow White Character Plaque	$50	$75
558	Celluloid Snow White & Seven Dwarfs	$350	$400
559	Large Celluloid Dwarf ea.	$100	$110
560	Large Snow White Bisque Set	$350	$450
561	Small Snow White Bisque Set	$350	$450
562	Boxed Snow White Bisque Set	$700	$750
563	Seiberling Snow White Figures Set	$450	$500
564	Windup Dopey	$250	$275
565	Dopey Doll by Alexander (Boxed)	$250	$300
566	Snow White Belgian Tin	$400	$600
567	Snow White Tin Tea Set	$250	$275
568	Snow White Belgian Tin	$400	$600
569	Snow White Belgian Tin	$400	$600
570A	Snow White Watering Can (small)	$100	$140
B	Snow White Watering Can (large)	$150	$200
571	Snow White Watering Can	$100	$140
572	Snow White Sand Pail	$120	$175
573	Snow White Sand Pail	$200	$275
574	Snow White Tin Tea Tray	$40	$75
575	Snow White Tin Set	$85	$125
576	Snow White Drinking Glass Set	$210	$225
577	Seiberling Seven Dwarfs	$280	$320
578	Snow White Soap	$100	$125
579	Seven Dwarfs Soap ea.	$50	$55
580	Snow White Safety Blocks (Small Set)	$100	$125
581	Snow White Safety Blocks (Large Set)	$150	$200
582-583	Snow White Game	$100	$150
584	Snow White Game	$100	$150
585	Snow White Tinkersand Pictures	$100	$125
586-587	Snow White Target Game	$175	$250
588	Snow White Cards	$95	$135
589	Snow White Card Game	$100	$150
590	The Game Of Snow White	$75	$125
591	Snow White Radio	$2,800	$3,500
592	Snow White Napkin Holders ea.	$85	$100
593	Snow White Bakelite Pencil Sharpeners ea.	$45	$75
594	Snow White Dime Register Banks ea.	$105	$110
595	Snow White & Seven Dwarfs Charms Set	$35	$40
596	Snow White Character Decals ea.	$35	$60
597	Dopey Playing Cards	$40	$65
598	Snow White Purse	$175	$195
599	Snow White Moving Picture Machine	$350	$375

Plate	Description	Good	Excellent/ Mint
600	Snow White Treasure Chest	$250	$275
601	Snow White Rocking Chair	$550	$600
602	Snow White Valentine Card ea.	$35	$40
603	Seven Dwarfs Valentine Card ea.	$35	$40
604	Snow White Valentine Card ea.	$35	$40
605	Snow White Character Pictures ea.	$20	$40
606	Snow White Coloring Set	$85	$125
607	Snow White Picture Puzzles	$100	$140
608	Snow White Composition Tablet	$60	$90
609A	Snow White Storybook	$50	$75
B	Snow White Jingle Book	$30	$45
C	Snow White Large Paint Book	$50	$75
610	Complete Story Of Snow White	$90	$130
611	Snow White Linen-like Book	$60	$90
612	Snow White Mirror	$35	$60
613	Snow White English Post Card	$25	$40
614	Snow White Paint Book	$35	$50
615	Snow White Storybook	$65	$90
616-617	Snow White Cut-out Book	$150	$225
618	Snow White Linen-like Book	$60	$85
619	Snow White Scrap Book	$65	$90
620	Dopey Linen-like Book	$50	$85
621	Snow White Framed Calendar Print	$100	$150
622	Snow White Big Little Book	$25	$45
623-625	Snow White Lobby Cards ea.	$45	$75
626A	Snow White Lobby Card	$45	$75
B	Ferdinand The Bull Doll	$250	$350
627	Ferdinand The Bull Pull Toy	$225	$300
628	Ferdinand Chinese Checkers	$75	$100
629	Ferdinand And Matador Windup	$650	$900
630	Ferdinand Windup	$130	$155
631	Ferdinand Crown Composition Bank	$100	$145
632	Ferdinand Chalk Figure	$65	$90
633	Ferdinand The Bull Cutouts	$145	$200
634	Ferdinand The Bull Linen Book	$60	$95
635	Put The Tail On Ferdinand Party Game	$65	$85
636	Braxton Ferdinand The Bull	$100	$110
637	Ferdinand Seiberling Toy Figure	$50	$75
638	Pinocchio By Ideal	$325	$350
639	Large Wooden Pinocchio	$750	$800
640	Wooden Pinocchio	$350	$375
641	Crown Toy Pinocchio	$350	$375
642	Composition Pinocchio	$400	$425
643	Pinocchio Doll By Crown Toy	$250	$325
644	Pinocchio Hand Puppets ea.	$110	$125
645	Pinocchio Windup	$350	$400
646A	Ideal Pinocchio	$350	$400
B	Ideal Jiminy Cricket	$350	$400
647	Chad Valley Geppetto	$900	$1,250
648	Wooden Jiminy Cricket	$400	$425
649	Fun-E-Flex Pinocchio	$175	$200
650A	Pinocchio Book	$60	$95
B	Ideal Pinocchio Doll	$200	$300
651	Jiminy Cricket Crown Bank	$100	$175
652	Pinocchio Crown Bank	$150	$225
653	Pinocchio Multi Products Figure	$125	$175
654	Pinocchio Seiberling Figure	$75	$125
655A	Geppetto Multi Products Figure	$65	$95
B	Pinocchio Multi Products Figure	$65	$95
C	Jiminy Cricket Multi Products Figure	$65	$95

Plate	Description	Good	Excellent/ Mint
656A	Gideon The Cat Multi Products Figure	$65	$95
B	Geppetto Seated Multi Products Figure	$75	$125
C	Lampwick Multi Products Figure	$65	$95
657A	Figaro The Cat Multi Products Figure	$65	$95
B	Small Pinocchio	$65	$95
658	Miniature Pinocchio Figures ea.	$30	$65
659	Fisher Price Pinocchio	$300	$350
660	Fisher Price Pinocchio	$275	$325
661-662	Pinocchio Mechanical Valentines ea.	$20	$40
663	Large Pinocchio Mechanical Valentines ea.	$20	$40
664	Pinocchio Better Little Book	$25	$40
665A	Bisque Pinocchio	$150	$175
B	Bisque Pinocchio	$175	$200
C	Bisque Pinocchio	$100	$125
666	Pinocchio Glazed Ceramic Planter	$40	$65
667	Pinocchio 3½" Bisque Figures ea.	$50	$85
668	Pinocchio Green Glaze Porcelain Figures ea.	$25	$50
669	Windup Pinocchio	$275	$325
670	Pinocchio The Acrobat	$500	$550
671	Cleo The Goldfish Character Glass	$10	$20
672	Jiminy Cricket Soap	$85	$95
673	Pinocchio Color Box	$20	$40
674	Windup Figaro	$150	$175
675	Pinocchio Tray	$50	$75
676	Pinocchio Tin Tea Set	$100	$150
677	Pinocchio Cardboard Figure	$20	$35
678	Pinocchio Lunchbox	$60	$85
679-680	Pinocchio The Merry Puppet Game	$65	$95
681	Pitfalls Of Pinocchio Game	$60	$85
682	Pinocchio's Circus Punch-out Set	$35	$60
683-684	Pin The Nose On Pinocchio Game	$100	$135
685A	Pinocchio Liberty Magazine	$15	$25
B	Pinocchio Ring The Nose Game	$50	$75
686	Boxed Set Of Six Pinocchio Books By Whitman	$200	$225
687	Pinocchio Character Story Paint Book ea.	$20	$35
688	Pinocchio Character Story Paint Book ea.	$20	$35
689	Pinocchio Character Story Paint Book ea.	$20	$35
690	Pinocchio Large Storybook	$35	$60
691	Pinocchio A Puppet Show	$75	$125
692	Pinocchio School Tablet	$25	$40
693	Pinocchio School Tablet	$25	$40
694-695	Pinocchio Die-Cut Picture Book	$65	$90
696-697	Pinocchio Picture Book	$50	$70
698	Pinocchio Soft Cover Book	$15	$30
699	Pinocchio Hard Cover Storybook	$40	$60
700	Pinocchio Picture Book	$25	$45
701	Pinocchio Small Linen-like Book	$20	$40
702A-B	Pinocchio Picture Puzzles (boxed)	$80	$110
703	Walt Disney's Pinocchio Book	$25	$40
704	Pinocchio Soft Cover Book	$20	$35
705	Pinocchio Theatre Lobby Card	$30	$45
706	Pinocchio Sheet Music ea.	$15	$25
707	Pinocchio Character Targets Set	$40	$65
708	Pinocchio Mask	$15	$20
709-712	Pinocchio Framed Prints, C. 1939 ea.	$60	$85
713	Mickey Mouse On Horse Windup	$4,000	$4,500
714	Mickey On Pluto Celluloid	$3,500	$4,000

Plate	Description	Good	Excellent/ Mint
715	Mickey Mouse Occupied Japan Celluloids ea.	$75	$95
716	Donald Duck Celluloid ea.	$75	$95
717	Donald Duck Boxers	$1,500	$1,800
718A	Mickey Mouse Celluloid Figure	$75	$95
B	Donald Duck Celluloid Figure	$75	$95
719	Crawler Donald Duck	$2,200	$2,500
720	Mickey Mouse Squeeze Toy	$350	$400
721	Sun Rubber Vehicles ea.	$95	$100
722	Sun Rubber Vehicles ea.	$95	$100
723	Donald Duck Baton Fisher Price	$225	$250
724	Donald Duck Choo-Choo	$175	$200
725	Donald Duck Doughboy Pull Toy by Fisher Price	$250	$325
726	Mickey Mouse Fisher Price Drummer	$175	$200
727	Donald Duck Xylophone Player Pull Toy	$200	$275
728	Donald Fisher Price Pull Toy	$225	$250
729	Mickey Mouse Choo Choo	$125	$150
730	Donald Duck Fisher Price	$225	$250
731	Mickey Mouse Viewer Film Display	$225	$350
732	Donald Duck Sweeper	$150	$165
733	Mickey Mouse Alarm Clock	$140	$155
734	Donald Jack-in-the-Box	$150	$165
735	Panchito Ceramic Lamp With Shade	$225	$300
736	Joe Carioca American Pottery Figure	$85	$125
737A	Snow White Leeds Planter	$25	$45
B	Snow White Leeds Bank	$30	$50
738A	Dopey Character Leeds Planter	$25	$45
B	Dopey Character Leeds Figure	$75	$125
739	Dopey Ceramic Lamp	$125	$160
740	Donald Duck Ceramic Lamp	$85	$125
741	Donald Duck Leeds Ceramic Figure	$60	$85
742	Donald Duck Leeds Ceramic Pitcher	$40	$65
743	Mickey Mouse Cookie Jar	$85	$110
744	Donald Duck Cookie Jar	$80	$100
745	Pinocchio Chalkware Figure	$20	$30
746	Donald Duck Chalkware Figure	$25	$40
747	Mickey Mouse Pincushion	$40	$45
748	Model Craft Set – Donald Duck	$40	$60
749	Gideon The Cat by Goebel	$85	$120
750	Joe Carioca Wood Composition Windup	$250	$325
751	(A through E) Large Bambi Figures ea.	$50	$90
752	(A through E) Small Bambi Figures ea.	$40	$70
753	Bambi Hankies Book (complete)	$85	$110
754	Bambi Paint Book (large)	$45	$65
755	Bambi Character Hankies ea.	$15	$25
756A	Thumper Storybook	$15	$30
B	Bambi Storybook	$15	$30
757	Thumper Leeds Planter	$25	$40
758	Flower The Skunk Miniature Planter	$40	$65
759A	Bambi And Flower Glazed Planter	$35	$60
B	Bambi American Pottery Pitcher	$125	$165
760	Thumper Fisher Price Pull Toy	$225	$300
761A	Small Steiff Bambi	$40	$70
B	Large Steiff Bambi	$60	$90
762	Minnie Mouse Schuco Mascott Doll	$150	$175
763	Minnie Mouse Schuco Windup Doll	$500	$750
764	Mickey Mouse Watch Box	$200	$225
765	Snow White Musical Sweeper	$100	$105

Plate	Description	Good	Excellent/ Mint
766	Dumbo Pitcher By Leeds	$40	$75
767	Dumbo Leeds Salt & Pepper Shakers	$20	$35
768	Disney Character Paper Party Hats ea.	$10	$15
769	Donald Duck And Mickey Mouse Crayon Box	$20	$35
770	Dumbo American Pottery Figure	$60	$85
771	Disneyland Safety Blocks	$90	$125
772	Donald Duck Doctor Kit	$30	$45
773	Library of Games	$80	$85
774	Mouseketeer Television	$80	$120
775	Donald Duck Electric Scissors	$75	$95
776	Scuffy Mickey Shoe Polish	$20	$25
777	Donald Duck Umbrella	$100	$110
778	Mickey Mouse Magic Erasable Picture Set	$95	$100
779	Mickey Mouse Club Newsreel	$75	$95
780	Disneyland Monorail Game	$20	$30
781	Disneyland Melody Player	$100	$110
782	Donald Duck's Tiddley Winx	$30	$45
783	Mickey Mouse Weather House	$60	$65
784	Donald Duck Ohio Art Pail, 3"	$35	$60
785	Donald Duck Sand Pail, Happynak	$50	$55
786	Donald Duck Ohio Art Tray	$25	$30
787	Donald Duck Sand Pails ea.	$50	$60
788	Donald Duck Bank	$85	$110
789	2nd National Duck Bank	$85	$110
790	Mickey Mouse Top	$60	$65
791	Dumbo Tin Windup	$150	$225
792	Marx Disney Plastic Walkers ea.	$20	$28
793	Jiminy Cricket Plastic Cups ea.	$8	$12
794	Schuco Donald Duck	$200	$225
795	Lars Donald Duck Doll	$300	$375

Plate	Description	Good	Excellent/ Mint
796	Donald And Nephews Plastic Windup, Marx	$65	$90
797	Donald Duck The Skier	$275	$325
798	Disney Parade Roadster With Box	$500	$550
799	Disney Parade Roadster Without Box	$375	$425
800	Marx Mickey The Driver	$650	$700
801	Line Mar Mickey The Driver	$750	$800
802	Disneyland Rollercoaster	$200	$225
803	Disneyland Ferris Wheel	$200	$225
804	Marx Donald Dipsy Car	$550	$600
805	Marx Donald The Driver	$375	$425
806	Walt Disney's Television Car	$650	$700
807	Line Mar Mickey Dipsy Car	$375	$425
808	Casey Jr. Disneyland Train	$175	$200
809	Goofy The Gardener Windup	$1,600	$1,750
810	Mickey On Scooter Windup	$300	$325
811	Mickey Mouse Scooter Jockey	$400	$450
812	Mickey Mouse Express	$300	$350
813	Disney Character Windup Train, Marx	$250	$325
814	Mickey Mouse Mechanical Tricycle	$550	$600
815	Marx Mickey Car	$300	$325
816	Marx Donald Car	$300	$325
817	Donald Duck Duet	$550	$650
818	Donald Duck Drummer	$600	$625
819	Donald Duck Whirling Tail	$575	$600
820	Minnie Mouse Knitting	$500	$550
821	Mickey Mouse Whirling Tail	$250	$275
822	Mickey On Pluto Windup	$1,400	$1,500
823A	Pluto Drum Major	$300	$350
B	Mickey Mouse Xylophone	$400	$450
C	Donald Duck Drummer	$400	$450
824	Mickey Mouse Meteor Train	$700	$725
825	Mickey Mouse Train	$200	$250
826	Mickey Mouse Unicycle	$900	$1,100
827	Mickey Mouse Skater	$1,400	$1,500

Plate	Description	Good	Excellent/ Mint
828A	Mickey Mouse Whirling Tail	$125	$150
B	Mickey Mouse Xylophone Player	$500	$550
829	Walt Disney's Donald Rocking Chair	$850	$900
830	Jiminy Cricket Windup	$350	$400
831	Goofy Whirling Tail	$350	$425
832	Line Mar Pluto Windup	$350	$425
833	Line Mar Pluto Friction Cart	$250	$300
834	Pluto Unicycle Windup	$750	$800
835	Pluto Lantern	$200	$250
836	Pluto Tin Windup	$300	$325
837	Mickey's Tin Delivery Cart	$325	$350
838	Mickey Mouse Carousel	$2,200	$2,500
839	Mickey the Magician	$850	$900
840A	Line Mar Pluto Friction Motorcycle	$100	$140
B	Line Mar Donald Duck Friction Motorcycle	$100	$140
841	Donald Duck Fire Engine, Line Mar	$1,600	$2,000
842	Donald Gym Acrobat	$500	$550
843	Pluto Gym Acrobat	$500	$550
844A	Ludwig Von Drake Windup	$200	$275
B	Ludwig Von Drake Go Cart	$175	$250
845	Donald Duck Gasoline Truck	$400	$450
846	Marx Pecos Bill Plastic Windup	$75	$110
847	Line Mar Windup Pinocchio	$325	$400
848A	Snow White Plastic Watch Stand	$12	$15
B	Cinderella Plastic Watch Stand	$12	$15
849	Cinderella Record	$5	$8
850	Cinderella And The Prince Windup	$150	$200
851	Cinderella Penney's Apron Pattern	$15	$20
852	Tweedle Dee And Tweedle Dum Salt And Pepper Shakers	$150	$200
853	King Of Hearts Ceramic Pitcher	$175	$235
854	Sleeping Beauty Paint By Number Game	$65	$80
855	Lady Platform Pull Toy	$75	$100
856	Mary Poppins Windup by Marx	$110	$150
857	Ludwig Von Drake Squeeze Toy	$10	$20
858	Mickey Mouse Bayard Clock	$200	$225
859	Pluto Bayard Clock	$225	$250
860	Pinocchio Bayard Clock	$275	$300

Books on Antiques and Collectibles

Most of the following books are available from your local book seller or antique dealer, or on loan from your public librar If you are unable to locate certain titles in your area you may order by mail from COLLECTOR BOOKS, P.O. Box 3009, Paducal KY 42002-3009. This is only a partial listing of the books on antiques that are available from Collector Books. Add $2.00 for postag for the first book ordered and $.30 for each additional book. Include item number, title and price when ordering. Allow 14 t 21 days for delivery. All books are well illustrated and contain current values.

BOOKS ON GLASS AND POTTERY

No.	Title	Price
1810	American Art Glass, Shuman	$29.95
2016	Bedroom & Bathroom Glassware of the Depression Years	$19.95
1312	Blue & White Stoneware, McNerney	$9.95
1959	Blue Willow, 2nd Ed., Gaston	$14.95
1627	Children's Glass Dishes, China & Furniture II, Lechler	$19.95
2270	Collectible Glassware from the 40's, 50's, & 60's, Florence	$19.95
1892	Collecting Royal Haeger, Garmon	$19.95
2352	Collector's Ency. of Akro Agate Glassware, Florence	$14.95
1373	Collector's Ency of American Dinnerware, Cunningham	$24.95
2272	Collector's Ency. of California Pottery, Chipman	$24.95
2133	Collector's Ency. of Cookie Jars, Roerig	$24.95
2273	Collector's Ency. of Depression Glass, 10th Ed., Florence	$19.95
2209	Collector's Ency. of Fiesta, 7th Ed., Huxford	$19.95
1439	Collector's Ency. of Flow Blue China, Gaston	$19.95
1915	Collector's Ency. of Hall China, 2nd Ed., Whitmyer	$19.95
2210	Collector's Ency. of Limoges Porcelain, 2nd Ed., Gaston	$24.95
2334	Collector's Ency. of Majolica Pottery, Katz-Marks	$19.95
1358	Collector's Ency. of McCoy Pottery, Huxford	$19.95
1039	Collector's Ency. of Nippon Porcelain I, Van Patten	$19.95
2089	Collector's Ency. of Nippon Porcelain II, Van Patten	$24.95
1665	Collector's Ency. of Nippon Porcelain III, Van Patten	$24.95
1447	Collector's Ency. of Noritake, Van Patten	$19.95
1037	Collector's Ency. of Occupied Japan I, Florence	$14.95
1038	Collector's Ency. of Occupied Japan II, Florence	$14.95
2088	Collector's Ency. of Occupied Japan III, Florence	$14.95
2019	Collector's Ency. of Occupied Japan IV, Florence	$14.95
2335	Collector's Ency. of Occupied Japan V, Florence	$14.95
1034	Collector's Ency. of Roseville Pottery, Huxford	$19.95
1035	Collector's Ency. of Roseville Pottery, 2nd Ed., Huxford	$19.95
2339	Collector's Guide to Shawnee Pottery, Vanderbilt	$19.95
1425	Cookie Jars, Westfall	$9.95
2275	Czechoslovakian Glass & Collectibles, Barta	$16.95
2024	Kitchen Glassware of the Depression Years, 4th Ed., Florence	$19.95
2379	Lehner's Ency. of U.S. Marks on Pottery, Porcelain & Clay	$24.95
1438	Oil Lamps II, Thuro	$19.95
2345	Portland Glass, Ladd	$24.95
1670	Red Wing Collectibles, DePasquale	$9.95
1440	Red Wing Stoneware, DePasquale	$9.95
1958	So. Potteries Blue Ridge Dinnerware, 3rd Ed., Newbound	$14.95
2221	Standard Carnival Glass, 3rd Ed., Edwards	$24.95
2222	Standard Carnival Glass Price Guide, 1991, 8th Ed., Edwards	$7.95
2347	Standard Opalescent Glass Price Guide, Edwards	$9.95
1848	Very Rare Glassware of the Depression Years, Florence	$24.95
2140	Very Rare Glassware of the Depression Years, Second Series	$24.95
2224	World of Salt Shakers, 2nd Ed., Lechner	$24.95

BOOKS ON DOLLS & TOYS

No.	Title	Price
2079	Barbie Fashion, Vol. 1, 1959-1967, Eames	$24.95
1514	Character Toys & Collectibles 1st Series, Longest	$19.95
1750	Character Toys & Collectibles, 2nd Series, Longest	$19.95
2021	Collectible Male Action Figures, Manos	$14.95
1529	Collector's Ency. of Barbie Dolls, DeWein	$19.95
2151	Collector's Guide to Tootsietoys, Richter	$16.95
1067	Madame Alexander Collector's Dolls, Smith	$19.95
2342	Madame Alexander Price Guide #17, Smith	$9.95
1540	Modern Toys, 1930-1980, Baker	$19.95
2343	Patricia Smith's Doll Values Antique to Modern, 8th ed	$12.95
1886	Stern's Guide to Disney	$14.95
2139	Stern's Guide to Disney, 2nd Series	$14.95
1513	Teddy Bears & Steiff Animals, Mandel	$9.9
1817	Teddy Bears & Steiff Animals, 2nd, Mandel	$19.9
2084	Teddy Bears, Annalees & Steiff Animals, 3rd, Mandel	$19.9
2028	Toys, Antique & Collectible, Longest	$14.9
1808	Wonder of Barbie, Manos	$9.9
1430	World of Barbie Dolls, Manos	$9.9

OTHER COLLECTIBLES

No.	Title	Price
2280	Advertising Playing Cards, Grist	$16.9
1457	American Oak Furniture, McNerney	$9.9
2269	Antique Brass & Copper, Gaston	$16.9
2333	Antique & Collectible Marbles, Grist, 3rd Ed.	$9.9
1712	Antique & Collectible Thimbles, Mathis	$19.9
1880	Antique Iron, McNerney	$9.9
1748	Antique Purses, Holiner	$19.9
1868	Antique Tools, Our American Heritage, McNerney	$9.9
1426	Arrowheads & Projectile Points, Hothem	$7.9
1278	Art Nouveau & Art Deco Jewelry, Baker	$9.9
1714	Black Collectibles, Gibbs	$19.9
1128	Bottle Pricing Guide, 3rd Ed., Cleveland	$7.9
1751	Christmas Collectibles, Whitmyer	$19.9
1752	Christmas Ornaments, Johnston	$19.9
2132	Collector's Ency. of American Furniture, Vol. I, Swedberg	$24.9
2271	Collector's Ency. of American Furniture, Vol. II, Swedberg	$24.9
2018	Collector's Ency. of Graniteware, Greguire	$24.9
2083	Collector's Ency. of Russel Wright Designs, Kerr	$19.9
2336	Collector's Guide to Antique Radios 2nd Ed., Bunis	$17.9
1916	Collector's Guide to Art Deco, Gaston	$14.9
1537	Collector's Guide to Country Baskets, Raycraft	$9.9
1962	Collector's Guide to Decoys, Huxford	$14.9
2337	Collector's Guide to Decoys, Book II, Huxford	$16.9
2338	Collector's Guide to Disneyana, Longest & Stern	$24.9
1441	Collector's Guide to Post Cards, Wood	$9.9
2276	Decoys, Kangas	$24.9
1629	Doorstops, Id & Values, Betoria	$9.9
1716	Fifty Years of Fashion Jewelry, Baker	$19.9
2213	Flea Market Trader, 7th Ed., Huxford	$9.9
1755	Furniture of the Depression Era, Swedberg	$19.9
2081	Guide to Collecting Cookbooks, Allen	$14.9
2340	Collector's Guide to Easter Collectibles, Burnett	$16.9
2278	Grist's Machine Made & Contemporary Marbles	$9.9
1424	Hatpins & Hatpin Holders, Baker	$9.9
1181	100 Years of Collectible Jewelry, Baker	$9.9
2023	Keen Kutter Collectibles, 2nd Ed., Heuring	$14.9
2216	Kitchen Antiques - 1790–1940, McNerney	$14.9
1965	Pine Furniture, Our Am. Heritage, McNerney	$14.9
2080	Price Guide to Cookbooks & Recipe Leaflets, Dickinson	$9.9
2026	Railroad Collectibles, 4th Ed., Baker	$14.9
1632	Salt & Pepper Shakers, Guarnaccia	$9.9
1888	Salt & Pepper Shakers II, Guarnaccia	$14.9
2220	Salt & Pepper Shakers III, Guarnaccia	$14.9
2281	Schroeder's Antiques Price Guide, 10th Ed.	$12.9
2346	Sheet Music Reference & Price Guide, Patik	$18.9
2096	Silverplated Flatware, 4th Ed., Hagan	$14.9
2277	Standard Baseball Card Pr. Gd., Florence	$9.9
2348	20th Century Fashionable Plastic Jewelry, Baker	$19.9
2223	Wanted to Buy	$9.9
1885	Victorian Furniture, McNerney	$9.9
2349	Value Guide to Baseball Collectibles, Raycraft	$16.9

Schroeder's Antiques Price Guide

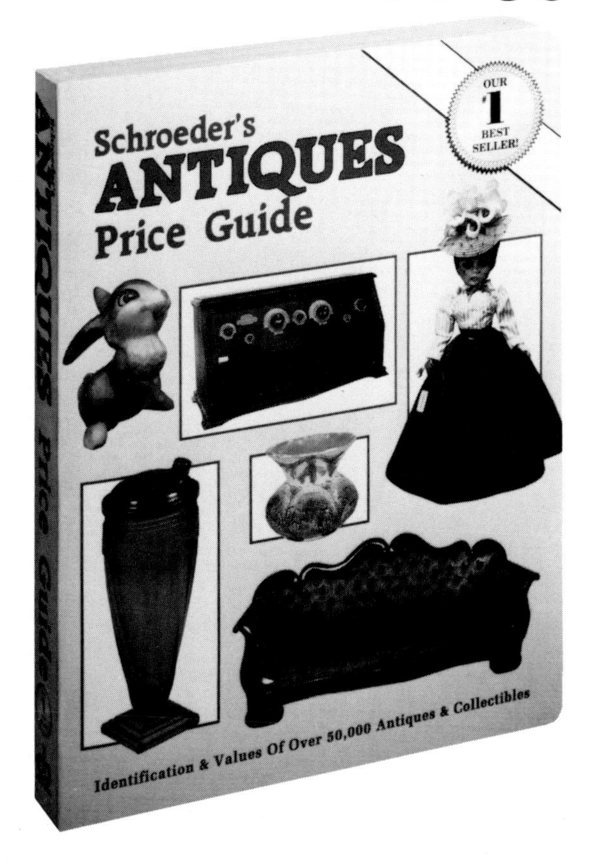

Schroeder's Antiques Price Guide has become THE household name in the antiques and collectibles field. Our team of editors works year-round with more than 200 contributors to bring you our #1 best-selling book on antiques and collectibles.

With more than 50,000 items identified and priced, *Schroeder's* is a must for the collector & dealer alike. If it merits the interest of today's collector, you'll find it in *Schroeder's.* Each subject is represented with histories and background information. In addition, hundreds of sharp original photos are used each year to illustrate not only the rare and unusual, but the everyday "fun-type" collectibles as well — not postage stamp pictures, but large close-up shots that show important details clearly.

Our editors compile a new book each year. Never do we merely change prices. Accuracy is our primary aim. Prices are gathered over the entire year previous to publication, from ads and personal contacts. Then each category is thoroughly checked to spot inconsistencies, listings that may not be entirely reflective of actual market dealings, and lines too vague to be of merit. Only the best of the lot remains for publication. You'll find *Schroeder's Antiques Price Guide* the one to buy for factual information and quality.

No dealer, collector or investor can afford not to own this book. It is available from your favorite bookseller or antiques dealer at the low price of $12.95. If you are unable to find this price guide in your area, it's available from Collector Books, P.O. Box 3009, Paducah, KY 42002-3009 at $12.95 plus $2.00 for postage and handling.

8½ x 11", 608 Pages $12.95

COLLECTOR BOOKS

A Division of Schroeder Publishing Co., Inc.